Educational
Policy-Making

by the same author

* *The Organisation of a Social Services Department*
* *Working Relationships within the British Hospital Service*
  The Government of Education
  The Politics of Education
  County Hall
* *Advisory Councils and Committees in Education*
* *The Challenge of Change (ed.)*

* Shared authorship

Educational Policy-Making

A Study of Interest Groups and Parliament

MAURICE KOGAN
Professor of Government and Social Administration
Brunel University

ASSISTED BY KATHERINE BOWDEN

London · George Allen & Unwin Ltd
Ruskin House · Museum Street

ISBN 0 04 370063 2 hardback
 0 04 370064 0 paperback

Printed in Great Britain
in 10 point Times Roman type
by Willmer Brothers Limited
Birkenhead.

Acknowledgements

Many people have helped in the production of this book. My colleagues in the Department of Government Studies at Brunel University, and particularly John Burnett, David Shapiro and Tim Packwood, made critical but constructive comments on our draft, as did Tony Becher, Helen Simons, Alan Evans, Brian MacArthur and Toby Weaver. Patrick Gallagher, of George Allen & Unwin Ltd, was a most encouraging and stimulating sponsor. And, at a critical time in the production of the work, the Nuffield Foundation gave a small grant which enabled much of the painstaking analysis of Parliamentary Questions, other parliamentary papers, and of local authority and teacher associations and press records, to be undertaken by Katherine Bowden. I am grateful to the trustees and to Patricia Thomas, Assistant Director to the Foundation, for their prompt and helpful treatment of my application for a grant. The librarians of the National Union of Teachers were unobtrusive and unstinting hosts for a great deal of our study of printed sources.

A large number of busy people in Parliament, in the main educational and related associations, in the educational press and in educational administration gave us time for what must have seemed to them somewhat long and tiresome interviews: Edward Britton (General Secretary), Alan Evans, Fred Jarvis and Max Morris (former President), of the National Union of Teachers; Terry Casey (General Secretary), J. D. Marsh, D. S. Wakefield, of the National Association of Schoolmasters; Sheila Wood, Secretary, the Association of Assistant Mistresses; Sir William (now Lord) Alexander, Secretary, the Association of Education Committees; Leonard Brown, Educational Officer, the County Councils' Association; Robin McCall (Secretary), Christopher Berry, Peter Sloman (formerly of the Department of Education and Science, now Education Officer), of the Association of Municipal Corporations; Jack Straw (also a former President of the National Union of Students) of the Inner London Education Authority; Anthony Becher of the Nuffield Foundation; Sir Kenneth Berrill, Chairman, and the late Ralph Fletcher, Secretary, the University Grants Committee; Geoffrey Templeman (formerly Chairman) and Brian

Taylor (Executive Secretary), the Committee of Vice-Chancellors and Principals; Tom Driver, General Secretary, the Association of Teachers in Technical Institutions; Stanley Hewitt, General Secretary, the Association of Teachers in Colleges and Departments of Education; Laurence Sapper, General Secretary, the Association of University Teachers; John Randall, President, the National Union of Students; Barbara Bullivant, Ann Sofer (also a member of the National Association of Governors and Managers and the ILEA), of the Confederation for the Advancement of State Education; Beryl MacAlhone, formerly of the Advisory Centre for Education; Richard Cunningham, Secretary, the Catholic Education Council; Dr Clifford Smith, formerly Secretary, the National Association of Labour Teachers; John Fairhall, education correspondent of the *Guardian*; Brian MacArthur, Editor, *The Times Higher Education Supplement*; Stuart Maclure, Editor, *The Times Educational Supplement*; John Scott, education correspondent of the Press Association; Max Wilkinson, education correspondent of the *Daily Mail;* Sir Toby Weaver and Harry French (Senior Chief Inspector), formerly of the Department of Education and Science; Victor Stevens, Joint Secretary, the Schools Council; Toni Griffiths, formerly of the National Foundation for Educational Research and the National Union of Teachers, now of the National Children's Bureau, and Alfred Yates, Director, the National Foundation for Educational Research; James Swaffield, formerly Secretary, the Association of Municipal Corporations; Sir Norman Lindop, formerly Chairman, the Committee of Directors of Polytechnics; James Boyden, George Cunningham, Eric Deakins, Professor Gerald Fowler, Roy Hattersley, Frank Hooley, Richard Hornby, Denis Howell, John Jennings, Frank Judd, Sir Gilbert Longden, Kenneth Marks, Timothy Raison, the Rt Hon Edward Short, the Rt Hon Michael Stewart, Edwin Wainwright, the Rt Hon Shirley Williams, Members of Parliament; Viscount Eccles, Baroness Phillips and Baroness White.

 We also interviewed a small group of former and present central government officials who, according to the present convention, may not be named, and who, while not revealing any information not publicly available, helped us by giving their perceptions of how interest groups and the parliamentary process impinged on the decisions which they make or participate in making.

Towards the end of the period of our study a group from the University of Illinois, led by Professor Myron Atkin, and collaborating with Tony Becher and Helen Simons of the Nuffield Foundation, was active in this country on a comparative study of educational government and administration. We had several meetings with them at which we exchanged constructive criticisms of each other's emerging findings. Our studies will complement each other, and we would like to express our appreciation of the mutual help that these exchanges gave.

Finally, my biggest debts are to Katherine Bowden, who did much of the detailed analytical work whilst keeping an eye on the wider social scientific implications of our work, and to Sally Marshall who produced successive drafts more quickly and efficiently than we could write them.

Contents

Charts

To battle! hark the trumpet calls,
The watchword flies along the walls:—
'For England, God and Truth,'
Lo, where for faith and fatherland,
Like marshalled hosts, for Britain stand
The guardians of her youth

From 'An "NUT" Gathering Cry', by Septimus G. Green.[1]

---

[1] The National Union of Teachers' Conference 1910: *The Book of Plymouth*, edited by C. W. Bracken (T. C. and E. C. Jack, 1910).

Part I

INTRODUCTION AND POLICIES

Chapter 1

Purposes and Scope

This book shows how a major zone of public activity, the British education service, developed, confirmed and changed its policies between 1960 and 1974, and who were the main agents of change. The approach is essentially historical, but the analysis is also related to the more general assumptions of political science and sociology about the nature of interest groups, the nature of the parliamentary system and of the decision-making process.

So as to keep the study within reasonable bounds it does not refer to Scotland or Northern Ireland, nor to the development of scientific, sports or arts policies, all of which have been, at various times, within the domain of the Ministry of Education and the Department of Education and Science.

To undertake the task properly we should have begun far back in the origins of the public education system, perhaps in the mid-nineteenth century. Instead we have chosen the period from the time, in 1960, when David Eccles was in the middle of his second period as Minister, to the time when Margaret Thatcher ceased to be Secretary of State on 4 March 1974. Although selective within that relatively brief period, we have analysed all the 'educational' Parliamentary Questions (some eight thousand), debates, and records of proceedings of parliamentary committees from 1 June 1960 until Parliament dissolved in February 1974. We have seen twenty-two present or former MPs who were active in that period. Of this number, ten were or are ministers.

We interviewed the leaders of most of the main interest groups: the Association of Municipal Corporations (now the Association of Metropolitan Authorities), the County Councils' Association (now the Association of County Councils), the Association of Education Committees, the Catholic Education Council, the Inner London Education Authority, the National Union of Teachers, the National Association of Schoolmasters, the Association of Assistant Mistresses, the Association of University Teachers, the Association of Teachers in Technical Institutions, the Association of Teachers in Colleges and Departments of Education, the National Union of Students, and the Committee of Vice-Chancellors and Principals.

We also saw eight present or former officials in the Department of Education and Science and the National Foundation for Educational Research, officials in the Nuffield Foundation, five leading educational journalists, and representatives of the Confederation for the Advancement of State Education, the Advisory Centre for Education, the ILEA and the London Comprehensive Schools' Association, the National Association of Governors and Managers, and the Committee of Directors of Polytechnics.

We have already acknowledged our debt to them in the Acknowledgements to this book.

Beyond these parliamentary sources and the interviews with some of the main actors, we checked on selected issues through the principal educational journals – *The Times Educational Supplement, The Times Higher Education Supplement, Education* – as well as in other weekly journals, particularly *New Society*, the *New Statesman* and the *Spectator*, as examples of the way the issues were presented to a relatively elite public. We looked at all the cuttings from *The Times* on educational matters from 1960 to 1974.

Other primary sources were used. We studied all the confidential education committee minutes from 1960 to 1973 of the AEC, CCA and AMC. We also looked at selected NUT papers. DES and UGC annual reports and copies of UGC quinquennial letters from 1946 to 1972 were consulted. The series of ministry and DES circulars was also analysed.

We made use of statements already collated by the author in his two brief books, *The Politics of Education* and *County Hall* [1], which give the perceptions of two former ministers and three chief education officers of what happened, and who helped it happen, in the education service within the 1960s.

METHODOLOGY

How usable are conclusions based on data such as these? There were many difficulties. We tried to see every parliamentarian who had been active in educational matters during our period, but we failed to get a full return because either many refused to see us, or we were unable to make sustained contact with them.[1] Most pleaded other commitments, although one former minister wrote, 'Why, pray, should I help you with your money making?' There is a general problem of making contact with MPs whose lack of secretarial and other facilities can make them unwittingly elusive. And they must feel themselves overworked by researchers and journalists. In spite of these limitations, however, MPs' views of the processes and the main issues proved to be so consistent with each other that interviews began to produce a diminishing return, although every individual added at least one new nuance to what has been said before and, at a minimum, confirmed other impressions. We feel that our perception of the MP's role in educational decision-making would not have been greatly extended if all interviews had been completed.

But the main systematic difficulty was not in tracing the main policies, which can be identified from printed sources, nor in tracing the actions of the interest groups. It was rather in determining relationships between interest groups; in seeing who impacted on whom and with what effect; in identifying those who made the decisions; in short, the process of policy formation. And this is why the interviews were essential although they needed to be supplemented by careful reading of evidence to parliamentary committees and the like. Many of the interviewees were concerned only with one particular area in education or had been involved during only one period. The main actors are busy men who have often been long away from the main events. Many could not have answered many of the questions of a structured interview. So the best we could do was to get intensities of feeling about what the main issues were and with whom they interacted by using free responses to some twelve key questions.

The best way of checking interviewees' perceptions might have been inspection of files. It was certainly helpful and illuminating to see confidential minutes of meetings of the AEC, AMC and CCA committee minutes. But even that might not give the full picture.

[1] Twenty-seven MPs declined to be seen or failed to answer our request, including three out of four of the Conservative ministers in office until February 1974 and both of the recent Liberal spokesmen on education. A further fifteen MPs or former MPs were approached and expressed willingness to be interviewed, but interviews could not be arranged with them. Five other interviews were frustrated in a similar way. Sixty-five interviews were conducted in all.

Officials do not disclose, even on official files, who or what influenced them in a course of action. And, in any event, the ministry and DES files of our period will not be open for research scrutiny for many years.

We have not been able to look fully at the relationship between central policy-making and the enormous change and drive deriving from local educational politics and administration except when it came through clearly from the central figures we interviewed. Fortunately, however, some of this is being tackled in Professor Myron Atkin's book which we hope to see published shortly after this volume.

This book is not, therefore, exhaustive in its evidence but it attempts to open up the field.

THE ARGUMENT

This book uses an orthodox model of the policy formation process and follows four main lines of description and analysis. It discusses first the multiple objectives of education, and analyses the main policies evident in the period and the ways in which they have changed over our period. This leads to an analysis and description of the main educational interest groups, and a preliminary classification of them into legitimised and non-legitimised groups. We attempt to assess the impact of some of the most important and to differentiate them in terms of their closeness to authority as represented primarily by the Secretary of State and the DES, and the extent to which they are in consensus or in conflict with national policy formation.

We then turn to a study of the role of Parliament, which shows how far national political activity affects and is affected by the major educational decisions made and enunciated through ministerial speeches, changes in law and other formal administrative action. And both of these sets of evidence are analysed against the national interest group activities.

The components of analysis – changes in values and policies, the role of the interest groups and of Parliament in relation to the central government decision-makers – are then brought together in accounts of how they interact in two areas of action which serve as case studies: the development of higher education and of comprehensive secondary education. We then try to generalise what is found in terms of the main literature on interest groups, elites and pluralism, incrementalism and gradualism, and the extent to which policy generation and maintenance are consensual or conflictual. Finally, we pose questions about the democratic quality and the viability of the British policy generation system.

GENERALISATIONS

The sources of policy generation are so difficult to locate, let alone place in any logical pattern, that detecting the changes in values, or the pressures by which change is effected, is more a matter of art than of analysis. The imagery of political science suggests too much precision: such words as 'power', 'structure', 'pressure', 'leverage' all suggest that political activity is analogous with predictable engineering systems. Softer and more modest imagery is needed.

Within these conceptual limitations, the issues which this study attempts to depict are as follows. To begin with, the British system for the government of education is generally assumed to be strong, largely continuous and consensual in its working and in its assumptions [2].

Many of the educational and institutional policies remained largely unchanged between 1960 and 1974 and, indeed, most of them were inherited from the first of the public education systems at the beginning of the twentieth century. The education service was expansionist, increasingly egalitarian and strongly devoted to liberal assumptions about the role of teachers and their relationships with students. A strong institutional fabric ensured continuity through which the main changes, which related less to the content and organisation of education than to ways of making it more redistributive, had to make their way. We seek to establish how consensus was broken, as the expansionist bubble burst, and scepticism took over; although, from what we have observed between 1960 and 1974, it may be that educational institutions and their interest groups are so strong that they will spring back and sustain the larger continuities which they support.

The institutional fabric depended upon interaction between three main sets of agents, central government, local authorities and teachers, who both sustained the continuity and produced change. For example, the setting up of the James Committee on teacher education was consistent with pressure from young teachers who thought that such reforms as the creation of the BEd were not adequate. The 1970 Act which transferred concern for the mentally handicapped from the health to the education authorities was partly the result of teacher insistence that no child is 'ineducable'. The creation of the Schools Council resulted from teacher objection to the attempt to create a Curriculum Study Group within the Ministry. If the central government, the local authorities and the teachers changed in many of their perspectives, the sanctioned changes came about not so much through a rational process in which all needs were pursued consistently and needs clarified but were, instead, caused by a few political leaders and permanent officials reacting at both the centre and within local authorities to a wider system of interest and pressure and imposing rationality later. At least two of the main movements during our period, towards comprehensive secondary education and towards mass higher education, based as they were on egalitarian values and also deriving from the pressures of the economy, were partly reactions to demographic pressure and to the pressures of an increasingly ambitious and consumer-orientated society. The education service responded within the limits of what it considered feasible in terms of resources and of educational politics.

In two major areas, higher education and comprehensive secondary schools, continuity was broken. In higher education the changes were structural – the development of polytechnics and the Open University and the expansion of universities – but had impact, too, on the content of education, and assumptions about academic freedom. But comprehensive secondary education was tackled incrementally, almost as a natural development from the tripartite system, rather than as a Swedish-style measure of social reform, though sporadic local pressures initiated the whole movement.

In analysing the place of the interest groups, representing the local authorities, the teachers and the various client groups, it is interesting to see whether some of the more powerful are, in the usage of the leading studies [3], more 'sectional' in their interests, defending the rights of the teachers or the local authorities, than 'promotional' of new causes, and whether this mode of classification is itself useful. While interest groups and their officials include some of the leading exponents of change (as, for example, more egalitarian policies, or the expansion of the higher education system to meet expanding social demand) they often reacted to, rather than initiated, the changes. It is to the less 'legitimised'[1] pressure groups, such as the National Union of Students, that we have to look for the more radical demands, such as their demands for changed relationships between teachers and students and reforms in the government of higher education. Other, and so far less successful, non-legit-

[1] This classification is elaborated in Chapter 4.

imised interest groups pressed for a greater place for parents in the schools. The NUS have been successful in becoming largely legitimised whilst outside the general consensus on many issues. It seems to be no longer true that only the interest groups that conform to the consensus have impact.

In our analysis of the role of Parliament in educational policymaking, our conclusion is not novel [4]. Parliament at most reviews, criticises and helps to aggregate and articulate feelings about policy. Essentially it reacts to, rather than initiates, policy. So far, indeed, are MPs from decision-making, that it is uncertain whether they have even enough authority to review and criticise effectively.

These issues – of what the changes were, of who caused them, of who brought about changes in patterns of authority and government, of who criticised policy – are the concern of this book.

v.
dear

Saud T playing the
discontinuous, reactive game
like Soc. of Ed.

Chapter 2

Some History: From Expansionism to Pessimism, 1960–1974

Educational policies and the values underlying them interact with the moods and fashions of their period. And the actions of politicians, interest groups and professions are both the products and the producers of changes in values and social needs. Education is perhaps the most socially volatile of all collective activities because it incorporates so much at once: the hope that man may change himself so as to be happier, more productive, and a good neighbour; and the hope that social arrangements can incorporate both the best of the past and the promise of the future.

The next two chapters, therefore, deploy many related themes. First, the policy analyst must remark the great changes that took place in a relatively short period: from 1960 when the Opportunity State was at its noon tide, when all seemed fair for economic expansion and the easing of social and personal relationships, to the time, now, when social and economic relationships are under attack if not in danger of dissolution. Against this theme of historical change, of which educational policies formed a part, we have to relate some of the ideological movements, which themselves formed part and were principal agents of social and economic change.

Chapter 3 defines educational policies, as they were changed between 1960 and 1974, and how far one can impute those changes to underlying values, institutional associations and the main interest groups which were involved in them.

Chart I records the main events in educational policy between 1959 and 1973. It shows how, between 1959 and 1973, the education service was concerned essentially with implementing the 1944 Act. At the beginning there was the repair of damage done by the war.

By 1960, the service was going full speed towards expansion, consolidation and improvement of the system within the terms of reference set by the 1944 Act. The Labour Governments of 1964 and 1966 created major reorientations of policy. By 1968, many of the underlying assumptions of the previous two decades had begun to be challenged. The challenges became sharper with the return of the Conservative Government in 1970.

The post-war Labour Government had had a difficult task at the beginning of our first period of reconstruction. Amidst steel and timber rationing, a recurrent shortage of building labour, a serious imbalance between pupil numbers and trained teachers, it did its best to implement the 1944 Act by providing secondary education for all up to the age of fifteen, by ensuring that there were at least roofs over children's heads, by remanning the schools through the emergency teacher training system, and by the first build-up of further education. When the Conservatives took office in 1951 they were not disposed at first to divert the products of growth, that were to begin to reach the private sector in the mid-fifties, into the public education system. Florence Horsborough was so well suited to the Treasury policies which she had been appointed to safeguard that her removal provided one of the few major victories of the educational pressure groups. The teachers persuaded Conservative MPs to revolt against her Teachers' Superannuation Bill, which touched on no great educational principle but attacked the income of badly paid teachers. She was, it is widely held [1], removed from office as a result of the unpopularity that the Bill incurred.

Sir David Eccles, who succeeded her in 1955, believed in success and expansion and, at the time when our analysis begins, in 1960, he was in the middle of his second term of office as Minister of Education. His policies more than any others represent the consensual, expansionist and ameliorist era of British education.

As Britain's relative position in the world declined, there was widespread optimism that nevertheless we might be a productive, benignly ameliorative society, in which tolerance and the good life would be both possible and desirable. From the appointment of Anthony Eden, and then Harold Macmillan after Suez in 1956, a long consumer boom began, punctuated and constrained though it was by recurrent economic crises. At the same time, an easy-going scepticism through which social relationships between different classes and generations were tested and softened became the prevailing norm. It seemed to be a time of a mobile and unrestrictive society, if one in which doubts about inequality were increasingly

Chart I: *main events in Education 1959–73*

Year	Minister	White Papers, Acts, Select Committees	Circulars	Other events, reports, etc.
1959	David Eccles	Education Act 1959. Mental Health Act 1959. National Insurance Act (Teachers' Superannuation).	1/59 Technical Education. 5/59 Further Education for Commerce Expansion. 7/59 Governing Bodies for Major Establishment of Further Education. 14/59 Extension of Teacher Quota.	National Council for Technological Awards set up. National Advisory Council on Further Education – Report. *Crowther Report* – (15–18 year olds).
1960	David Eccles	Charities Act 1960.	1/60 The Future Development of Management Education and Business Studies. 3/60 Youth Service – building programme. 6/60 Expansion of all Building programmes. 8/60 Nursery Education – minor concessions. 11/60 Courses for Youth Leaders.	*Albemarle Report* – published (youth service): recommendations accepted immediately. *Anderson Report* – published (students' awards). *Crowther Report* – second part published. *Robbins Committee* set up (higher education). United Kingdom Advisory Council on Education for Management established. National Advisory Council on Art Education – Coldstream Report (First report – new Diploma in Art and Design). National Council for Awards for Art and Design set up. National Advisory Council on the Training and Supply of Teachers – recommended the establishment of a second full time training course for teachers of the deaf and partially deaf. Royal Commission on Local Government in Greater London – Report published. Local Government Commission for England – published draft proposals for the East and West Midlands.
1961	David Eccles	Education Bill introduced on the implementation of some of the recommendations by the Crowther Report. White Paper (1/61): 'Better Opportunities in Technical Education'. White Paper: 'Provision for Old Age'. White Paper: 'London Government' (government proposals for reorganisation). Select Committee on Estimates – detailed examination of school buildings.	3/61 Regional Colleges. 9/61 Changes in GCE Exams. 17/61 Youth Service Buildings.	National Council for the Supply of Teachers Overseas set up. Introduction of secondary school examinations below O-levels on a regional basis – *Beloe Report* – published (CSE). National Advisory Council on the Supply and Training of Teachers – enquiry into the shortage of maths teachers. Central Advisory Council for Education (England) reconstituted under Mr J. Newsom – enquiry into full time courses either at schools or colleges of further education for 13–16 year olds of average or less ability. National Advisory Committee on Education for Industry and Commerce reconstituted under Sir H. Pilkington – sub-committee on organisation of sandwich courses. Standing Advisory Committee on Grants to Students. Creation of (short-lived) curriculum study group

Year	Minister	Acts/Bills	Dated items	
1962	Edward Boyle	Education Act 1962 – some recommendations of Crowther Report. Select Committee on Estimates – school dental services. White Paper: 'Industrial Training Government Proposals'. Local Government Bill. Pensions (Increase) Act.	1/62 Awards for First Degree – university courses. 3/61 Regional Colleges. 9/61 Changes in GCE and A-level Exams. 17/61 Youth Service Buildings.	National Advisory Council on Art Education – second Report. National Advisory Council on Education for Industry and Commerce – Russell Report on sandwich courses. Sub-committee set up under Mr W. F. Crick. Higher awards in business studies. National Advisory Council on the Training and Supply of Teachers – 'The Demand and Supply of Teachers 1960-1980: The future pattern of the education and training of teachers'. A major inquiry into the effects of streaming in junior schools by the NFER. *Anderson Committee Report* – published. *Henniker Heaton Committee* set up (day release).
1963	Edward Boyle	London Government Act, Remuneration of Teachers Act. Children and Young Persons Act, Industrial Training Bill.	1/63 Industrial Building and Consortia. 4/63 Uniformity of all Advanced Course Grants. 5/63 School Dinner and Mid-day Supervision. 9/63 CSE.	Reconstitution of the English and Welsh Central Advisory Councils. *Plowden and Gittins Committee* set up (primary education). *Robbins Report* – published. *Newsom Report* – published ('Half our Future'). NFER Report on Secondary Education. National Advisory Council on Education for Industry and Commerce – two reports. Working Party under Sir John Lockwood to look into a proposed Schools Council. First Report of the National Advisory Council on Art Education (post-Diploma courses).
1964	Edward Boyle	Industrial Training Act.		Schools Council for the Curriculum and Examinations created to replace the Secondary School Examinations Council – *Lockwood Report.* National Council for Diplomas in Art and Design set up.
March	Quinton Hogg	Public Libraries and Museums Act, Remuneration of Teachers Bill.	10/64 CNAA. 13/64 Schools Council.	*Henniker Heaton Report* – published. National Advisory Council for Education for Industry and Commerce Reports – *Crick and Alexander Reports.* Two further committees set up – further education in agriculture, and the most effective use of technical college resources. CNAA Royal Charter granted. Edward Boyle announces intention to raise school leaving age to sixteen.
October	Michael Stewart	Education Bill (permitting middle schools).		
1965	Anthony Crosland	Remuneration of Teachers Act. Teachers' Superannuation Act. The Pensions (Increase) Act. The Science and Technology Act. Education Act.	7/65 Education of Immigrants. 8/65 A Policy for the Arts. 10/65 Organisation of Secondary Schools.	NFER research into methods of organising comprehensive schools. First Public Schools Commission set up under Sir John Newsom. SSRC created. Woolwich speech on the binary system. Advisory Committee on a university of the air – report. Royal Commission on Medical Education under Lord Todd.

Year	Minister	White Papers, Acts, Select Committees	Circulars	Other events, reports, etc.
1966	Anthony Crosland	Education Bill (voluntary schools). White Paper: 'A Plan for Polytechnics and Other Colleges'. Local Government Act. White Paper: 'University of the Air'. National Insurance Act.	2/66 Management Studies in Technical Colleges. 9/66 Co-ordination of Education Health and Welfare Services. 11/66 Technical College Resources, Size of Classes, and Approval of Further Education Courses. 27/66 Overseas Students.	*Hunt Committee* established (immigrants and the youth service). A Committee on Manpower Resources for Science and Technology set up under Sir Willis Jackson. *Dainton Committee* – set up (supply of candidates for higher education in science and technology).
1967	Anthony Crosland	Education Act. Teachers' Superannuation Act. PAC Report: Parliament and Control of University Expenditure.	8/67 Immigrants and Youth Service. 11/67 School Building Programme in EPAs.	National Libraries Committee set up. *Seebohm Report* published. *Plowden Report* – published.
September	Patrick Gordon Walker	Education Bill. Devaluation.		Creation of National Council for Educational Technology. *Hunt Report* – published. *Sutherland Report* – published (creation of council for scientific policy). Government announcement: Planning Committee. Open University set up.
1968	Patrick Gordon Walker		1/68 Corporal Punishment. 6/68 Education Building Programme. Raising of the school leaving age deferred.	*Gittins Report* – published (primary education in Wales). Central Advisory Council for Education (England) Report – 'Children and their Primary Schools'. National Advisory Council on Art Education – special committee under Sir William C. Coldstream. Summerfield Report – published (psychologists in the education service).
April	Edward Short	Education (No. 2) Act (character and size of colleges of education). Race Relations Act. Public Expenditure and Receipts Act (milk). White Paper: 'Local Government in Wales'. Select Committee on Education and Science – HMIs.	14/68 Milk in School Schemes Withdrawal from Secondary Schools. 15/68 Abolition of Non-qualified Teacher Categories. 19/68 Urban Programme.	The responsibility for education of mentally handicapped children in England and Wales transferred from Department of Health and Social Security to the Department of Education and Science. *Weaver Report* – published (students and universities). First Report of Public Schools Commission – published. *Todd Report* – published (medical education). Committee of Enquiry into Education of Handicapped Children set up.
1969	Edward Short	First White Paper: 'Plans for Public Expenditure up to 1971/72'. Pensions (Increase) Act. White Paper: 'Superannuation'. Children & Young Persons Act. The Family Reform Act.	2/69 Urban Programme Phase 2. 8/69 Withdrawal of Qualified Status for Untrained Graduates.	National Libraries Committee Report – published. Com mittee of Enquiry into the Speech Therapy Service. *Haslegrave Committee* set up (committee on technician courses and exams). Open University Planning Committee – published and Royal Charter granted. *Russell Committee* set up (adult education). Dainton Report – implemented. Youth Service

		School leaving dates. Select Committee on Education and Science (students and their relations).		Development Council Report – published ('Youth and Community Work in the '70s'). NFER – survey on eleven and fifteen year olds. Report made to the Schools Council and the SCUE on the reform of sixth form examinations.
1970	Edward Short	Education Bill (to empower the Secretary of State to submit plans for the reorganisation of secondary education on comprehensive lines – still considered when Parliament was dissolved in May). Education (School Milk) Act (junior school children in middle schools to have free milk). Select Committee on Education and Science (training of teachers – did not have time to report). Expenditure Committee Report.		Second Report of the Public Schools Commission published.
June	Margaret Thatcher	White Paper on public expenditure in education put into effect in 1971. White Paper: 'Transfer of Functions (Wales) Order 1970' (Sec. of State for Wales responsible for primary and secondary education). Education (Handicapped Child) Act. Chronically Sick and Disabled Persons Act. Education (Superannuation) Bill.	5/70 School Milk. 7/70 Government and Conduct of Establishments of Further Education. 10/70 Replace 10/65. 17/70 Integration of Special Education with other forms of Education. 9/70 Third Phase of Urban Programme.	James Committee set up (education, training and probation of teachers). Haslegrave Report – published and accepted. Coldstream Report – published.
1971	Margaret Thatcher	Education (Milk) Act. White Paper: 'The British Library'. Green Paper: 'A Framework for Government Research and Development'. White Paper: 'Public Expenditure 1975-76'. The Pensions (Increase) Act. Select Committee on Education and Science – teacher training. Select Committee on Expenditure – control and educational expenditure.	3/71 Revised Arrangements for School Meal Charges. 13/71 School Milk for Under Sevens Only. 8/71 Raising the School Leaving Age to Sixteen.	Advisory Committee on Handicapped Children Report – published. James Report – published. Two reports: (1) 'Organisation and Management of Government' – Rothschild Report. (2) 'The Future of the Research Council System' – Dainton Report.

Year	Minister	White Papers, Acts, Select Committees	Circulars	Other events, reports, etc.
1972	Margaret Thatcher	White Paper: 'A Framework for Expansion'. Local Government Act. White Paper: 'Public Expenditure 1976-77'. White Paper: "A framework for Government Research and Development'. Superannuation Act. Education Act (Further Education).	3/72 Provisions of Milk & Meals (Amendment) Regns. 1972. Remission of School Dinner Charges. 4/72 Education: A Framework for Expansion.	Report of the Committee of Enquiry into the Education of Visually Handicapped Children - published. Committee of Enquiry into Reading and the Use of English set up - *Bullock Committee*. Committee into the Speech Therapy Service - published.
1973	Margaret Thatcher	Select Committee on the Education of Immigrants reported. Education (Work Experience) Act. Employment and Training Act (establishment of manpower services commission). Education Act (charities and religious education). NHS Reorganisation Act. Child Employment Act.	1/73 & 8/73 Reorganisation of Local Government. The Education Function and the Establishment of Education Committees. 2/73 Expansion of Nursery Education. 7/73 Plans for the Expansion of Higher Education in the Non University Sector by 1981.	*James Report* - qualified acceptance. *Russell Report* - published. New Advisory Board set up to replace the Council for Scientific Policy.
1974			1/74 School Health Service.	
March	Reg Prentice	Takes office.	4/74 Withdrawal of 10/70. 7/74 Work Experience.	Pelham Report - published (scales of salaries for the teaching staff of colleges of education).

Source: Annual Reports from the Ministry of Education and the DES.

felt. These attitudinal and social changes were reflected in education by the circulars announcing the expansion of further education, by the building of as many as two new schools every day, by the changes in government of institutions and demands for public participation.

Eccles rode on this tide. He wanted to improve rather than to radically change the system. He found that expansion was favoured in general terms but that no one was clear about how to use the money [2]. But the improvement was remarkable: 'The school building programme for 1960/61 marks the beginning of five years' increased effort to improve the quality of primary and secondary education. Large building programmes are in hand for technical education, for the training of teachers and for other educational services' [3]. In 1956 he had announced plans for the reorganisation of rural schools, a relatively cheap reform (perhaps £50 million in capital expenditure) which appealed to him as a county member. Technical education was more important although hardly a vote catcher except for the self-made man then entering Conservative politics, but it had appeal for a government nervous about Britain's competitive position. He persuaded Churchill to let resources flow by telling him that the Russians had twenty times as many places in technical education as did Britain [4]. From the 1956 White Paper onwards, there was a persistent flow of circulars on virtually every aspect of further education. And from the circulars issued in 1960 [5] one can see a procession of policies – of more teachers, of provision for the youth service, of better awards for students, of larger building programmes. In his period of office, the first thoughts about expanding higher education were expressed.

Eccles, as did Edward Boyle later, widened public interest in, and Conservative support for, education. They talked to the constituencies about the levelling-up of opportunities. Eccles provoked a warning from the Prime Minister to be more careful when he told a Conservative Party Conference, 'all those women in hats', that they should send their children to maintained primary schools.

Eccles worked comfortably within the 1944 Act, which was both expansionist and non-partisan. To him, teaching standards were more important than structure and he sponsored the boom in teacher supply and the large building programme. Even in retrospect, in 1974, he thought that the eleven-plus was an issue only in the towns; and that the farmers liked secondary modern schools and preferred them to the 'rat holes' of old-fashioned and small grammar schools.

C

As Eccles put it, during the debate on the Crowther Report (1 March 1960):

'... I expected [the Report] would tell us that the post-war revolution in employment and the spread of wealth should modify, perhaps radically, the pattern of educational advance which seemed right at the beginning of the war. But the Council did not take that view. The report endorses, with the utmost conviction, the principles of educational reform laid down in the 1944 Act.'

And so it did [6].

So Eccles was able to give an optimistic account of progress in the service. Voluntary staying-on in the secondary schools was on the increase. The people were voting for education with their feet: 'HM inspectors are repeatedly telling me of schools where staying on suddenly becomes a fashion. First, the able children and those from the more responsible homes take the lead and set the example. It catches on.'

There were, indeed, a few premonitions of changes to come. In the Crowther debate, Eccles referred to 'the race to get to university which is doing great harm ... the conclusion is inescapable. Many more university places must be available ... even if it means sacrifices in other directions, the money must be found for education ... education is the response which a free society makes to the claims of each individual child to be cared for, not for what he produces, but for what he is. We must remain a strong nation.'

In the same year, there were other indications of changes to come. Jo Grimond demanded a royal commission on the universities [7], as did Eirene White later in the year, and Eccles promised an inquiry. George Thomas thought 'that the sixties are bound to be the teenagers' decade'. Eirene White, indeed, was the most systematic critic of the time of the Government's refusal to plan educational advance: 'activity is no substitute for policy', she said, and was particularly critical of the lack of coherence in policy as between universities, teachers' colleges and colleges of advanced technology. Other criticisms were sporadic: James Boyden on maintenance allowances for older school pupils, Eirene White on the size of classes, Fergus Montgomery on the raising of the school leaving age, Anthony Greenwood on sanitary conditions in primary schools and the proportion of the national income spent on education, the supply of teachers, expansion of further education for industry, expansion of nursery education and equal opportunity.

There were sporadic attacks on the independent schools and an eccentric attack on school design by Sir Frank Markham (about this time British primary school design was acclaimed at the Milan Triennale). There was a flurry of attacks on political inquiries made about pupils at the William Ellis school and a debate about the supply of text books.

But towards the end of the year [8] the Parliamentary Secretary could express the Government's expectation for education. 'We are now having to reinforce the success of the earlier education drive which began some years ago and which is now producing as its fruits an intensified demand for more and better education everywhere in the country.' Earlier Eccles had predicted that poverty would be abolished in the next decade.

Thus the debates recall several concerns in the whole society – for more teachers, for better buildings, for more university places. The objectives were those of economic advancement and of personal development. What was missing was the plea for redistribution and any clear analysis of the relationships between the economy and educational advance.

It has been recalled elsewhere [9] how Edward Boyle became Minister in July 1962 in a period of determined expansion, although dominated by economic crisis. The relationship between education and economic growth was not doubted. In 1962 educational expenditure exceeded £1,000 million for the first time. It increased from 3·2 per cent of the gross national product in the mid-1950s to 5 per cent in 1965 and 6 per cent in 1969 [10]. Boyle assumed that curriculum and organisational development could meet changes in social needs and that the schools could develop to meet the expansion of knowledge.

Additional money for teacher training, the appointment of the Plowden and Gittins committees on primary education, a large increase in the Ministry's research fund and in school building programmes (including nearly £30 million to be set aside for improvements in primary and secondary education), the adoption, in 1963, of the recommendations of the Robbins Report 'as an opportunity to set the course of higher education in this country for a generation': all these were evidence of general expansion. 'Courses of higher education should be available for all of those who are qualified by ability and attainment to pursue them', said Robbins and, in 1964, the Government announced its intention to raise the school leaving age to sixteen.

Boyle was essentially non-doctrinal about the key issue of selection in secondary education. 'We no longer regard any pattern of organisation as "the norm" compared with which all others must be stigmatised' [11]. It was not, of course, so radical a policy as his own critics thought, for comprehensive education is indivisible. But he was the last minister in the first of our major periods, from *1955 to 1964,* which was one of expansion, consolidation and optimism, in which the policies of the 1944 Act (with the exception of nursery education, compulsory day release, county colleges and adult education) were systematically pursued, and without too many doubts about social and economic objectives.

The second phase, from *1964 to 1968,* begins with two important episodes: the Robbins Report and all that it implied for the scale and structure of higher education, and the advent of the Labour Government in 1964. Robbins built on the simple concept of opportunity and social redistribution by proposing expansion without completely sponsoring mass, let alone universal, higher education. Although not overwhelmingly radical in its assumptions, the change in the scale of higher education affected the government of education both in terms of the relationships between institutions and central government and in terms of the internal government of universities and colleges. Indeed, the expansion of higher education had more dramatic effects than the potentially more radical policies of comprehensive secondary education promulgated in Circular 10/65 or the proposals for educational priority areas and urban aid.

In expanding higher education and establishing the binary system, through which thirty university-level polytechnics were placed in the public sector in an uncertain parallelism with expanded universities, the Labour Government established an uneasy amalgam of belief in public utility, as stated by Crosland and the more fervent protagonists of the polytechnics [12], and elitism in the universities. The growth of student numbers brought consequences in terms of costs, institutional size and, perhaps, student behaviour that flared into the troubles of 1968, the declining student demands of the 1970s, and the rupture of long-held understandings between government and the universities in 1973 and 1974.

The universities, so long the 'pampered darlings' [13] of Whitehall, which were allowed to cater for an elite and not to account in any detail for the cost, became larger and costlier and, at the same time, subject to challenges about their purposes. The sense of being an elite was diluted by their own growth in student numbers and, indeed, of universities. Their monopoly was challenged by the polytechnics. MPs and Whitehall became progressively questioning about their accountability.

As we record in Chapter 10, the DES and the UGC became more directly prescriptive from 1966, and by 1974 the resource control over universities had become at least as firm as that of the DES over polytechnics.

Higher education was a major zone of change. The expansion of it and the creation of the polytechnics, and the promotion of the comprehensive school and the first attempts to create educational priority areas, all demonstrate how the Labour Government took up expansionist policies already prepared by their Conservative predecessors but also how in terms of policies relating to social distribution they broke the consensus of two decades. The continuities were those of education being an indisputed good. The new and discontinuous policies were based on contentious social and economic rather than received educational premises. And with the Labour Government there were, at least under Crosland, premonitions of change in style. The interest groups were fully consulted but so was the social science intelligentsia. The Central Advisory Councils which had sustained educational liberalism for forty years were discontinued, though not before they legitimised educational sociology and its redistributive connotations. The planning branch of the DES began work if on an admittedly weak start.

It is true that economic difficulties, the fact that expansionist programmes were already under way so that new thinking was less evident, and the change of ministers all had their effect once Crosland had gone. From the list of DES circulars (see Chart II) it is clear that demands for teachers' control over corporal punishment [14], on the banning of untrained teachers in the schools [15], on the negotiations for a teachers' general council, were being met as Edward Short, after a brief period when Patrick Gordon Walker was in office, got into his stride.[1]

Finally, when Mrs Thatcher came into office in 1970, there was a further breaking up of the elements of consensus. Free school milk and subsidies for school meals were abolished or reduced, and the parties divided again on the issue of comprehensive education. At

[1] 'For Edward Short had been a serving teacher, was an NUT member and a Union-sponsored MP. Only his personal commitment to improving the status of the profession opened the way to a Teachers' General Council, and this in spite of continued opposition to any loss of Departmental power among his own permanent office staff.' – R. D. Coates, *Teachers' Unions and Interest Group Politics* (CUP, 1972).

the same time, rigour of a new sort was reaching Whitehall. The 1970 White Paper on central government reorganisation [16] set the stage for programme analysis review and the 1972 White Paper was framed in much the same style of analysis [17]. It was not inherently restrictive, but within it higher education manifestly had to make its case for resources; programmes were to be related to explicit purposes. And in 1973 the most severe economic blizzard since the war finally brought the movement of educational optimism and expansion to an end. Not only did higher education have to justify its place but also live within tighter margins, and this at a time when the numbers getting A-levels and student demand for places were reduced reciprocally with the downturns in economic activity.

Thus we remark four divisions within our period: from 1946, but more particularly from 1955, to 1964 was the period of growth and consolidation; from 1964 to 1968 was the period of new types of expansion and egalitarian policy; from 1968 to 1970, Labour consolidated itself but pessimism became apparent; and from 1970 to 1974 the favourable climate surrounding education came to an end.

CHANGING VALUES

The main policy movements related to major changes in ideology and values. The concept of educational equality responded to changes in assumptions about educational testing, about the nature of measured intelligence (particularly as it affected selection for secondary education), concepts of educability in the population, and related assumptions about the power of the environment over educational performance. The movements in thought about the relationship between education and the economy, and about participation in institutional government, were all evident in the 1960s and early 1970s.

These changes in thinking justified changes in policy on access to higher education and on the organisation of secondary education, and encouraged the growth of policies of positive discrimination through educational priority areas, and the changes in staff, student and parent representation in the different types of educational institutions.

Others have recounted well [18] how the concept of the 'G factor' (general intelligence which can be identified despite the environmental husks within which it is hidden) was taken to justify eleven-plus tests and, more broadly, the 'soft' concept of equality

which allows for equal opportunity but not for equalisation of provision. It seemed natural, until the early 1960s, that few pupils
should be selected for full academic secondary education and an
even smaller minority go on to higher education. These assumptions
were attacked vigorously first by Fred Clarke, a friend of Karl
Mannheim, and the first chairman of the post-war Central Advisory
Council [19]. Later in the 1950s, the sociologists, particularly Jean
Floud, A. H. Halsey and Michael Young [20], were showing that
testing caused even more grammar school places to be taken by
children from the higher socio-economic groups, and that children
responded to teacher expectations and the judgements incorporated
in selection.

Psychologists took up the same theme in showing how measured
intelligence was variable for individuals as between times of testing
and that a margin of error of fifteen points shows itself between the
ages of seven and fifteen [21]. This evidence was fundamental to
the Plowden Committee's proposals for positive discrimination.

On educational testing and selection, social scientists were among
the agents of change. But teacher opinion also had an effect.
Teachers within the Labour Party [22] tried to impress ministers
in the late 1940s and Labour Party annual conferences until Labour
were returned in 1964. The Labour Party document *Learning to
Live* (1959) was drafted by Michael Stewart and others before the
election. Yet some MPs, including apparently Harold Wilson, did
not really support comprehensive schools which were still 'vote
losers' [23]. Earlier on, neither Ellen Wilkinson nor George
Tomlinson in the late 1940s had disturbed the development of
secondary education as a tripartite, selective system. A few local
authorities such as Middlesex in the late 1940s and London,
Coventry, Birmingham and Manchester tested the Government by
putting up comprehensive schemes, few of which were allowed to go
through unchanged. Comprehensive schools became thinkable when
a few London comprehensive schools, under such distinguished
heads as Margaret Miles and Molly Green, showed what they could
do. Even Barbara Castle, usually on the left of the Labour Party,
argued for a better grammar school rather than for a comprehensive
school in her constituency. She raised, on the Adjournment on 1
March 1960, the question of the building of a technical grammar
school in her constituency, Blackburn, and said:

'The big discrepancy between standards in our own state technical
and grammar schools and those obtained at the independent Queen

Elizabeth Grammar School was part of a very bad principle that the
state grammar school should be the "Cinderella" of education compared with the independent school which is getting resources from
private industry for its educational needs.'

In this, she participated in the general failure to attack divisiveness
[24].

THE ENVIRONMENT OF SOCIAL AND ECONOMIC POLICY

One commentator on comprehensive education [25] has typified
the period from the 1920s to the early 1950s as the period when the
psychologists were in power, and the period from the early 1950s to
the end of the 1960s as the period when the environmentalists took
over.

The environmentalists' arguments affected policy in two ways.
First, they laid the foundation for the ending or softening of selection on the grounds that those not selected for grammar schools or
for higher education were the victims of their environment rather
than their genes, and that, by the same token, good educational
environments could enhance their educational performance by giving them an opportunity 'to acquire their intelligence', in the words
of Sir Edward Boyle's preface to the Newsom Report. Secondly,
they opened up the arguments for educational priority areas
through which positively discriminatory policies, as first described
in the Plowden Report, would give children an opportunity to redress
the disadvantages of poor general environments. This led to the
schemes administered by A. H. Halsey and others, and financed by
the DES and SSRC.

Now, in the 1970s, Eysenck, Jencks and Jensen in the USA,
arguing from different points of view, have cast doubts on the
ability of the environment to determine performance, and Jencks
has maintained that the school is not able adequately to manipulate
life chances without a far wider set of changes on the whole fabric
of the economy and social distribution. But it was on arguments
such as these, as well as those of the economists, that the Crowther
Report (1959) argued in favour of raising the school leaving age, the
Plowden Report (1967) proposed a large expansion of nursery
education, and the Robbins Report (1963) established student
demand as the firm imperative guiding admission for higher education. And all at a time when the education service itself was
buoyant about its successes. Repeated surveys of reading ability

showed how the onset of more 'progressive' methods in the schools were accompanied by better reading ability in children of seven, eleven and fifteen tested in 1948, 1956 and 1960 [26]. In Robbins's words, the pool of ability was a 'widow's cruse' [27]. The pressure for expansion until the system reached the level of take up predicted for, say, California thus seemed irresistible. No MP or prominent educationalist during our period was prepared to argue for a slowing down of the rate of expansion. The Robbins proposals were soon seen as conservative estimates of the legitimate demands for places and Kingsley Amis's declaration that 'more means worse' was thought to be eccentric and reactionary. Only perhaps some vice-chancellors were uncertain as to what expansion might do to the universities, but no explicit caveats were entered. In 1963, a Year of Education was celebrated by the Council for Educational Advance, a movement largely stimulated and run by the NUT, which had begun during the war and was revived in 1960.

Education thus fed on euphoric optimism about man's perfectibility, on a belief that collective effort could advance social and personal happiness and wellbeing. Even now backbench Labour MPs regard it as an inalienable right [28].

If, however, the sociologists and psychologists made most of the running in finding arguments for educational expansion, it was the economists, always confident of their judgements and the overriding importance of economic argument, who made the policy respectable. The Crowther Report contained the first discussion in official literature of the economic arguments in favour of expanding a social service when it analysed the benefits of raising the school leaving age. The Robbins Report contained a major essay on the relationships between education and economic growth. The Plowden Report tried to justify the better provision of primary and nursery education on the grounds of its likely contribution to a flexible labour force and the benefits of an increased contribution from working mothers.

But by 1968 uncertainty began to be strong and arose from several sources. The first was doubt about the relationship between education and economic growth [29] – whether, for example, the concept of the formation of human capital was useful and, if so, whether education could be related directly to capital growth. Moreover, planners who had assumed that manpower needs could be calculated, and thus used as the framework for detailed educational planning, were shown to be wrong. The behaviour of the labour market and of the economy at large made such predictions unreliable. Doubts began to grow as to whether education did not act more as an incentive to consumption than to production. And the costs of education were seen to be enormous. There were also doubts stemming from concern about the impact of economic expansion on the quality of life [30].

EDUCATIONAL DOCTRINES

At the same time, doubts about the progressive ambience of the British education system became more clamant. An influential group of teachers at the London University Institute of Education [31] expressed doubts about the developmental approach implicit in the Plowden Report. They did not attack informality but the reliance on children's innate curiosity, and argued for a more instrumental concept of education. Their book coincided with the less analytic and better publicised Black Papers which expressed opinions overly anti-egalitarian in favour of a formal, elitist and differentiated pattern of education [32]. As one Conservative front-bencher put it [33], the arguments about comprehensive education seemed different in 1974 than they had in 1964. Why not improve selection rather than destroy it?

The reaction to consensual liberalism was at least in part a result of individual preferences of ministers. One backbench MP [34] thought that ministers had always been more in favour of comprehensive education than had their Conservative backbenchers. Tory MPs believed, it was said, in a system which would retain selective elements but not predominantly so [35]. Such a minister as Edward Boyle became regarded as a 'soft' Conservative who had led policy into channels not consistent with underlying Tory ideals. There should be a strong move towards restricting comprehensive education to schemes related to adequate and perhaps purpose-built school buildings. Large schools were, in any event, no longer acceptable – a movement of opinion widely shared. One former Labour minister had, in fact, been uncertain about them in the early 1960s [36].

While Tory MPs accepted the received wisdom that the curriculum was not the business of ministers nor the DES nor even LEAs but head teachers, there was now a general swell of opinion against permissive methods and open schooling, as revealed particularly in the press in 1973 and 1974 [37].

The general mood, reacting against the optimistic reports of successive ministers and Central Advisory Councils, was accentuated by reports of difficulties, if not breakdown, in the secondary schools. Some London schools reported pupil absences of up to 50 per cent in the fifth and newly compulsory year. Stories of playground riots, vandalism in schools and, indeed, out of it as well, during school hours, added to the belief that liberal doctrines needed to be reversed.

INSTITUTIONS AND GOVERNANCE

Further doubts resulted from changes in the uneasy area of educational governance. When education was unchallenged as a social and economic good, or as a conveyor of personal autonomy, the client was prepared to accept the political assumptions of a formal education system. Well-intentioned parents were willing that their children should be socialised, and instructed, in the best ways of making a living through the agency of the school. As certainty faded, and as more general participative trends got underway, the school's right to prescribe education came under challenge from those who believed that parents should have a strong voice in the government of schools.

Other doubts were the product of those who challenged the fundamentals of institutionalised education. Some of the more extreme doubts were the product of an unreflecting and dour neo-Augustinianism that saw no good in any earthly institution held together by ties of shared, and hence limiting, commitments, or by the ties of institutional authority. Some, deriving from the new sociological criticism, raised important issues about the viability of the knowledge and skills that were handed on, and about the ways in which knowledge is affected by the ways it is created, transmitted and legitimated through examination systems, teacher control and other status systems. Teachers have a virtual dictatorship over the curriculum [38] and some, including liberal rather than radical parents, think it time to loosen their hold. The schools are seen to hand on and inculcate social values concerned not only with moral and religious precepts but also with children's futures in a bureaucratised and industrialised society [39]. The educational process's part in socialisation and bureaucratisation became the commonplace of sociology teaching throughout the universities and polytechnics. These doubts about the educational process affect concepts of institutional power, membership and roles of governing bodies, and teacher–pupil relationships.

These radical doubts have always been present in radical thinking in Britain. They troubled the Left in the 1930s. But they took on a peculiar power in the late 1960s and early 1970s because they could be mediated through a vastly expanded student population in far less well defined and more uncertain higher education institutions. It is not surprising then that, as we shall see later, the National Union of Students, in initiating challenges to institutional authority on the place of students in governing institutions and on the examination and admission processes, should prove to be one of the most potent of the interest groups. The assumption that the education system will maintain itself under the loosely-prescribed controls of the local authorities and the DES or the governing councils of universities has been tested by student politicians in the universities and in the polytechnics and, to a lesser extent, in the colleges of education.

Finally, the whole expansionist egalitarian movement of the 1960s was changed by the appointment of Margaret Thatcher. In the words of one of her former colleagues, 'she was not disposed to listen' to the unalloyed liberalism of the education service. Her appointment brought in more rigorous testing of purposes, as in the explicitly analytic approach of the 1972 White Paper, which was part of general government trends. And she decisively moved priorities from higher to primary and nursery education.

These changes of sentiment and policy were important challenges to the predominantly liberal Conservatives who dominated educational debate throughout the late 1940s and 1950s.

In setting the historical background to the analysis of policy and interest groups which follows, we have attempted to relate the official events recorded in Chart I to the changes in values and to the changes in intellectual, and particularly social science, perceptions of education and its institutions. These changes took place at great speed in the 1960s, and were no doubt hastened by the advent of a Labour Government after thirteen years of Conservative rule. If many of the changes were articulated and identified by the intelligentsia, we emphasise that less clearly identified forces within the teaching profession, within the ranks of the local and central government administrators, and within the inspectorates, also played their part. And both government and intellectuals interplayed with politicians in Parliament and in local authorities and with the main educational interest groups. Changes in value thus reflected as well as activated changes in events.

Chapter 3

The Objectives and Policies of Education, 1960–1974: A Classification

Between 1960 and 1974, then, there were several movements in educational policy which can be read in the speeches and public acts of ministers, in circulars and in reports. These policies can now be classified and related to the parts played by the main actors in educational policy-making.

A CLASSIFICATION OF POLICY

Chart II contains a list of policy themes: Column 1 shows the underlying values and objectives of educational policies; Column 2 shows some thirty-five policy trends in our period which the values underlie; Column 3 shows the detailed events through which the policies were effected.

The basis of these statements should be made clear. Interviewees were asked what they considered to be the main policy movements in this period. The results of these interviews were somewhat selective and arbitrary but gave a wide range of perspectives. Then some selected and particularly knowledgeable witnesses were asked whether Charts I and II seemed to them to be an adequate depiction of movements in the period.

Every Parliamentary Question and ministerial announcement and statement made in Parliament during this period was analysed (*see* Chapter 9). These were not an exhaustive indication of policy movements although, of course, they have an intrinsic importance of their own (which we discuss later), and they helped build up the inventory of policies for us. The most reliable statements at the national level (and determinants of major policies at the local level),

Chart II: Values, Policies and their Supporters

Types of policy	Policy trends	Main events	Supporters	Opponents	Period of impact of policy
Educational and social	1 Development of adult education	Ashby Report (1954). Russell Report (1973).	All. But no action sanctioned	None	Continuous
Educational and social	2 Expansion of nursery education	Ministry's refusal to expand (Circular 8/60) – minor concessions.	DES official policy. NSA, NUT, local authorities, parental pressure		1945 onwards
		Plowden Report (1967) – plan for expansion. White Paper (1972) – decision to expand.		Local authorities and NSA against government boost to voluntaries	1967 onwards Continuous pressure leading to a favourable policy
Educational and social	3 Development of youth service	Circulars 3/60 and 17/61 – Building programmes. Circular 11/60 – the establishment of courses for youth leaders. Circular 12/62 – training of part-time youth leaders.	All	None	Select Committee on Estimates – criticism of ministry's cynicism (1957). Albermarle Report (1959) leads to changes in policies Continuous
Educational, social and institutional	4 Development of special education	Increased provision to meet the new identification of needs, e.g. Circular 10/62 – Children with Impaired Hearing. Integration with other forms of education, e.g. Circular 15/70 – Transfer of Mentally Handicapped Children to Education from Health; and transfer of handicapped sixteen to nineteens from social services to education (both covered by 1970 Act).	All, NUT	None	Continuous since 1950s
			Special education association biennial conferences, teachers' associations		Relatively recently (much post-war building for specialist treatment)
Educational, social, economic and institutional	5 Expansion of technical and other further education, and organisational consequences	Percy Report (1945). White Paper (1956). Circular 1/59 – Technical Education – the Next Step. Circular 5/59 – Further Education for Commerce Expansion; representatives of industry and commerce on governing bodies. Circular 7/59 – governing bodies to include	General support from local authorities, ATTI, CBI, TUC, APTI	No dissent	A continuous set of policies deriving from the Percy Report. A period of strengthening, of a relatively new institutional structure

Policy area	Events / description	In favour	Doubts / opposition	Dates / notes
	commercial and industrial representation. White Paper (1961) and Circular 1/61 – Better Opportunities in Technical Education – technicians and craftsmen education. Circular 3/61 – Regional Colleges; an infra-structure under the CACs. Circular 10/64 – Establishment of CNAA. Circular 14/64 – Henniker-Heaton – Report on day release. Administrative Memoranda 4/64 and Industrial Training Act 1964. Circular 2/66 – Management Studies in Technical Colleges. 1965 Woolwich speech – the binary system.	Crosland quotes ATTI, local authority associations	Doubts in Labour Party	Discontinuity of policy as higher education expansion raises issues about the 'top end' of the system
	Circular 8/66 – A Policy for Polytechnics and Other Colleges. Circular 11/66 – Pilkington Report. Circular 7/70 – Government of Colleges of Further Education.	ATTI, local authority associations		
	White Paper (1972 – continued expansion; and Circular 7/73.	ATTI, DES	Local authority associations doubts	
6 Educational and institutional School building expansion and planning	Circular 6/60 – expansion on all fronts in building programmes. Architects and Buildings Branch bulletins on design. Circular 1/63 – Industrial Building and Consortia.	Everybody (from mid-1950s)	More or less quiescent by mid-1950s	1950 onwards
7 Educational and institutional Teacher supply and distribution planning. Expansion of teacher force	Creation of teacher quota system. Circular 14/59 – extension of teacher quota. NAC reports and the development of teacher supply policies and administrative structure; Reports 1–9 concerned with wholesale expansion of service. Circulars issued regularly on policy for supply and distribution of teachers.	All main interest groups are in favour		1956 onwards
	White Paper (1972) – reduction and structural assimilation of teacher training.	NUT, ATCDE, CHUDE, UCET		1972 onwards

Types of policy	Policy trends	Main events	Supporters	Opponents	Period of impact of policy
Educational and institutional	8 Content and status of teacher education	McNair Report (1944) – recommended 3 year courses. Extension to three years (1960). Robbins Report (1963) – Creation of B.Eds. Plowden recommended enquiry (1967). Select Committee on Teacher Education (1970). Edward Short's ATO enquiry (1970). James Committee set up (1970). James Report (1973). Closure of colleges proposed (1974).	DES	ATCDE, NUT, university education departments, CHUDE	1963 onwards Discontinuous: 1972 onwards
Educational and social	9 Raising the school leaving age to 16	1944 Act. ROSLA (1948). Boyle's announcement (1964). 1972/73 decision – Cabinet deferral (1969).	Successive CACs, TUC, CBI. All local authority associations, NUT, Joint Four, all political parties	NAS (from late 1960s). Some other educationists had doubts	From 1944 Act, but recommended in pre-war reports. A continuous policy
Educational	10 'Open schooling'. Child-centred learning	No specific formulation of policies, but Plowden, Newsom and Crowther confirmation of assumptions.	NUT and NSA, colleges of education, local authorities (as in evidence to Plowden), HMIs, ACE, CASE	Black Papers, Association for the Defence of Academic Standards, NAS, *Perspectives on Plowden*, R. S. Peters, ed. (1968)	A policy gaining strength from the 1930s A continuous policy
Educational	11 Introduction of more structured school curriculum	(i) Introduction of Nuffield Science, Mathematics and Modern Language Teaching. Teachers' Centre (from mid-1960s). Taken up by the Schools Council. (ii) EPA curricula and Halsey's seven points for disadvantaged and associated action research. *See* 18.	Nuffield Foundation, the science establishment, DES, HMIs. (Later Schools Council) DES, EPA researchers (Bernstein, Halsey, Midwinter)	Some early doubts in teacher associations Plowden. Doubts in 'Froebelian' educational group	1961 onwards New From 1967 to present
Educational and institutional	12 Reformulation of art education	Summerson Report (1944). Coldstream Report (1970). Gann Report (1974).			A 'new' policy

		Policy measures	Interested parties / pressures	Comment
Educational	13 Establishment of middle schools	Circular 7/73 – Absorption into Polytechnics. Education Act (1964) and Circular 12/64.	West Riding made the running, Plowden Report recommendations	From Leicestershire Plan onwards (late 1950s) (rephasing of primary and secondary phases)
Educational and institutional	14 Secondary examinations	Circular 9/61 – consolidation of policies on GCE O and A levels. Beloe Report on CSE (1961). Circular 9/63 – establishment of CSE and regional structure, Modes 1, 2 and 3. Butler and Briault proposals (1970) – one examination at 16.	Ministry and SSEC reluctance. Teachers pressing for CSE examinations. Some local authorities not wanting a centralised system	The issues embodied in these movements have been a recurrent preoccupation of the service. Institutionally important because of questions of university and teacher control, and of local authority place in CSE arrangements
Social	15 Comprehensive education	Moves from late 1940s by Middlesex, London, Manchester, Birmingham and other local authorities. 'Learning to Live' (1959) – Labour Party Policy Statement. House of Commons motion against selective education (21 January 1965). Circular 10/65. Circular 10/70. Reg Prentice's announcements of policies (1974). Circular 4/74.	Labour local authorities, Labour Party teachers, Labour Party from 1959, NUT from 1966, Campaign for Comprehensive Education. All change. Local authority associations opposed action in 1970 because consultation was thought to be inadequate	Conservative Party, Campaign for Educational Standards. From 1940s period of slow advance until Crosland's circular of 1965 and its reversal in 1970. A strongly discontinuous policy
Social	16 Control or abolition of private education	Implementation of Part III of the Act (1955). Crosland sets up Public Schools Commission (1966). Proposal for removal of direct grants and tax concessions (1974).	All, Section III of 1944 Act. Labour Party, Fabians, NUT. HMC, Conservative Party, CBI	No impact as yet. Labour Party policy since 1930s. Discontinuous

D

Types of policy	Policy trends	Main events	Supporters	Opponents	Period of impact of policy
Social	17 Awards to students	Anderson Report (1960). Education Act (1962) and Circulars 4/63 and 9/62 – uniformity of all advanced course grants. Circular 7/63 – awards to students on advanced sandwich courses. HND/DIP. H.E. mandatory (1974).	NUS, DES, MP pressure	None, but ministers worked with local authority associations to secure agreement from racalcitrant authorities	Progression since the 1944 Act Continuous
Social	18 Educational priority	Plowden Report (1967), Chapter VI. Seebohm Report (1967). Circular 11/67 – EPA Building Programme. Halsey research programme. Circular 19/68 Urban programme.	Virtually total support	Some disagreement about methods and teachers' role	1967 to the present
Social	19 Education of immigrants	Circular 7/65 – suggests between 1/3 and 1/5 of school population optimum. Select Committee on the Education of Immigrants (1973). White Paper (1974).	DES	At first, teachers reluctant to make special provision at all	From mid-1960s
Social and institutional	20 Creation of polytechnics within a binary system	Woolwich Speech (1965). Lancaster Speech (1967). Circular 8/67. Proposal for Higher Education Commission. White Paper (1972). Circular 7/73.	Labour Party (but divided). ATTI (changed attitudes). Directors of polytechnics, Eric Robinson. Bi-partisan and all denominational	Labour Party (but divided). AUT, NUT, DES. ATTI. Some non-conformist opposition but not systematic	1966 onwards
Institutional	21 Settlement concerning the control and financing of voluntary schools	1944 Act – tripartite system. 1958 Act, 1959 Act – 75% grant for buildings and repairs of transferred and substituted. 1967 Act – schools and colleges of education get increased grant.		None	A continuous policy since 1944 Act
Institutional	22 Teacher control over curriculum and internal school organisation	(i) Defeat of Curriculum Study Group (1964). (ii) Creation of Schools Council (1964); Lockwood Report; Circular 13/64. (iii) Freedom to use corporal punishment sustained – Circular 1/68. (iv) Teacher control over examinations, particularly CSE	Teacher and local authority associations. Teacher and local authority associations. Teacher associations	DES. Plowden Chapter, STOPP, 'liberal' opinion	Since abolition of payment by results in 1898. Sustained by successive Committee and other CAC reports. 1898 to present. A strongly continuous set of policies.

	Objective	Documents / events	Interests	Interests / reactions	Timing
Institutional	23 Freedom and/or accountability for higher education teachers	Student troubles (1968). Craig, Blackburn, Atkinson affairs. Annan Report, 1974.	CAFD, AUT, NUS in favour of difference. CVCP uncertain. MPs' questioning of universities' accountability		1968 onwards
Institutional	24.1 Student demands for participation	1968 disruptions, concordat between vice-chancellors and NUS. Subsequently repudiated by NUS. Select Committee on Student Affairs (1969).	NUS, CAFD	CVCP, AUT have some doubts. Questioning by MPs	A 'new' issue 1968 onwards
	24.2 Student insistence on contractual rights	NUS debates early 60s.			
	24.3 Politicisation of NUS	Presidency of Jack Straw onwards (1968) – see Weaver Report above.			A 'new' trend
Institutional	25 Increased prescription of student numbers and of types of higher education courses	Changing content of quinquennial allocation letters to universities (1966 and 1972). PAC Reports on Audit (1966). Select Committee on Expenditure, Control of Educational Expenditure (1971). White Paper (1972). Education planning paper, and Circulars 7/73 and 7/74.	DES, UGC, local authorities	Universities, AUT, NUS	Arguments begin in 1960s. Policies explicit from Robbins (1963) onwards
Institutional	26 Development of managerial responses to unionisation of the universities	Creation of salary negotiation machinery for non-teaching staff in universities (1968). Creation of salary negotiation machinery (Committees A and B) for university teachers (1970).	CVCP, AUT, technicians	None, but some regrets	From mid-1960s
Social and economic	27 Expansion of the universities	Pressure from intelligentsia (unspecific); SSEC Reports (1962 and 1963). Robbins Report (1963). Successive quinquennial allocations. White Paper (1972).	All interests except for some academics	Some academics. Some unspecified doubts among MPs	From 1963 until 1973
Institutional	28 Supervision of mid-day meal	Circular 6/63 – discussions of conditions under which teachers supervise. Still continuing in 1974. NUT strikes (1969). Broader implications for professional commitment are taken up.	Ministry, teacher associations, local authority associations		Continuous pressure for changes such as this

Types of policy	Policy trends	Main events	Supporters	Opponents	Period of impact of policy
Institutional	29 Insistence on teachers' qualifications	Circular 15/68 – abolition of non-qualified teacher categories. Circular 18/69 – withdrawal of qualified status for untrained graduates.	NUT (Edward Short's support)	Local authorities reservations	Continuous pressure for changes such as this
Institutional	30 Teacher participation in government of higher education	Circular 7/59 – governing bodies (said nothing about teacher or student representation). Circular 2/67 – colleges of education; creation of academic boards, teacher and student representation. Weaver Report (1968). 1968 (No. 2) Act – governing bodies no longer sub-committees of local authorities. Circular 7/70 – government and conduct of further education. Teacher and student representation. AUT a party to salary negotiations (1966).	(Of increased participation) AUT, ATTI, ATCDE		1967 onwards
Economic with social implications	31 Free school milk and subsidised school meals reviewed	Circular 3/71 – Revised arrangements for school meals. Charges increased. Circular 13/71 – School milk for under sevens only.	Conservative Government	Labour Party, teachers' associations	Conservative Government 1970-1974 Discontinuous
Economic	32 Differential fees for overseas students Welfare of overseas students in technical colleges	Circular 2/63. Circular 27/66.	DES responding to treasury pressure	CVCP, NUS	From 1966 Discontinuous
Educational and social	33 Extended school day	Successive CAC Reports.	All but some doubts about increased pressure on teachers		Continuous
Institutional and economic	34 Increased unionisation of teachers	Teachers' strikes increased (from 1961). NUT Rank and File Movement (1968). ATTI (1967), NAS (1968), NUT (1971) joined TUC.	Some teachers' associations	Local authority associations and Joint Four	Discontinuous
Institutional and social	35 Broader participation in local government	Parental and teacher membership of governing and managing bodies.	ILEA decisions in 1970s		

however, were the flow of ministry and DES circulars and administrative memoranda during the period, and they, too, were analysed. Nothing, except in the area of university government, that appears in parliamentary papers fails to appear in circulars and administrative memoranda – which are, of course, considered and determinant statements of ministry intentions. Every White Paper, for example, is promulgated to the educational system by circulars, except when local authorities are not involved. We concluded, therefore, that we were safe to take circulars and administrative memoranda, and equivalent ministry or DES and UGC statements on universities, as the main source of our analysis of national policies.

These empirical data were then related to broad categories of values and major objectives. Such categories are evidently both arbitrary and open to any test of falsification that the reader may wish to apply. The summary of values and objectives was based in part on some of the main authorities in this field – at the analytical level on Paul Hirst and Richard Peters [1] and, more recently, on Julia Evetts [2], as well as on our own reading of consultative committee and CAC reports over the period [3].

From statements of values, policy and policy events the Chart analyses, in Column 4, the reaction of the main educational interests and Parliament to the policies enunciated by the central government. Column 5 shows the time pattern involved, a point relevant to our classification.

CLASSIFICATION OF VALUES

The classification of policies was related to four groups of value bases – 'educational', 'social', 'economic' and 'institutional' values.

Here we must pause to clear the way on a theoretical point that is also important to the values analysis. There are many ways of classifying values and for our purposes we find it useful to distinguish between *basic* and *secondary* (or instrumental or consequential) values [4]. A basic value is one which requires no further defence than that it is held to be right by those who believe it. The concepts of equality or freedom or defence of society or the sanctity of the family may be held as basic values. Basic values may have several defences in terms of, for example, evidence that they lead to good or otherwise desirable consequences, but these are not necessary for their statement or support. Secondary values are defensible by reference to basic values. Thus democracy is a set of instrumental assumptions about how to conduct human transactions that relies for its defence on such basic value assumptions as the desirability of freedom (and democracy safeguards freedom), and the right of the individual to self-expression. The basic values are self-justificatory 'oughts'. The secondary values are concepts that carry the argument into the zone of consequences and instruments and institutions.

Many of the values held in the education service, such as teacher freedom to create the curriculum, are unclear in status. Is professional power a self-justificatory ought, a good in itself? If not, to what basic value does it address itself? Freedom of the teacher, or the creation of conditions in which such self-justificatory oughts as the right of pupils to individual development, freedom of life-style, defence of society, equity of treatment of pupils (which might otherwise be at the whim of political or bureaucratic forces) are furthered, might be the defence. In making our analysis of educational policies we need refer to only a selected group of basic values and their instrumental consequences. In another publication, the author proposed a tentative list of the values basic to general social policy as follows (it is slightly amended here): helping the inadequate; equality; equity; worth of the uniqueness of the individual; sense of community; family; interpersonal values; defence of society; individual effort; self-determination; minimum living standards; choice of life-style; retribution; progress and change; freedom. And the following are instrumental concepts: public burden; selectivity; universality; participation; democracy; social control; residualism; increase or preservation of national resources; punishment; incentives; alienation; institutionalism; deviance. Each of these is defended by one or more basic value.

To return now to our classification of educational policies, it will be seen that the first three – educational, social and economic – relate directly to the basic values, whilst the institutional values require basic values beyond themselves for their defence. This point will be taken up again more fully later.

MIXTURES OF VALUES

Policies may be underpinned by more than one value and it can be difficult to identify the leading value. For example, all 'educational' values have social and economic connotations when they are translated into operational statements of policy. Comprehensive and selective education can be defended on educational or economic or social grounds. But the arguments for comprehensive education in the last twenty years have been predominantly social, and, as a result, its protagonists have been different from, though not necessarily in conflict with, those arguing for an expansion of technical education ('the economy needs it') or open primary schooling ('it makes children happier and educates for freedom and creativity').

TWO CHARACTERISTICS: INSTITUTIONAL ASPECTS AND CONTINUITY

From the analysis of values, we argue, it is possible to reflect on two characteristics important to a discussion of policies: their institutional aspects and their relative continuity.

Policies are the operational statements of values – 'statements of prescriptive intent', 'the authoritative allocation of values', 'programmatic utterances'. We have identified thirty-five of them in our period.

It is possible to see from the list of circulars, administrative memoranda, White Papers and ministers' speeches in Chart II that some policies are continuous, either from the beginnings of the public system or from the 1944 Act; such policies are, for example, the flow of expansionist and consolidating provision for further education, or the continuing actions in defence of teacher control over curriculum or examinations. Others are discontinuous or innovative, such as comprehensive education or educational priority areas or the expansion of universities and the creation of the polytechnics.

If a policy is continuous it can be asked whether this is because it relates to values that can be regarded as immutable in society (because, perhaps, it is related to universal human instincts or needs), or whether it is intrinsically no more 'eternal' or axiomatic than others but has found support in either a strong institutional fabric, such as a system of government or administration, or in a strong profession. For example, policies associated with 'educational' values, which we discuss later, are continuously sustained. This could be either because individual development or autonomy is inherent to British society or because it is reinforced by a fabric of consensual relationships between the DES, the local authority and teacher associations. These relationships have made it possible for values relating to teacher control over curriculum, and professional recruitment over the institutional structure incorporated in local authority power, to stand as continuities against which other new policies have to make their impression.

There are 30,000 educational institutions in England and Wales which have much autonomy and freedom. The heads of them are public figures whose names are on the school note paper and the notice board outside the school. Each of them is allowed to develop organisational and educational styles of his own, and chief education officers are resistant even to the notion that they 'manage' the heads and their schools [5]. This system of delegated authority carried with it a corresponding power system which enables values to be stored and maintained at points sufficiently distant from and impervious to central government or other mechanisms by which society is governed. Pluralism thus sustains educational policies in their continuity in a way not evident in more general social or economic policies, which have to rely on different power connections if they are to make their way in the education service.

Social and economic policies have been discontinuous. Whilst egalitarianism has been a major value throughout British educational history, it took particular forms as policies changed in 1964. Although it is being advanced through means which are educational rather than social in form, such as the EPAs or comprehensive education, it relates explicitly to the 'hard' concept of equality which the Labour Governments of 1964 and 1966 deliberately introduced. Their main purpose was the redistribution of life chances – a social objective. As a result, different power networks came into play. The education service had to contain and assimilate issues coming from outside its own institutional setting. It responded to the policies generated by intellectuals, politicians, researchers and journalists. One example is that before economic and social issues became a key part of arguments about education, *The Times* newspaper hardly carried a report on educational matters before 1967 except for systematic coverage of major reports, university and public school appointments and other announcements, degree classification lists, and open scholarships at Oxbridge colleges. From the Enfield case, in 1967, it eased into the educational field until, in 1974, a political commentator, Ronald Butt, wrote several articles attacking comprehensive schools. The network of interest widened perceptibly. As we will discuss later, R. D. Coates has shown [6] that teacher politics exploded the normal framework of negotiation with the DES and local authorities as salary negotiations became part of general wages and incomes policies.

The other main area of discontinuity or innovation was in the application of economic arguments to education. The Percy Report of 1945, on which the binary system of higher education was eventually built, argued for expansion with no supporting economic arguments or data [7]. As we have seen, fourteen years later the Crowther Report defended the raising of the school leaving age by reference to the need for skilled manpower [8]. Later the Robbins Report (1963) and the Plowden Report (1967) on primary education contained economic justifications for their proposals.

By the late 1950s John Vaizey [9] and other economists had made the case for education as an investment. David Eccles won support for all his policies on the grounds of the nation's needs for competitive advantages in world markets. Now in the 1970s, as the economic justifications for education flake and disintegrate, so does the support of the Treasury-led government economic network. Economic values thus operate in a highly discontinuous fashion and they certainly refer to a network and power system beyond that normally encountered by the DES and the established educational interest groups.

VALUES AND POLICIES IN THE EDUCATION SERVICE

So far, values underlying education have been grouped into over-lapping educational, social, economic and institutional categories. These are not boundary-definable categories but any of the thirty-five policies can be classified in terms of a predominant, rather than an exclusive, value base, or a conjunction involving more than one value base. And congregations of values underlying a single policy (or group of policies) relate to both its continuity or discontinuity and its institutional backing: continuous policies are those which are maintained primarily by the established educational interest groups; whilst generally the discontinuities or innovations which have come largely in the social and economic zones are the results of external interventions. Where the educational interest groups have joined the quest for innovation, particularly in the social area, they have had to do so cautiously so as to sustain internal consensus, and their own institutional assumptions have had to move so as to keep up with new social policies.

Educational Values
Educational values and policies have developed a particular form and institutional framework because of the nature of the basic values themselves, and the technological ways in which they are expressed and put into effect. Educational values which affect the

curriculum and organisation of the educational process, including the internal organisation and relationships of the school, are forms of *basic* values listed on page 54 concerned with the worth of the unique individual, individual effort, self-determination, choice of life-style, progress and change and freedom. This wide range of generality simply emphasises that it is inherently difficult to state the aims of education, and that such statements are particular, or critical, or ambiguous, and potentially in conflict with each other, or at least non-convergent [10]. But teachers must, to survive in their roles at all, be able to hand on, consistently and continuously, what they consider to be the values normal in society. This consistency is not absolute, and not all teachers conform to the prevailing norms of the society that employs them. The consistency is, however, institutionalised through their work organisation, which is that of a large institution, in which the head has a lot of authority, which is established by law and maintained by a publicly elected body, and at which attendance is compulsory. The consensus and consistency are not as strong as in, say, medicine, although health care, more broadly, is as uncertain about its values as is education. And education is not explicit or certain about the desirable qualities it should produce. It also cannot hope for perfect conformity with its clientele, because it 'often consists of putting people in the way of values of which they have never dreamed'. All the same, teachers are more concerned to know where they and their pupils stand than are many other key groups in society.

So teachers and the interest groups which represent them have to select among a wide range of values and policies. In doing so, and in producing an educated person, they inevitably seek to produce a person with knowledge or values that they think to be right. Their associations will defend 'educational' values, which might well be in conflict with those aims of the education service which are related to economic or social or, say, civil rights assumptions.

Thus, to take the example of policies for the educationally deprived – a social rather than an educational set of policies – all can subscribe to the general intentions of educational priority areas. These seek to reinforce educational processes for the deprived so that their life chances will be improved. But, at the operational level, divisions of policy become apparent. For example, the Plowden Report wanted specific material provision for educational priority areas and schools, but assumed that the educational processes which were good for most children, such as in terms of our basic values, would be best for deprived children as well. By contrast others would argue, at one extreme, for the operant conditioning advanced by some American theorists and practitioners [11] and, indeed, some of these assumptions were built into the earlier experiments in educational priority areas in this country. So at this point the *educational* and *institutional* policies of 'an integrated service' – of providing integrated procedures for all children, or encouraging freedom of life style, individual effort and good interpersonal relations – came into conflict with *social* assumptions about ways in which provision might be differentiated for those in most need. When this type of division becomes overt, a second set of differentiations becomes apparent. For the Plowden Committee, and the interest groups which are concerned with the interests of the teachers and of the local authorities, would maintain that teacher interaction with individual pupils is the basis of the best educational practice and should, therefore, determine the decision-making process in education. Institutional values then become divided between those who would maintain that teachers have the know-how and should have the authority to cater for the deprived, and those who maintain that broader social considerations ought to lead to a wider diffusion of authority over the educational decision-making process.

The educational values and policies are thus those of the teachers and their associations, the local education authority administrators, inspectors, and advisers at both central and local levels. The DES officially takes no view on educational matters as such, but will generally support the assumption that authority should rest with the teachers, the schools and the local education authorities in determining educational policies.

The 'educational' values and policies came up for severe testing in the 1960s, particularly from the mid-1960s onwards, when social and economic assumptions began to assert themselves. To make these generalisations a little firmer, some of the values are described in more detail. Within the 'education' values, for example, *individual satisfaction and autonomy* is an imputed doctrine in British education, but particularly in primary schools and universities. It derives from a long tradition of acceptance of the thinking of Froebel, Montessori, Dewey, Susan Isaacs and Piaget as the philosophical pace-setters of the British educational scene. Individual autonomy and personal satisfaction are basic values in their own right. These are things that people want for themselves and care about. But they also are stated as technological precepts about the nature of the educational process and the ways in which children best learn to be skilful and inventive [12]. Thus, as critics of the Plowden Report have pointed out [13], its famous Chapter II evinces a particular biological view of child development which is dominant in British primary schools. It assumes that children bring with them a genetic programme which will enable them to develop only if the environment in which they work is right.

From this, several important consequences flow. Children's interests become central to good education. The world of learning must come to meet them, rather than children coming to meet the world of learning. Pre-ordained curriculum patterns cannot be laid down by an educational system or, for that matter, by teachers, who should provide stimulating environments and resources on which children can draw. These aspects of educational values derive, of course, from wider social values such as freedom. They also help to determine the role structure of the education service. They explain why British schools are less tied to the predetermined, non-developmental, prescribed curriculum of, say, French schools or any other of the European systems, and thus provide the basis for institutional as well as educational values.

This educational set of values and objectives and the related institutional policies are displayed in those policies listed in Chart II which, for example, avoid central prescription of curriculum (No. 22), allow maximum freedom for schools and colleges within the local authorities (Nos 10 and 22), teacher freedom and informality in higher education (Nos 23 and 30), 'open schooling' in teacher–pupil relationships (No. 10), and teacher control over examinations (No. 22(iv)).

Those who hold these values strongly are the teachers' associations, the colleges of education, the dominant group of educational psychologists, HM Inspectors of Schools and, indeed, the whole liberal educational establishment. They are continuous and have a strong institutional base.

Between 1960 and 1974, the major overt statements of policies concerned with educational content and form were declared in reports made to ministers by the CACs. No reader of Crowther, Newsom or Plowden can fail to see that two precepts predominated in them: education shall relate to the pupil's own interests, and relations between pupil and teacher shall be open and free.

In Julia Evetts's terms, the approach was progressive rather than idealist [14]. The policies were affirmed by the main teacher associations in their evidence to the councils.

If, as we have argued, these precepts about pupil–teacher

relations are the technological argument for teacher power, they reinforce policies that are both explicit and operationally important. They account for teacher reluctance over parents' participation or control in the schools, the uncertainties (even among the reformers) about the role of governors and managers in the control of curriculum, and, most resoundingly, the defeat of the Ministry's intention to have a Curriculum Study Group (*see* Chapter 8). These precepts are explicit in examinations policy, as in the creation of the third mode of the Certificate of Secondary Education examinations introduced in 1964, which provided for internal assessments by teachers with external moderation.

So freedom for children becomes freedom for teachers and the schools. This, in its turn, reinforces the more separatist policies which the teacher interest groups created, such as Edward Short's decision to deprive untrained teachers of their jobs, and to allow decisions on the administration of physical pain as a method of control in schools to remain in the hands of teachers [15]. The educational values thus become inextricably tied up with more instrumental concepts of institutional and professional authority.

Social Values

But if teachers are defended in their pursuit of educational values, they are also concerned with processes of socialisation. This, however, bifurcates in its underlying values, for socialisation is concerned with such varied basic values as helping the inadequate, equality, equity, creating a sense of community, family, defending society, increasing national resources and also with creating interpersonal relationships.

In this shadowy area between social and educational values, the institutional framework of education inevitably comes under strain. So some maintain that 'the child living in Britain learns to be a performer of roles, which are not only applicable to his age and sex, but also to his position in the society to which he belongs' [16]. Others within the education service, however, maintain that education should and does socialise for freedom and social mobility, and that its predominant mode is concerned with instilling personal autonomy. Thus the assumed objectives of education as represented in the Gittins Report on Welsh education, in discussing a society where a high value has been placed on education, are those of high social mobility and personal advancement [17].

This set of values, therefore, is subject to a wide range of opinions. 'All schools reflect the views of society, or some section of society, about the ways children should be brought up . . .' [18]. The Plowden Report continues that one obvious purpose is to fit children for the society in which they will grow up. The denominations would certainly urge this as an objective of the education service, so would the Confederation of British Industry, and so would the great majority of parents, who expect their children to 'learn to behave', or even to be disciplined into patterns of behaviour, as surveys of parents' attitudes to corporal punishment have shown [19]. Within the system, the assumptions of socialisation are strong. Attendance at school is compulsory and the period has twice been increased since 1946. Religious education and acts of worship are compulsory so that non-believers have to contract out. Teachers are assumed to be *in loco parentis*. In higher and further education this institutional assumption has been challenged and this is a significant change of the 1960s.

These assumptions of control and socialisation constitute part of the institutional power of the educational system. But they are being challenged from the point of view of a widely diverse series of social values. There are those who now oppose compulsory schooling, the distinctive role of teachers and the authority they carry, and the imposition of productivity values on what should be, they maintain, autonomous educational institutions run by those who study in them [20]. Of the thirty-five policies listed in Chart II, some fifteen have social value bases. And of the social policies, those associated with the social value of *egalitarianism* have been, perhaps, the most important in our period. Social class and other socio-economic factors such as income, housing and the size of family are firmly associated with poor educational performance; although the mechanics of association have been poorly elaborated, so that teachers have little guidance on what to do about them even when they are given more resources. It is now recognised that schools reinforce rather than arrest relative disadvantage even though the performance of the whole school population might have improved. Not all share egalitarian assumptions. For example, while most parents believe in comprehensive schools for the whole population, most want grammar school places for their own children [21]. The ILEA plans for a more effective comprehensive school structure have drawn more protest than support from the upwardly mobile.

In spite of these doubts, however, the studies made in the 1950 and 1965 Douglas Reports, the CAC Reports and the National Child Development Studies [22] all reinforce the substitution of the 'weak' concept of equality by the 'hard' concept. From assuming that society could pay off its obligations to the disadvantaged by equalising opportunity, both political parties accepted policies of positive discrimination, which will give equal provision or even better provision to offset environmental disadvantage.

The policy implications of these views have been major. Selection has begun to be ended at all stages of the system. Educational priority areas first suggested in Chapter VI of the Plowden Report were boosted by both Labour and Conservative Governments, and proposals that underprivileged applicants should have preferential treatment in university entrance have also been advanced [23].

Until recently, egalitarian policies have been accepted by the education service with disagreement about degree rather than principle. Because some of the movements affected existing structures and the interests embodied in them, even the more egalitarian of the established interest groups, such as the NUT, followed rather than led the move towards comprehensives, which began with individual local authorities until Labour ministers took up the policy. But no single interest group opposed the expansion of higher education, the move towards comprehensives, the provision of more nursery education or of educational priority areas. A reaction came well after the policies were accepted and then from quite small groups who were concerned about the quality of education resulting from the rejection of elitist assumptions.

All attempts at social engineering bring unpredictable complications. Firstly, they sharpen problems of role relationships. Just as the assumption of personal autonomy leads to informal relationships within the schools, so egalitarianism can lead to attempts to structure curriculum, perhaps to induce operant conditioning and thus reduce teacher discretion. These tendencies conflict with the liberal tenets of the British educational system. Secondly, although the school, unlike medicine, is compulsory, 'the new poverty', that is the failure of parents to take up what the school offers because of attitudes or lack of confidence, gets in the way of the schools becoming an equalising force. When these difficulties are overcome and parents become involved, social differentiation ceases to be so important a factor [24]. Yet empirical attempts to generate parental interest in the school have failed [25]. Nonetheless, egalitarian policies are explicit and important, as shown in Chart II.

Economic Values

Economic values relate closely to some of the social values. By economic values we mean those which are concerned with increasing the productivity of the society and defending it against the effects of poor economic performance.

These values are overtly stated in the 1956 White Paper on technical education, the Crowther, Newsom and Robbins Reports, and the 1972 White Paper on educational policy which assumed this objective without defensiveness or uncertainty. Many further education circulars were explicit in relating the work of the colleges to the needs of industry and commerce, and their importance in our period can be seen from Chart II (No. 5) which lists a veritable procession of them.

These objectives can conflict with the values of personal realisation and autonomy. The conflict is recognised so that, for example, there is a cautious use of secondary school curriculum for narrowly vocational education (Newsom Report, Chapter XIV): HM Inspectors of Schools have always resisted the inclusion of shorthand and typing as school subjects on the grounds that this may involve reiterative skill training and not the development of the mind or spirit. The same arguments partly account for the decline of technical schools. Conversely, it is maintained, as in the Plowden Report, that good education, that is, liberal education, increases flexibility in manpower. The working population thus learns how to learn and adapt itself to changing economic and social demands and, at the same time, prepare itself for the good life.

The economy and manpower values are in a variable relationship with egalitarianism and personal freedom. For example, in the expansion of higher education, society simultaneously provides for improvement of the economy and the trained manpower to service it, for opportunities for personal development and freedom, for the creation of an elite, and for a more equal society. There is no automatic economic argument justifying all the places in higher education on the grounds of productivity. Instead it is argued that social and economic demands should not be in conflict. Social demand has become the imperative – a good to be provided – but education may be so structured that it will also accommodate economic imperatives by providing, where necessary, higher education within categories that mould student preferences to economic needs.

In this value there have been great fluctuations. Economic growth is no longer so certainly the main objective of developed countries;

equality, a better quality of life and high employment rates are now thought more important objectives to pursue than untrammelled growth. These policies have been present throughout our period, though intensified since the mid-1950s. The whole system and its interest groups believes it is helping society to be more productive. But lack of confidence in productivity, and uncertainty about its social effects, make them uncertain policies now.

Institutional Values

Institutional values are particularly important in the analysis of educational policies and government because much of the activity of the main interest groups is taken up with their promotion. For this reason, it is too easy to assume that they are inherently defensive of professional or bureaucratic interests. If construed objectively they can be seen to relate to such basic values as equity or freedom or a sense of community, as well as the defence of society or the interest groups themselves. They relate to such wide-ranging policy issues as the defence of local authority rights against centralisation, the place of parents on governing bodies, the status of teachers, the freedom of the universities or the rights of students. For the most part they are secondary or instrumental values because they do not, as do the other values discussed here, relate directly to the desired outcomes of the educational system.

Of the institutional values, *participation* or *generation of community* values have been among the newest, and are also strongly related to developments wider than education itself. It is argued that schools should be 'more open' to the community and to parents. The participation objective is ambiguous. It can maintain that schools should be pervious to review by their clientele, or that parents should have a place in school government, or simply that parents should be active in their children's education. The problem is less one of principle than of role conflict – is it possible for parents to participate in their children's education and to allow for the growing professionalism of the teaching staff? Is participation by parents in conflict with government by parents? The move towards participation has two main sources. There is a general concern about the anonymity of public service organisations and their inability to be responsive to client needs. Secondly, there are technological assumptions about the ways in which parents' attitudes and participation improve children's performance. The Plowden Report more than any other document tried to promote these assumptions. These attitudes relate to other more general

E

participative issues, as have been brought to notice by the Maud Report on local government, the Skeffington Report on participation in planning, the Seebohm Report on social services, and the documentation on the reorganisation of the health service. They became pressing in the activities of the Confederation for the Advancement of State Education, the Advisory Centre for Education and the National Association of Governors and Managers.

Of the *institutional maintenance values,* the *professional values of teachers* are important. These may relate to the individual autonomy and satisfaction objectives, but have a life of their own. It is maintained that there are educational processes, which can be typified in precepts from applied educational and social psychological studies, about the nature of the developing child that constitute the base of the teacher's professional expertise. This assumption of professional expertise and the rights that go with it, so vigorously attacked by Musgrove and Taylor [26], can conflict with attempts to open up the educational processes to help the deprived and, more generally, to use the schools for radical policies of social engineering. Indeed, teachers' objections to positive discrimination assumptions are analogous to social workers' objections to the way in which some have formulated their role, as being mainly that of social control, as if the person-to-person relationship is not a matter of practised skill and professional knowledge, and as if more generally applied and structured procedures might be more beneficial. Social engineering is antipathetic to traditional liberal professional assumptions. Social engineering implies measurement and it implies the wholesale applications of generalised policies. Teachers fear that examination results will be used as the obvious indicator of success. And they are frightened as well that educational technology will bite into their ability to run their own schools.

These 'professional' assumptions are important to the maintenance of the power structure for it is not only teachers, but also local educational administrators, inspectors, organisers and teacher educators who hold the power and help them face confidently both the attempts of lay administrators to control education from the outside and the attempts of laymen, including parents, to get into the act.

Again we should relate these general descriptions of values to the policy events listed in Chart II. Of the participative policies, we refer to changes in the governing bodies of schools, colleges and universities which have increasingly brought in the employees and students of these institutions. The examples of institutional policies concerned with defence of the fabric include the negotiation over local government reform, the increasing unionisation of teachers, the defeat of the proposals for the Curriculum Study Group, the insistence on teachers all being trained, and many others.

CONCLUSION

In this chapter we have tried to show how policies can be identified from published official and interview material. We have also classified them in such a way as to enable them to be aligned with the analysis of historical continuity or discontinuity contained in Chapter 2, and to the allegiances which divide roughly between those internal to the institutional structure and those external to it. To determine our classifications and relationships more formally we should have had to analyse the negotiations leading to each policy and produce a more detailed micro-analysis of the sentiments, motives and circumstances of each move. And we should have taken that analysis deeply into the zones of decision-making – the DES and the Treasury and local authorities. But whilst conscious of the limitations of what we have done, we strongly assert the need to make these linkages. For policy analysis and a usable study of politics are at present frustrated by the failure of the main authorities to move from general analyses of values through to specific policies and then on to the institutions which create and sustain the opposing policies. Linkages must be studied and not merely inferred.

Part II

THE INTEREST
GROUPS

Chapter 4

Policy Changes as Perceived by Those Involved

In the previous chapters some of the policies of the period as represented by interviewees, ministers' speeches, circulars, administrative memoranda and other public events are drawn out. But the objectives and values underlying policies are not explicitly stated in Britain. The Education Act, 1944, is so general in its statement of intentions, in Section I, as to be meaningless. It simply refers to the intention to provide 'a comprehensive and varied system of education'.

Those interviewed shared our belief that the setting of objectives had long been implicit and unsystematic. In the view of one senior official [1] it was only in recent years that the systematic review of purposes and programmes was undertaken. The main events in this development were the establishment of the Public Expenditure Survey Committee and of Programme Analysis Review undertaken by senior officers and HMIs in the DES who fed them into a central point in the Treasury. This trend can be documented from such documents as the Report of the Select Committee on Expenditure, 1970, and the 1972 White Paper on educational policy.

The first explicit attempts to make these changes began with the creation of the planning branch under Crosland in 1966, although earlier the development of teacher supply planning was an important start towards defining purposes and the resources that need go with them, as were the planning for the emergency training scheme and the raising of the school leaving age to fifteen (HORSA).

Government might now be more systematic but it is hardly more open in its statement of objectives. While the White Paper is precise about the Government's intentions, there was no open consultation leading up to it. Except for its unusually explicit statement of the purposes of higher education it contained no open declaration of what the underlying values might be.

If the centre is uncertain about the value bases of its policy, or perhaps evades the values issue altogether, there is, as will be seen in the next three chapters, no simple set of assumptions that typifies the perception of policy in any other group.

Thus, the local authority interest groups can be seen to be concerned primarily with the institutional values relating to the freedom of local authorities from central control and the insistence on due process in central government's dealing with them. They are generally concerned, too, with ensuring that the services which they administer are in good shape and expand in relationship to general social needs. But their views on the larger social issues as embodied in the egalitarian policies of the mid-1960s are neutral and indeterminate (*see* Chapter 6).

The teachers' interest groups are concerned with the advancement of the teaching profession, both for the welfare of its members and because they maintain that what is good for teachers is good for the children. They are concerned with perpetuating the main liberal educational policies which we have described, and the system of teacher and school freedom and authority which sustains those policies. They have been more prominent in advancing social and egalitarian policies than have the local authority associations, but only when they felt that there was sufficient consensus in the profession and in society as a whole for them to be able to move (*see* Chapter 7).

Policies as perceived by the newer interest groups which formed in the 1960s emerge very differently from those of the established groups. The role of parents in decision-making, the enhancement of the role of governors and managers, the status, contractual rights and participative power of students, the right of teachers to participate in institutional decision-making, the belief that schools should help mould a more equal and undifferentiated society – all these values came from outside the system and cut deep into the institutionalised educational policies and values.

The continuous assumptions were, therefore, sustained by an authority and power network not easily paralleled in any other area of public life. For example, the health service, the social services and social security policies have been more susceptible to externally conditioned organisational and policy changes. Some would argue that where the education service responded to social and economic argument it was also responding to continuous and preservative themes.

This section describes the interest groups which substantiated the continuous educational policies. It is also concerned with showing how changes in social attitudes towards education were mediated through other, and new, interest groups, and the extent to which the parliamentary process both recorded and conveyed, as well as helped substantiate, some of the major changes in policy.

In discussing the interest groups we bear in mind our values and policy classification. The sectional and promotional groups differ from one another in their value bases. And our distinction between legitimised and non-legitimised interest groups also relates to degrees of institutional power and legitimacy, and the values backing them.

Chapter 5

The Place of Interest Groups in the Decision-Making Process: An Analytical Framework

TYPES OF INTEREST GROUPS

If policies changed in the 1960s and 1970s, who caused the changes? We can identify virtually all the parts of the educational policy-making process. The difficulty will be, however, to allocate power and authority to any particular part. In the next two chapters, therefore, we assume a preliminary classification of interest groups before describing the more important of them in some detail. At the end of this book we attempt to classify the interest groups in terms not only of the obvious interests which they represent, but also in terms of the values and policies described in Chapters 2 and 3 and the classifications that can be derived from them.

The main parts of the decision- and policy-making system are: parliament; central government; local government, teachers, the centres of academics and research work, students and their interest groups; and the newer interest groups which are so much concerned with parents.

There is an extensive literature on interest groups, and this has concerned itself with two main issues. First, how internal organisation and the purposes of groups and opposition parties change as they become depoliticised [1] and bureaucratised; it is assumed that they begin to take on the same characteristics as the governments and other organisations on which they put pressure [2]. The second issue is whether interest groups are affected by the different purposes for which they are created, as, for example, between groups pursuing members' collective interests ('sectional') [3] or some more altruistic ('promotional') cause.

A further classification can be added which relates to the

question: 'What authority and what power in the decision-making process does an interest group possess?' The interest groups accepted by government as part of decision-making are different from those which attempt to influence a system of which they are not recognised as a part.

It is possible to distinguish between the *legitimised* and the *non-legitimised*, or non-accepted, pressure groups. The legitimised groups are those which have an accepted right to be consulted by government and by local authorities, and by public organisations concerned with education such as universities, before policies are authorised. Some interest groups are consulted as a matter of statute, as with the consultations about the amount and distribution of the rate support grant.

While the right to be consulted often has a legal base it is never specific and the decision to consult is in the gift, formally, of the Secretary of State. This is true of the right to be consulted on the salary of teachers. Two important examples of the Secretary of State's power to legitimise are the way in which the National Association of Schoolmasters, after a long and fierce campaign, was admitted to the Burnham Committee, and the way in which Mr Reg Prentice removed the Association of Education Committees from the Burnham Committee (*see* Chapter 6). But although authority to legitimise rests with the central government, it takes a major dislodgement of the power system for an identifiable interest group to be disregarded on any decision affecting its membership.

. The non-legitimised pressure groups have a somewhat different role from the legitimised ones. All the legitimised interest groups represent accepted parts of the education system, legally constituted public bodies or groups of employees, or those who have rights to legal provisions of grants or status, such as students or denominations. The non-legitimised groups have a different role which is to challenge accepted authority and institutions until policies are changed, as with the campaign against physical punishment (STOPP) or the campaign in favour of comprehensive education.

THE LEGITIMISED INTEREST GROUPS: DIFFERENCES

Interest groups are legitimised if they have a statutory or conventional right to be consulted by government on matters affecting their members, or on the development of the education service as a whole.

The fact that some interest groups, such as the local authorities and the vice-chancellors, not only put pressure on government, but themselves represent important parts of educational government, affects their stance and their role. The local authorities maintain the schools. The vice-chancellors administer the self-governing universities. They are unlikely, therefore, to press for major changes that are in conflict with the continuing elements of government policy. They follow the consensuses which they believe government has the right to interpret and promulgate, but become all the more anxious when consensual assumptions about consultation procedures or financial relationships are disturbed: a point affecting vice-chancellors since 1973 when the conventions of the quinquennial settlement of grants were suddenly changed.

These interest groups differ, however, from government when they promote and defend the interests of their own members, or when they press the DES to expand or maintain the standards of the education service.

The teachers' associations are not the same as the other legitimised associations in this respect. But even they are more a part of the authorised system than they themselves might recognise. They represent the professionals who run public institutions. They represent heads as well as rank and file teachers; and teachers themselves are, in any event, concerned with the maintenance of a system which carries authority and is part of the social control mechanism. Moreover, the teacher's ultimate managers, chief education officers, are themselves almost, if not quite, all former teachers. So the teachers do not argue for the same position as do industrial trade unions. They also face employers who are elected representatives, with the backing of those who elect them, rather than private employers. Moreover, the breadth of their membership restricts their ability to be decisive, let alone aggressive. The broader the membership, the less easy it is for them to get agreement on policies other than generalised sectional policies on salaries or working conditions. And even on those points there can be quite sharp internal differences. These characteristics soften their relationships with government, though, obviously, they are not equivocally a part of management.

The legitimised pressure group which demonstrates best the dynamics of the system is the National Union of Students. It is far more in the style of a conflictual interest group than any other. As will be discussed later, it moved during our period into legitimisation but yet kept up an aggressive and critical role.

A further characteristic is common to the educational interest groups: none holds any real sanction. The most that can be threatened is a teachers' strike, which is a serious irritant to parents, but not at all comparable with industrial action by miners or railwaymen. And it is not a sanction at all in the hands of university teachers, or vice-chancellors, or local authority associations.

Chapter 6

Local Authority Associations

SOME RECENT HISTORY

While we were making our study, major transformations took place in the local authority associations. Throughout the whole of our period, five major local authority associations dominated the flow of advice to, pressure on, and co-operation with, the government. In April 1974, with local government reorganisation, the Association of Education Committees (AEC) continued to exist only in an attenuated form, and only after a struggle in which it was nearly killed, and not for the first time, by the other associations [1]. In particular, the AEC was excluded from one of the areas of its greatest influence – salary negotiations. The ILEA decided to join the newly-formed Association of Metropolitan Authorities.

The two newly-formed English associations, the Association of Metropolitan Authorities (AMA) and the Association of County Councils (ACC) remained in the headquarters of the former AMC and CCA, but there were two important changes in internal structure. The ACC emerged with a clearer dependency on party political majorities than had the CCA, its predecessor, since the delegate system (in which only one member was a voter) gave way to an allocation of three, four or five delegates to each authority. They may thus become more responsive to general political movements within their areas. Secondly, the AMA decided to have a distinctive educational secretariat, partly to make good their word that they were, and would become even more, competent to handle the matters abrogated by the Association of Education Committees. The CCA already had an education officer.

The Defeat of the AEC

There was never a time when the other associations did not feel that their position was strongly usurped by the AEC. No other local government service had its own association with such powerful representative rights, and the CCA and the AMC felt that it was wrong that multipurpose local authorities should have special representation as to only one, albeit the largest, function by a specialist body. They felt that education was never adequately represented in terms of its financial or general aspects in relation to the other multiple aspects of local government. Even a minister (Eccles) who had warm regard and respect for Sir William (now Lord) Alexander, Secretary of the AEC, felt that it was a mistake to have one service so strongly and separately represented [2]. Here their views were in line with the movements towards corporate management eventually heralded by the Maud Reports on local government and the Bains Report on local government structure. The fact that the AEC had got away with it, in taking the lead particularly in salary negotiations, and on many other issues, was some indication of the special position that the Government was prepared to accord education over other services. The AEC had survived the perils of the Local Government Act of 1958 which substituted general for specific grants for education along with other services, and also required local authority associations to negotiate for the general grant.

The fight over the continuation of the AEC was fierce. The Secretary of State, Reg Prentice, however, removed it from Burnham and told the annual conference in 1974: 'It cannot be disputed that the responsibility for education rests by statute upon the LEAs and not education committees.' The new Association of County Councils and Association of Metropolitan Authorities formed a Central Council of Local Education Authorities (CCLEA) which soon represented every local authority in England and Wales. Within a few weeks, the AEC retained only 35 education committees out of a possible 104 [3].

COMMON FEATURES AND CONTRASTS

In the next few pages we shall draw out some of the common aspects of the local authorities' ways of working, and the impact they have on policy. It will be convenient to discuss them comparatively first, and then briefly refer to their organisational and individual characteristics.

Consultation by the DES

The local authority associations have a continuing relationship with government. They are consulted on every issue of relevance to local authority educational functioning – changes of law either by legislation or by subordinate legislation (statutory instruments and statutory orders), and on every circular, administrative memorandum and DES branch letter before it is sent out. They are consulted formally on some scores of issues a year.

They have a statutory right, once they are selected by the Secretary of State as 'bodies representative of local authorities', to be consulted on the determination of the rate support grant[1] and on teachers' salaries – by virtue of the Local Government Act, 1958, and of statutory instruments. They form part of the triangular system which determines teachers' and other local authority salaries through the Burnham, Pelham and Whitley committee system which they have shared with the DES and the teachers since 1963, when Edward Boyle caused the DES to become a party to salary negotiations instead of simply approving or rejecting suggestions made by the two main sides.

Giving Evidence

They give evidence to every council, committee and parliamentary committee that affects education. They have members on every educational council and consultative committee, except the Central Advisory Councils where, however, they are, in fact, informally represented by members chosen on a 'personal' basis [4].

They can also assert pressure through the local government press. In education, the most important of these is the journal of the Association of Education Committees, *Education,* which for many years has had weekly contributions from the Secretary to the AEC, William Alexander. Such journals as the *Local Government Chronicle* also comment on educational matters.

Relationships with MPs

Apart from their relationships with the DES, they have relationships of varying intensities with MPs. Thus, the AMC ensures that their view is put adequately by the simple device of making a large number of MPs and members of the House of Lords its vice-

---

[1] Rate support grant (RSG) is the general grant for almost all local government services paid by the Department of the Environment, in consultation with the other central departments, to local authorities after consultation with their associations.

presidents [5]. One MP who asked to be allowed to receive briefing materials from the AMC was told 'Oh, we'll make you a vice-president' [6]. They do not necessarily act directly as spokesmen for the AMC, particularly since some of them are certain to be ministers for part of the time, but they constitute an information and briefing network through which the local authority point of view can be asserted. The AMC had seventy-seven member authorities covering over two hundred parliamentary constituencies before the February 1974 election. For the most part, they feel that their consultative arrangements with the Government are and should be adequate so they do not seek support from Opposition speakers as such, even when they are threatened by major changes, although officers of one association thought that they were known to have the capacity to cause difficulties in the Commons if their views were wrongly discarded [7].

Alexander in the AEC can get matters raised in Parliament. The Vice-President is often an MP. When, for example, Alexander believed that the denominations were being given too large a control over schools in return for the contribution they made under the terms of the 1946 Act, he had access to the Chief Whip and was able to get the matter raised internally in the Government [8]. But, in general, he, as with the other association leaders, would reckon to go to officials first, ministers second (and usually in that case in attendance on the AEC's Chairman), and to MPs only as a last resort. There is little legislation on education compared with that for other local government concerns, and the general associations relate more closely to the Department of the Environment than to any other department.

Their Impact

Was their relationship with the DES and its ministers close and important? The testimony of former ministers is clear. Boyle [9] agreed that Sir William Alexander, Secretary of the AEC since 1946, had great influence. He must have been in the DES building about three times a week. He was at every meeting of importance and his expertise on every issue affecting local authorities or the education service was great. He had been consulted about every important issue since the war and had produced a view on each, often spontaneously, and in the places where it counted.

His own role and views can be most easily seen from the journal *Education*. It had editors with minds of their own and one of them, Stuart Maclure, became the most influential and respected of all educational journalists. But *Education* also carried Alexander's weekly columns and evinced his influence in many other ways.

Crosland testified to the way in which it was necessary to secure agreement with the AEC and the other associations [9]:

'I was greatly influenced by what the NUT said in my consultations with them on the draft of circular 10/65 about the need for local authorities genuinely to consult the teachers; and I was influenced by much the AEC said about the draft ... their role, among other things, is that of continually commenting on policy as it developed. Sometimes you accept their advice and sometimes you don't. The Association of Teachers in Technical Institutions, for example, had a lot of influence on the development of the binary policy ... I always kept in very close touch with national bodies. I would often, for example, meet Alexander and an informal group of directors of education and I kept in close touch with the leaders of the teachers' associations.'

Boyle said they had [9]:

' "a very considerable effect" [on policy making] ... it was quite a limited number of officials who had a major impact. Sir William Alexander had a wide knowledge of the education system. He was constantly in the Department as a visitor. He had the advantage, with his editor, Stuart Maclure, that they had a weekly paper *Education*, the Journal of the Association of Education Committees, [which] was not just a sounding board but it was read by everybody who was "in" the maintained school world, and the world of the local authorities. And I think I emphasise most Sir William's great knowledge of the system.... For example, I can remember the time when he was against middle schools and then, later, he was inclined to think that nine to thirteen schools, or else the sixth form college both had merits, but one could often try things on him knowing here was somebody of enormous knowledge and experience of how the whole complicated mechanism of government and local authority, how this worked from the local government side.... One had to be careful ... as a minister, after talking with Sir William, or with some other people in local government ... not to sound too much like the spokesman in Parliament for the maintained schools.'

Not all associations rated the same in the view of the DES and its ministers. We cannot, for obvious reasons, quote official opinions on this, but Edward Boyle had no doubt about the differences [9]: 'Now and then rather absurd attempts used to be made by other association leaders to be a sort of equal with Sir William. Well, I mean, they just weren't.' Boyle went on to say that there were other people, too, who carried weight – Sir Ronald Gould, the General Secretary of the NUT, and the chief and deputy education officers of London. 'London, to a Minister of Education, is like a self-portrait – it's always there when you want it.'

There are, of course, different views on impact. When three chief education officers were asked whether such bodies as the AEC or the AMC affected decision-making one thought that the local authorities influenced the AEC rather than the other way around, and that the AMC, to which the local authority belonged, 'did not concern itself with education very greatly' [10].

Evidence of Impact and Interplay

In order to get a more detailed view of the interaction between the local authority associations and national policy-making, we met senior officials of the AEC, AMC and CCA, who helpfully put the minutes of their committees at our disposal. We were thus able to see which issues they initiated, at least at the recorded and formal level, and on which issues their role was primarily reactive.

The CCA education committee meets on average six times a year and the AMC education committee meets somewhat less regularly – between five and nine times a year. Occasionally both the AMC and CCA have special meetings to discuss particular issues such as teachers' salaries or the Industrial Training Bill, or have extra meetings to complete long agendas. Both bodies deal with about a dozen different topics a meeting, ranging over such issues as foreign language teaching in primary schools, secondary school organisation, evidence to advisory committees such as Robbins or Plowden, local authority expenditure on education, building costs and car parking policy in schools. It is not possible, of course, to tell from the minutes how much detailed discussion took place on each subject.

We analysed the minutes of the CCA from 1960 to 1972, the AMC from 1962 to 1972 and the AEC from 1960 to 1973, these being the sequences made available to us.

Of the two general associations, the CCA showed itself to be more active educationally during our period. It had a full-time education officer and two administrative officers concerned with education whereas until 1974 the AMC did not have an education officer but only an officer concerned with education, housing and social services.

The major issues considered by the CCA were the school meals service, school transport, building programmes, further education (particularly the binary system), problems associated with universities and students, schools and teachers, the Schools Council, the National Foundation for Educational Research (NFER) and agricultural education.

All problems concerning teachers were treated in great detail. These included teachers' pay, superannuation, conditions of work, part-time teachers, retirement, training, employment and distribution. The problems connected with schools also covered a wide area, such as the size of classes, use of audio-visual aids and facilities for music.

The AMC dealt with similar topics although naturally it hardly discussed anything connected with agiculture but was instead more concerned with industrial training or further education, and particularly with the running of the binary system. These differences faithfully reflect the differences in educational interest between rural and city areas.

But there are some surprising omissions from the papers, particularly those of the AMC. There is barely any discussion of the principles of comprehensive education, or major educational issues such as positive discrimination or educational priority areas.

The issues that occur most frequently in both groups are problems connected with salaries, conditions of service, supply, and the organisation of the training of teachers in both primary and secondary education. These topics come up in both groups on average twelve times a year. Other topics that arise regularly, such as school equipment, car parks and playing fields, are discussed only, on average, two to three times a year.

The emphasis on teachers' matters reflect the major area in which negotiations take place – teachers' salaries and conditions. Both the major associations react here to moves made on salaries by the teachers' associations, or react because the DES has sent a circular or a letter concerning teachers for comment, or because Questions have been raised in Parliament about teachers, although such questions do not often trigger off action by an association.

This raises the question whether the associations initiate policies. In general, it is clear that they react rather than initiate and this is confirmed by some officers we have interviewed. Our detailed evidence is not absolute on this point because few of the letters from the DES are published in the minutes of the AMC or the CCA, and they do not say whether the matter was brought to the DES's attention by the NUT or any other group representing the teachers. It is only when the NUT or NAS have actually taken strike action, or threatened it, that the topics discussed in an education meeting can be seen to be a result of action by a particular pressure group.

Yet it is clear that the majority of topics are raised, if not first initiated, in response to letters or circulars or memoranda from the DES, or as a result of a request to give evidence to advisory committees, or in response to Bills being placed before Parliament, or to the activities of select committees. Sir Toby Weaver [11] told us that the local authority associations' contribution was not that of initiating action. Michael Stewart summed it up for us as 'over major controversial issues, they follow, rather than lead'. Indeed, some MPs told us that local authorities are mainly conditioned by concern about the level of rates and that they inhibit rather than promote expansion – a point we cannot confirm or refute. And on our evidence it seems to be true that the CCA and AMC rarely seem to have totally disagreed with anything raised by the DES and seek to modify to only a limited extent. They are concerned about inter-authority expenditure and the level of general expenditure, and such institutional relationship issues as how much control local authorities will have over expenditure for school buildings, for example. This concern for expenditure is less evident with the AMC, perhaps because in further education it is the AMC authorities which run the more expensive institutions to which all local authorities contribute on the pool.

Other connections become clear from the papers. The two associations are involved in the Schools Council and the NFER. They periodically meet the NUT, ILEA, Welsh Joint Education Committee, NUS and Committee of Vice-Chancellors, or take note of issues raised in letters from these groups. They frequently meet the AEC. There are more general meetings presided over by the DES. Joint statements are made and these are usually connected with teachers' salaries but occasionally with further education salaries and conditions.

The CCA also receives many letters from local authorities on the same issues as occur in their minutes. These topics are minuted more carefully by the CCA than by the AMC. The CCA also comes under more pressure from a large variety of interest groups. In the minutes considered, thirty-eight approaches from pressure groups reached the CCA as compared with twelve to the AMC. These included the Open University, the British Standards for School Furniture Committee, the Council for Colonial Holidays for School Children, the National Institute for Adult Education and other somewhat more heterogeneous groups. The CCA evidently deals with a much broader variety of educational or para-educational issues than does the AMC.

The AEC is different from the AMC and the CCA in many of its ways of working and of making impact. Its executive committee meets approximately eight times a year. It has an educational advisory committee and a general purposes committee which meet about six or seven times a year. Normally all the recommendations of the two-sub-committees are accepted by the executive committee although they are occasionally amended. The executive committee also discussed more important resolutions passed or matters raised by the AGM as, for example, part-time teachers in further education (1971).

When compared with those of the two other local authority associations, the minutes and discussions are detailed. As might be expected, the AEC deals with a greater number of educational topics and the range covers all aspects of higher, further, secondary, primary and nursery education, as well as such subjects as the school health service, decimalisation, purchase tax on books and career education. But again there are surprising omissions, the most notable being comprehensive education which is barely touched upon except in response to DES circulars or letters from local authorities, and the binary system which is totally ignored. The issues which occur most frequently are similar to those of the CCA and AMC, although more peripheral issues such as field study centres, speech therapists and training of librarians are dealt with in greater detail. The AEC, as can be seen from Chart IV, relates to no less than 136 miscellaneous groups. These include not only the main groups concerned with education, but also the Central School of Speech and Drama, the British Council of Churches, the National Book League, the British Families Education Service, the Association of Navigation Schools, the National Institute of Houseworkers, and the National Youth Brass Band of Great Britain. Most of them had only one contact with the AEC in our period. Usually the approach is by letter. In 1960 the Royal National Institute for the Blind sent a letter pointing out that there were few piano tuners in schools. In 1961, the National Institute of Houseworkers Ltd requested that the AEC should see that students were sent to their centres. From the AEC minutes one senses the wide spectrum of educational concerns. Of all the local authority groups, and probably the other interest groups too, it covers the widest range of subjects connected with education.

Compared with the CCA, the AEC is under greater pressure from individual local authorities; the topics discussed range from local to broader issues, such as the future structure of the Youth Employment Service.

Chart IV shows the outside groups which initiated discussions within the local authority association committees. This is not an exhaustive indicator of interaction with outside groups, but a least shows the formal interactions which might have affected their policy attitudes.

All three associations have a great deal of contact with the DES through letters, circulars, draft circulars, administrative memoranda, meetings with officials, both informal and official, as well as meetings with the Secretary of State for Education. They are also in contact with other government departments, such as the Home Office and the Department of Employment, although surprisingly the AEC seems to be approached by these departments more often than the CCA and AMC. Both the CCA and the AEC are under a great deal of pressure from individual local authorities and also from a wide range of groups which are on the periphery of the education world. The AMC is the odd one out in this respect, but this will probably change with the appointment of an education secretariat.

The minutes record discussions of evidence to be given to government and parliamentary committees. They seem, however, to take little note of parliamentary activity, although they fully consider relevant Bills and Acts, White Papers and Select Committee reports. For example, the Industrial Training Act, 1964, occupied a lot of time. The AEC spent a great deal of time discussing all the official reports on education, whereas the CCA and AMC only discussed the more important ones, such as the Crowther, James and Plowden reports. The AEC also had more detailed discussions about the Public Schools Commission. It did not seem to be so concerned with the Schools Council and the NFER and, on the whole, took little interest in educational research matters.

The AEC is the only group to have recorded joint meetings with the AMC, CCA, NUT, Joint Four, ATTI, ATCDE, UGC and NUS, which take place formally at least three times a year. Official letters to each other and joint letters initiating action do not seem to occur regularly and the AEC seems to respond to action and letters from the NUT more frequently than it does to any other group.

Chart IV summarises outside initiators of the discussions in committee; Chart III summarises virtually all the issues discussed because few subjects are introduced into discussion unless they are initiated directly or indirectly from the outside. And that is an important characteristic of these principal legitimised associations. It implies participation in a consensual process of decision-making.

THE THREE MAIN ASSOCIATIONS: INDIVIDUAL
CHARACTERISTICS

The Association of Education Committees

The Association of Education Committees has had a peculiarly strong position in educational policy-making. Until 1974 it represented all the education committees in England and Wales other than the Inner London Education Authority which represented itself at the national level. Its secretary, Sir William Alexander, was appointed to this post in 1946 after being Director of Education, Sheffield. The whole work of the Association rests on Alexander

Chart III: *Main Topics Discussed by the CCA, AMC and AEC*

Topics	CCA (1960–72)	AMC (1963–72)	AEC (1960–73)
Teachers (training, conditions of service)	127	83	248
Educational building costs and programmes	35	42	56
Further education	37	47	93
Schools Council, NFER	50	63	45
Universities and students	65	39	90
School meals and milk	30	36	57
Schools (libraries, equipment, valuation of sites)	69	49	a
Agricultural education	30	1	10
Interauthority expenditure	34	2	16
Polytechnics	11	33	8
Youth leaders and community wardens	4	0	39
Industrial training (including day release and the Industrial Training Act)	19	26	35

a It is difficult to compare the AEC with the CCA and AMC as they discuss a greater variety of 'school' subjects.
Source: Committee Minutes.

Chart IV: *Initiators of Committee Discussions*

Groups which Initiate Action by the AMC, CCA, AEC	CCA (1960–72)	AMC (1963–72)	AEC (1960–73)
1 DES letters, circulars, memos	175 (13·6)[a]	123 (12·3)[a]	384 (27·5)[a]
2 Evidence to government and parliamentary committees	48	41	43
3 Acts/Bills	13	14	39
4 Parliament	7	5	13
5 White Papers	16	18	20
6 Government and DES committee reports on education	24	29	67
7 Local authorities (individual)	77	—	351
8 CCA (letters)	—	1	7
9 AMC (letters)	44	—	5
10 AEC (letters)	10	7	—
11 NUT (letters and actions)	5	4	21
12 Other groups (main groups that are mentioned in the text)	45	29	69
13 Miscellaneous groups	48	17	136
14 Schools Council/NFER	33	43	21
15 Burnham	12	8	22
16 Public Schools Commission	1	8	11
17 Other government departments	11	8	38
18 Initiated indirectly from outside	207 (15·7)[a]	159 (15·9)[a]	344 (24·5)[a]

[a] Average per year.

and a staff of eight. Until 1974 it was governed by a committee of forty of whom twelve were chief education officers.

Much of the strength of the Association rests on the personality and effectiveness of Alexander himself. He has been able to negotiate with the Department and the teachers' associations in the knowledge that his committee will usually back him, and that he probably possesses a greater understanding of the main issues than any other single full-time official in the education service.

Although close to some ministers, Alexander's main working relationships are with under-secretaries at the DES. They consult him before formal communications are sent from the Department and he is able to contact officials in the branches for information or for discussion of an issue. There are regular but formal meetings with the Secretary of State when, for example, conference resolutions are brought to his or her attention. His working rule is never to attack an individual officer but to reserve any attack, on behalf of the AEC, for the policies or for the ministers who are accountable for them.

Whilst he is an extremely powerful official, he, in common with all the other officials responsible for interest groups, defers to the executive committee and to the annual conference, and differences between him and his committee are not visible to the outside world. Committee resolutions have occasionally been voted down at the annual conference.

Alexander's way of working is informal and quick. He is not in his office for more than an hour a day. The AEC is in membership of a large number of committees covering every conceivable interest in schools, policy and administration. He is able to reply to most of the letters which come to him from the DES, from local authorities and from other associations, off the cuff. It is this speed and clarity which has placed him and his Association in such a strong position.

There are thus regular, well-understood and mutually accepted mechanisms with the DES. This is not, perhaps, surprising since the AEC represents the one set of institutions which have a clear statutory obligation, with the central department, for education. There is hardly any difference in the main attitudes on educational policy between most local authorities and the centre. Both press for an expansion of the service although, clearly, the DES has to withstand the more exuberant demands on behalf of central government. Both are concerned with the pursuit of efficiency.

An illustration of this 'efficiency' norm is Alexander's personal attitude [12] towards comprehensive education, which he does not believe will give an adequate deal to the ablest children. Whilst the Association as such has no official views on the subject, he says that had selective education been retained for the ablest 5 per cent, genuine comprehensive schools could have emerged without distress to the vast majority of parents. But in 1968 it became plain to him that comprehensive schools were here to stay and that it was his dury to accept this as a political fact of life. Since then, therefore, in speeches and in his own book *Towards a New Education Act* [13], he has maintained that, as the largest secondary schools are too large for adequate educational and social performance, post-compulsory age education should be provided in a new tertiary stage of education, or in colleges in which excellent sixth-form facilities as well as technical and other forms of further education can be offered for the sixteen to nineteen age group. He thus goes against many of the long-standing assumptions of the teaching profession, such as those held by the Association of Assistant

Mistresses (*see* page 122), that the sixth form, as painted in, for example, Chapter XXI of the Crowther Report, is what makes a secondary school into a major educational institution and provides incentives for excellence in teaching.

On some of the major logistical issues such as those of teacher supply he maintains that he, and his association, have been pragmatic rather than political. He argues for differentiation between those sources of teacher supply which are inflexible – the colleges of education in particular – and those which are flexible because they can be reduced or increased at short notice and without large capital expenditure, such as one-year training for graduates and the encouragement of the return of married women teachers to schools. He also argues that since education is and will be constrained by economics, the profession needs to look far more critically at its own demands for the reduction in the size of classes and not go, without careful consideration, towards such general policies as 'a profession of half a million' to which the NUT is committed.

This is the policy flexibility which can be expected of those who manage the system. These policies do not, of themselves, explain the tenacity with which either the DES or the other mangement interests held so firmly to the tripartite system of education as sanctioned by the Education Act, 1944. At the same time as they are promulgated and advanced, they have the appearance of neutrality. Over the longer perspective, no policy proposed by management appears radical, or critical of the system being managed.

In what sense, then, is the AEC an interest group? It is an interest group inasmuch as it argues cogently for distribution of power and authority in the education service between the centre and the local authorities. Yet in arguing for this, Alexander has not been particularly respectful of the existing pattern of interest within his own Association. He argues, for example, that larger local authorities will be able to sustain their own inspectorates which can check on the efficiency of education whilst HMIs become a *corps d'élite* who can put out advice, built up on knowledge of the national range of experience [14].

Local government should carry the full responsibility of spending its own money, as well as that allocated to it by the centre. He argues, in his book, for delegation to governing bodies within budgets as well. He somewhat dramatically argues, both in his evidence to the Select Committee on the inspectorate and in his book, that a centralised system might lead to dictatorship (curiously enough he seems to assume that centralised education is not a characteristic of the democratic West – the contrast between centralised France and Sweden and decentralised Yugoslavia would seem to belie this). He believes that the main movements come from local authorities – for example, nursery education as established in Bradford or the youth employment service in Birmingham. He even throws doubt on the propriety of MPs approaching ministers rather than councillors on the way in which the education service is run.

He sees no clear role for the centre in education. Central government must be concerned with the flow of national monies into education, with the establishment of common national policies and with the prescription of minimum standards for buildings, staffing ratios, provisions for health and so on. National governments should equalise opportunity throughout the country. 'However, it is important that national policy should be restricted to those questions where it really is essential to adopt a national line.'

The AEC can claim to have seriously modified the Department's attitudes and functions. Thus, in the late 1940s when the Department went for fast recruitment of teachers and the raising of the school leaving age, Alexander urged that it should be concerned with the bulge in the birth rate which would demand more women primary than men secondary teachers. He made a speech on it at the AGM in 1947 and George Tomlinson instructed the Deputy Secretary of the time, Sir William Cleary, and a protagonist of raising the school leaving age, to cause a change in teacher supply balances. A skilled official of an interest group outside the DES must, in fact, take a broader view than any single official other than the Permanent Secretary. Alexander stands by consensus, however, and the flying of kites and the pushing of ideas through regular and well-accepted mechanisms. He has been remarkably successful in developing precedents and procedures for salary negotiation and when a matter has interested him and his committee, such as getting expenditure on books improved, he has had his way [15].

The AEC has benefited from having this formidable man who has exercised a leadership role in the local education service throughout its boom years. It must now be expected that the Association will decline in importance as education itself gets more generally on the defensive both nationally and locally.

The County Councils' Association
The County Councils' Association has represented the counties of

England and Wales since the turn of the century. It gave way, in April 1974, to the Association of County Councils.

Its offices are in Eaton Square in Belgravia and the impression of social status is enhanced by the list of presidents, most of whom have been peers, and of chairmen, most of whom have been knights, on the board in the hall where there is also a tinted engraving of Queen Victoria receiving the Association's council.

The declared aim is to watch over the rights and privileges of local authorities, and countries in particular. The committee structure is organised to these ends and replicates the divisions of functions of a county authority: there are agricultural, civil defence, education, finance, housing, libraries, parliamentary and general purposes, planning and social services committees, and a selection committee which chooses members for the other committees.

The orientation of the Association may well change as it becomes the ACC because of its new methods of appointing committees. The CCA did not distinguish between large and small counties: all had four representatives on the executive council, and each county had a recognised spokesman and a 'voter'. The ACC will allow three, four or five voters according to the size of the authority. This may lead to sharper politicisation, a process likely to be the more accentuated by the main political parties' increasing interest in local politics as a source of power [16].

The education committee, as others, is chosen by the selection committee which consists of committee chairmen. Once appointed to a committee a member tends to remain on it. Again, powerful continuities may now be broken, for of the forty members of the education committee in January 1974 only three will return to the equivalent committee within the ACC.

County education officers advise the education committee and form a society of their own. They meet before the education committee meetings, and about half of them usually attend. All CEOs of authorities in membership receive copies of agendas. There are now twenty advisers nominated by chief officers but, it should be noted, three are county clerks, three treasurers, one a medical officer and one a director of social services.

This reflects an important element of CCA policies – that education is the most important of the local authority services but should be administered as one of several related services, among which local authorities may have to adjudicate. This would be its view when it adjudicated on the classic borderline cases such as the location of school welfare and health services, or on the balance of power between different local authority services. It does not believe that authorities should be required by statute to have an education committee, even if it believes that most ought to have one. Hence the antagonism towards the Association of Education Committees which has certainly 'usurped' many of the CCA and AMC's functions. The AEC was explicable from the CCA perspective at a time when there were over three hundred education authorities (if we include the pre-1944 Act, Part III authorities), which did not necessarily relate to other authorities or their functions. The CCA could thus only speak for some of the larger rural authorities at that time. With the trend towards all-purpose authorities the need for a separate AEC diminished, although the AEC is seen as having provided a valuable lead on such major issues as teacher supply and salaries.

The CCA is overtly non-partisan on such issues as the development of comprehensive education because it must speak for authorities of all political persuasions. As county authorities become more sensitive to general political movements (because hitherto Labour municipalities will amalgamate with Conservative rural areas and thus reduce the number of safe majorities on both sides), neutrality should become even more apparent if internal peace is to prevail.

The CCA claims to have affected policy in specific ways, as well as exercising vigilance against DES attempts to squeeze local authority discretion. The pooling of local authority advanced further education expenditure, the creation of general rather than specific grants in the 1958 Local Government Act, the rationalisation of awards to university students, (which came about by negotiation in the latter 1950s), and the making of the school meals service into a genuinely local authority service instead of one for which the central government paid in full and thus prescribed costs and standards are among the issues it claims to have pressed.

On such matters as building programmes, the CCA was concerned not so much about size as about the ways in which they are administered by the DES and the lack of local authority freedom to see their own projects through within total limits, as well as the rigours of control over costs. The CCA was strongly in favour of the binary system of higher education, as is clear from its evidence to the Royal Commission on Local Government, on the grounds that local authorities could only undertake education effectively if they administered all stages of education. It would be fair to say that while it does press issues, as its proposals for a new education bill published in 1969 show, the issues pressed are all of a mildly reformist or of a technical nature.

The Association of Municipal Corporations

The AMC was virtually identical to the CCA in its impact on education policy-making. Its ascribed role was the same and any difference in influence probably reflects the impact of different sets of personal and political relationships. Thus one Labour Secretary of State had no time for what was then a predominantly Conservative group of local authorities, whilst Mrs Margaret Thatcher was immediately able to resume close relationships with Dame Katherine Ollerenshaw, who was Chairman of the AMC education committee and a prominent Conservative Manchester alderman [17].

The AMC shares the CCA's doubts about education's special treatment, about the mandatory requirements on local authorities to have an education committee and teacher membership of education committees and about statutory requirements to have a chief education officer but not a chief executive. It also shares the attitudes to the AEC recorded in previous pages.

On educational policy generally its officers agree that it is reactive [18]. It was, indeed, created as a reaction to central government insistence that there should be town polls in the Borough Funds Act, 1872, and it explicitly exists to protect local authorities' interests and rights. It does not claim to take a lead in the creation of educational policy and feels that the DES must make the running on such issues as raising the school leaving age rather than the local authorities. At the time when the interviews with officers took place, the officers were inevitably concerned with matters of structure rather than educational policy, since this was the time of local government reorganisation. In their view local authorities create style and quality, not overall policy [19].

The AMC could not hold all its members together on educational policies although it provided a network for consultation and collective support for those who otherwise might be isolated chairmen of local authority committees. It fell apart on the detailed geographical recommendations of Redcliffe-Maud and never achieved clear agreement on more fundamental issues of local authority structure and functions. It came together, however, in challenging central government in any attempt to abrogate the powers of local authorities.

Its role and status are revealed by its attitudes on certain issues.

It supported the movement from specific to general grants in the 1958 Act. It was opposed to the requirement that short lists of those applying for appointment as chief education officers must be submitted to the DES, and the statutory requirement that there must be education committees. It was mainly in favour of the binary system of education, but had become alarmed at the propensity of the large authorities to expand polytechnics at the expense of the local authority pool. It was thus behind the creation of the Local Authority Higher Education Committee which sought to collate views on such matters. It related regularly to the DES but even more to the Department of the Environment, which its Secretary might visit perhaps two or three times a week for meetings. Relationships were mainly informal and correspondence was regularly exchanged on circulars and administrative memoranda, but a great deal of discussion centred around the Burnham negotiations.

Relations with the teacher associations became more active as teachers have become more militant. Indeed, the picketing of local authorities by the NAS and NUT strengthened the coherence of the AMC. Apart from this, however, discussions about teachers' conditions of work and school meals' issues, for example, were fairly continuous. The AMC had a controversy with the teachers over fees for marking CSE examinations. The AMC felt that it was able to be authoritative on behalf of all authorities, although the DES might bounce ideas against individual chief officers.

The AMC was, therefore, clearly part of the management system, and the main differences with central government were on the role of local authorities. As far as distinctively educational issues are concerned it was less interested in say, the principle of comprehensive education, than the way in which the DES allow local authorities to carry through schemes. The AMC was opposed, in evidence to the Select Committee, to the proposal of a higher education commission. It felt that the retention of teacher education and the polytechnic sector was right since only local authorities could have expanded higher education as quickly as they did.

The AMC believed, as did the CCA, that it must be vigilant towards government, and thus is a prime example of 'non-decision-making' – of the process whereby influence and power rests in the ability to constrain and veto as much as to propose and act. The other main educational relationships were with teachers, which were amicable in spite of recent sharper unionisation.

As can be seen from the analysis of the role of the AMC, education was not given priority. Indeed, out of a membership of 300 local authorities, only 100 were local education authorities. The structure of the newly-formed AMA is greatly different from the AMC. Its membership includes all the local education authorities of the municipal authorities as well as the ILEA. The areas are similar both in size and in composition, and they all share the urban problem [20]. The political composition of the AMA is solidly Labour, whereas the ACC is predominantly Conservative. The AMA now has an educational secretariat consisting of one chief officer and a deputy. A group of advisers has also been nominated, consisting of eight chief education officers, two chief executives and two treasurers. Both the ACC and AMA sit on a joint body of eighteen members, the Central Council of Local Education Authorities (CCLEA), where they have equal representation. It still remains to be seen what the exact function of CCLEA is going to be and whether it is going to speak to the DES with a single voice.

Thus the AMA ought to be in a better position to harness its expertise than it was before local government reorganisation. Indeed, it will be better able to speak for the problems in urban centres, such as the deprived areas, and will also be able to develop trans-departmental policies. This gives it an added advantage when dealing with Whitehall, where there are four departments concerned with different aspects of local government.

At the very least, the AMA has changed its structure for creating policy concerning education, giving it far more importance than did the AMC. And given that urban social matters are a key area of national policy it would be surprising if the new arrangements did not quickly move the AMA into a more positive and active role.

THE INNER LONDON EDUCATION AUTHORITY

The last of the associations to which we will refer is the Inner London Education Authority (ILEA). This is not properly an association, yet it is a major local authority interest group in its own right. It has always been separate from the other associations, although it has now joined the newly-formed AMA.

Nonetheless, it is likely to retain its direct relationship with the Government. At the same time, because it was controlled by the party in oppositon to the Government for quite long periods – although this has not been so since the February 1974 election – the ILEA was an important element in the dynamics of change as it wrestled with national policies it disliked. Government regards it as a mirror of the general educational situation in the country, as Boyle testified [21].

London was one of the few major local authorities which helped change educational policies. Because from the 1930s it was controlled by the Labour Party, except for a brief period of Conservative rule in the 1960s, the London County Council and the ILEA were able to promote the cause of comprehensive education, even when Conservative governments would not allow existing grammar schools to be merged with non-selective schools.

This experience, which it shared with Middlesex, Manchester and Birmingham, demonstrates an important general point about the interest groups. Local authority associations represent common denominators of local authority interests – the status of local authorities and the ever-present demand for more resources for education. They cannot, however, aggregate opinion on some of the most sensitive educational issues which are, as we have seen, related to broader social or economic considerations. Individual local authorities have deployed these issues most sharply.

Interest Groups Within the ILEA

The ILEA is significant in demonstrating a further aspect of interest groups: the way in which they cause change more effectively at the local rather than at the central level. The very existence of the ILEA testifies to the success of interest groups. A campaign launched by the LCC, in which it was strongly joined by the National Union of Teachers and other bodies, was launched to preserve an education authority for inner London. The LCC was dismembered by the London Government Act of 1964. In no other part of the country was a single-purpose education authority allowed to remain. Pressure was put up by London MPs and teachers, who organised meetings which as many as 400 parents and teachers attended to protest against the Government's intentions. The issue will undoubtedly come up again. Conservatives do not want a single-purpose education authority which is likely to be dominated by Labour virtually in perpetuity. The inner London boroughs would like education to join the other social services under their control.

As it is, London makes its representatives directly to the DES as, indeed, the Greater London Council raises its loan finance with Treasury agreement. It submits evidence directly to advisory committees and to parliamentary committees. And its building is across the road from that of the DES by Waterloo Station.

The ILEA itself relates to interest groups. Before Labour lost control in 1967 there was consultation on the reorganisation of secondary education. There is no doubt in the view of one ILEA leader [22] that, by building up negotiations and consultation with parents and governors and other interested people, the ILEA encouraged the development of pressure groups. A series of meetings took place at which leading councillors had to stand up to attack from people opposed to the changes. The ILEA responded by changing its plans several times. It did this partly out of self-interest; for by creating pressure against itself it demonstrated to the DES that it had consulted public opinion, and that it took into account views about freedom of choice which Conservative ministers would want to be able to say they defended best of all.

The ILEA not only goes out to the general body of public opinion with its consultative documents and its public meetings, but it also has a strong network of relationships with the Inner London Teachers' Association (NUT), the ATTI and many other bodies. There are several consultative committees. The links between ILEA officers and the main officials of the unions are strong. It was for this reason, presumably, that the NUT and ATTI did so much to keep the ILEA in being. There are good relationships with such bodies as NAGM and CASE, if only because several leading members of these informal interest groups are also leading members of the dominant Labour party in London.

We have thus seen that between the different local authority associations there are differences in perspectives and attitudes. Individual local authorities, as most strongly exemplified by London, take distinctive viewpoints on matters both social and educational. The more general local authority associations find it difficult to aggregate opinions on the more sensitive issues which are on the edge of social rather than educational policies. But, nonetheless, in terms of our classification of values, the local authorities can be seen to have common attitudes and ideologies.

What attitudes and ideologies do the local authority associations advance? First, it is clear that they are nearest government because they share the management of the education service with the DES. They, too, are on guard against generous pay settlements for teachers, and have the more direct role of safeguarding public monies as they are actually spent even if central government continues to meet the bulk of the cost through the rate support grant. Secondly, they do not conflict with central government on many of the main purposes of education. They represent a wide range of political opinions and are compelled to follow national policies created by the DES such as comprehensive secondary education or the establishment of polytechnics. They cannot be sure of securing a common view among their own members on any issue with serious social consequences and thus cannot seriously challenge the centre on them. They are thus primarily 'reactive' on educational policy. But they differ from the DES in two significant ways. First, they defend the role of the local authorities against what they may consider as the centralising tendencies of the DES. They argue that this is the best way for the education service to be administered. This leads them to resist the DES's attempts to force through policies even if the majority of the members are of the same political party as the minister. Thus Mrs Margaret Thatcher's withdrawal of Circular 10/65 and its somewhat peremptory replacement by Circular 10/70 drew unanimous protest from the local authority associations – it was not what she did but the way she did it that was objectionable.

The local authorities do not deny a Labour government the right to create comprehensive education but become restless if it should 'require' rather than 'request' local authorities to act on a matter on which there is no specific statutory stipulation. This primarily sectional aspect of their functions takes on sharper importance when functions are to be allocated between local authorities and other statutory or charter bodies. So they will support, perhaps retrospectively, any government move that will strengthen the role of the local authorities in, say, the development of the polytechnics.

A second aspect on which they might disagree with the DES is not so much on differences of policy as on differences of intensity – how fast and far will the level of expenditure on education be allowed to rise so that more school buildings are permitted or all-age schools closed?

They are concerned, therefore, to advance the assumption that education is a service which springs from local rather than from central government.

The same sectional interests led their feelings about the broader educational issues. They wanted to make sure that universities were brought into regional planning. They asserted not only local government of schools but the importance of preserving the freedom of the school to develop its own way of working. And this, to their credit, they would assert even against their own members who might wish to be more prescriptive about the running of schools.

The local authority associations are divided among themselves inasmuch as they have different interest bases: the problems of rural schools have no high priority in the AMC or the ILEA. The AMC and CCA as the two 'general' associations have been worried about the 'kidology' – the assertion that there should be a special place for education within local authorities at a time when clerks and treasurers were increasingly concerned to develop corporate planning. Not all councils want to expand education at the expense of the ratepayers, although CCA and AMC minutes are surprisingly silent on any local resistance to expansion.

How effective have they been as interest groups? On our somewhat biased sample of interviews, ministers seem to have found them more effective than did officials. But this may be because political leaders are likely to be more receptive to external pressures.

One former minister thought them more interested in the status of local government than anything else and not, therefore, very influential in educational policy-making as such. They were divided on the introduction of general grants in 1968 and took no initiative on the introduction of the binary system. The DES promoted it and they approved of it once it was put through. They were more active on matters of collective concern such as the pooling arrangements for further education, the agreement of conditions of service and salaries of teachers, and on DES proposals that lead to any change in expenditure patterns for local authorities or changes in local authority powers. But they have not changed educational objectives on the national scale. This pressure for change might well be the role of individual local authorities rather than the role of their associations, although new alignments might change this stance.

The associations are explicitly and unashamedly reactive rather than innovative. They are an important example of the consensual network and inasmuch as they break consensus it is for obvious sectional interests.

Chapter 7

Teachers' Associations

The main schoolteachers' associations which we have studied are the National Union of Teachers, the Joint Four (associations representing teachers and heads in predominantly selective secondary schools) and the National Association of Schoolmasters. Once again, we shall discuss general characteristics before describing three of the more important in more detail.

STATUS AND INTERACTION

These associations are formally recognised interest groups. They are only a wafer away from the local authority associations in consultative status. Although local authorities are statutory bodies performing duties and exercising powers under legislation which confer on their associations a stronger role in formal decision-making, teachers' associations are party to many of the most important decisions. They do not see every official promulgation in draft but certainly they are consulted about most of those which affect the interests of their members or the running of the education system in general, although under Mrs Thatcher the DES was thought to have been less consultative [1]. We have already quoted Crosland's consultation with them on the place of teachers in the reorganisation of selective education. In some matters directly concerned with conditions of work, such as the supervision of school meals, circulars refer to explicit agreements reached with them [2].

As with the local authority associations, the main teachers' associations are always invited to give evidence to official and parliamentary committees on education. They have a formalised and established place on negotiations for teacher salaries. Over a period of time they maintain a firm position about the profession's control over its membership and standing, the pattern of teacher education, the raising of the school leaving age, the role of inspectors and advisers, the quality of school buildings and the place of the profession generally, and have opportunities to state that position. The distribution of power has changed between the various teachers' associations. The strongest, oldest, and most powerful is the NUT. During our period, however, the National Association of Schoolmasters found its way to full consultative status.

The teachers' associations are powerful bodies. Their memberships in 1960 and in 1973 are shown in Chart V below.

Chart V: *Membership of Teachers' Associations: 1960 and 1973*

	1960	1973
NUT	237,964	320,000
Joint Four	40,953	80,000[b]
NAS	22,651	60,230
ATTI	13,121[a]	40,094

[a] 1962 first available figures.
[b] Approximate number.

What particular programmes and ideologies have they been concerned to advance? First, plainly, they have a clear trade union role, advancing and negotiating salaries and conditions of work for their members. This role is not as straightforward as it seems, for it can be elevated to discussion of the role of the teacher and discussion of different philosophies of education within different parts of the educational process. For example, many of the status struggles have centred upon arguments about the relative importance of the primary stage of education, and adequate allowance for teachers who pursue in-service education. Generally, too, the associations assume that what is good for teachers is good for education: small classes, good salaries and relief from non-teaching chores.

Secondly, the associations are a strong force in creating opinion about the style, organisation and content of education. By their membership of successive committees and commissions [3], on all of which they had some members even when, as with CAC appointments, these were 'personal', they were part of the progressive, liberal and child-centred movement which has predominated in British education and which has affected official policies on school examinations, as with the Secondary School Examinations Council reports from Norwood onwards which regarded examinations as at best a necessary evil, and as in the 'new orthodoxy' which assumes that open schooling in the primary schools is best. Herein lies the importance of the emergence of the National Association of Schoolmasters. For whereas the NUT in particular has been concerned to argue that, given their freedom, the schools and their pupils will establish good standards of work and conduct in the schools, the NAS has not been reluctant to break consensus in expressing its pessimism.

If, indeed, we look at the main policy movements stated in Chart II it is clear that the teacher associations have been first of all concerned to maintain and advance those policies which are typified as educational and institutional and which are the continuous themes of British educational policy. They have not resisted the social and economic policy intrusions of the mid-1960s and, indeed, have often supported changes in policy for social reasons. But because they cannot focus opinions on such an issue as comprehensive education easily, they have had to wait for political determinations by ministers or by local authorities before coming out openly behind the more contentious social policies.

THE NATIONAL UNION OF TEACHERS

Founded in 1870, the National Union of Teachers is the most important of the teacher associations. In 1973 it had nearly a third of a million members in schools and establishments for further education, which made it the largest in Europe. It represents the majority of primary and secondary school teachers.[1] Its financial assets are formidable. It is, generally, a major public institution, with all the characteristics and resources of one.

It has an excellent library. It has one of the best-established legal departments in the British trade union movement, with a staff of seventeen headed by two lawyers. It is reputed to have spent £5,000

[1] The NUT has associations or partnerships with the ATTI, the Association of Teachers of Domestic Subjects, the Youth Service Association, the British Association of Organisers and Lecturers in Physical Education, the National Association of Youth Service Officers, the Association of Educational Psychologists and the British Association of Art Therapists.

in representing members' interests in the Maria Colwell case, although the main burden of defence fell on social workers rather than on the teachers involved in it. Its offices stand formidably in the middle of the education interest groups' square mile in London.

Organisation

We are mainly concerned here with the Union's impact on policy and will describe only briefly the overall organisation structure. There are about 560 local associations which elect delegates to conference, put forward resolutions and have a primarily political function. There are 104 divisions which correspond to local authority areas and have primarily educational functions. The supreme authority is the annual conference which consists of representatives of local and county divisions. An executive consisting of fourty-four members, which includes four representatives of the ATTI and two representatives of the ATDs, is elected every second year from twenty-seven electoral districts. The divisions are coterminous with the areas of local education authorities and act as the negotiating bodies. They nominate or elect teacher representatives to local education authorities and are the principal organs of representation to local authorities.

The work of the Union on individual teacher matters is mainly carried out by twelve highly experienced regional officials based in regional offices throughout England and Wales. Their salaries were over £4,000 a year in 1974; they have a car and a secretary and are expected to represent individual members on such matters as injuries sustained at work, wrongful dismissal or other conditions of service questions. They refer matters of principle to Union headquarters and make use of the Union's legal education and salaries departments.

The executive committee of the union devolves much of its work for detailed consideration and scrutiny to committees concerned with finance, general purposes, membership and organisation, law and tenure, salaries and supernanuation, education, publicity and public relations, and international relations [4].

Objectives

The NUT's declared objectives are: (*a*) 'to secure improvement in the education of the child'; and (*b*) 'to achieve a higher status for the teaching profession'. Its prospectus quotes with approval a statement that it is 'neither an incorporated professional institute nor a trade union, but a teachers' professional organisation which combines the best features of both, with functions peculiarly its own'.

The NUT argues that it is predominantly concerned with the advancement of teachers' standards of work and with the establishment of professional standards which will distinguish their members, by virtue of qualification and training, from those who are not members. It also says that the larger aims are 'the unity of all teachers and ... the establishment of an integrated system of education'. Hence the hostility to the National Association of Schoolmasters with its overt competition for recruitment and what the NUT regards as a disruption of unity. The moves towards a unified profession have been persistent [5].

The NUT's claim to be concerned as much or more with educational advance as with trade union matters accounts for the emphasis placed on the work of the education department. It had four senior officials, a total of twenty-five staff, and an education budget of £84,000 (net of overheads) in 1973. The salaries department had a smaller staff but a similar salaries bill. Its educational policy statements have become more numerous – perhaps four a year now – and effective over recent years. Some are on purely educational matters such as work experience and the schools (1973), others are concerned with structural issues, as in a pamphlet on the reform of teacher education (May 1973). In that document, for example, the Union claims to have played a prominent part in the debate and, 'in conjunction with some of the other interested organisations such as UCET and the ATCDE, was responsible for a number of the constructive alternative proposals that were eventually incorporated into the White Paper' (1972). The same pamphlet also expresses the Union as being 'at a loss to explain why' Circular 7/73 suggested a 40 per cent cut in initial training places without consulting the Union. The pamphlet claims that 'the initiative of the union, together with the partners of teacher education, was able to synthesise the opposition to the James Report into a constructive policy for reform', and argues that the area training organisations should be replaced by 'new administrative organisations which should not be dominated by the universities'.

On the certificate of general education (1972), raising the school leaving age (August 1972), the safeguarding of teachers' rights when schools are reorganised (1971), the reform of local government (undated), the Butler and Briault reports (1973), the supply of teachers (July 1973), the employment of children (1973), and a prospective education act (1969), the union produced clear, well-documented and cogent statements. It, too, has commissioned outside researchers in its survey of teacher supply [6], where they argued for the substitution of range forecasting for single value forecasting and for tests of the sensitivity of calculating teacher requirements. Sophisticated stuff this, but relevant to teacher supply policy. This survey is significant because while the NUT may not like universities it retains academics to help expand procedures and techniques.

The pamphlet on *Raising the School Leaving Age* co-ordinated a great deal of research conducted locally on the preparations made by local authorities for the raising of the school leaving age. The pamphlet is interesting from many points of view. First, it demonstrates a somewhat uneasy relationship with some individual local authorities. Fifty-seven did not reply, and nine refused to provide the Union with copies of reports on the grounds that they were confidential and available only to the Secretary of State and the Department of Education.

Secondly, it shows the Union at work on activities which certainly affect the working conditions of teachers, but also have a broader educational canvass. The Union maintained that the success of the five-year secondary course would 'depend on such factors as the concentrated build-up of techniques, curriculum development, projects, staffing, equipment and buildings and upon the adequate provision of in-service education'. The replies showed great variations in school building between authorities. One city quoted in the NUT document 'is being forced to delay new programmes in the curriculum of its schools because of an accommodation crisis. The other city highlighted, contrary to this approach, is trying, despite its scarce resources, to co-ordinate its entire secondary school development and building programmes.' The NUT identified two basic approaches – that of a local authority that caters for extra numbers of children simply by adding the necessary amount of additional accommodation while the other meets the problem by a much more thorough reorganisation of its total secondary provision.

On curriculum, it found that only 61 per cent of local authorities were contemplating changes in curriculum structure. No education authority mentioned any plan for initiating or expanding work experience in its schools – a policy urged both by the union in its document *Work Experience and Secondary Schools* (July 1971) and by the Newsom Report (1963). The returns also showed important information about staffing and in-service education. While many local authorities were plainly being hampered by financial stringencies, the union survey indicated that this was only a partial explanation.

'The inadequacy of their preparations may be equally attributed towards attitudes towards raising the school leaving age. As a result the Executive urges the Secretary of State to withdraw restrictions on school building improvements and to find additional financial support for the critical years 1972–3 and 1973–4, to ensure that there was a revised rate support grant to take account of additional staffing needed, that in-service courses should be provided far more generously and vigorously and that local authorities provide additional finance to enable teachers to participate in a considerably expanding "on-going programme".'

The Union thus puts out statements of policy and urges its members to put pressure as best they can both locally and centrally. In this the NUT uses its two main journals, *The Teacher* and *Secondary Education*.

NUT policy on conditions and salaries is unsurprising. It wants more money for its members and a greater uniformity of salaries between different sectors of the service. A poster, now somewhat out of date, on the walls of headquarters, reads:

> *Full time teacher wanted,*
> *starting salary £13 a week*

The Union has always pressed hard for more in-service training. In its evidence to James it suggested that one year in ten should be devoted to it. It maintains that the schools have to settle for teachers who spend twenty hours a week for perhaps forty years in the classroom with no opportunity for further study, and no inducement towards self-evaluation. As a result, able potential teachers either never join the profession or leave quickly. And for those who remain, defensive attitudes such as a strong belief in tenure rights become the norm.

The NUT inevitably faces ambiguity as between its professional and trade union objectives. NUT conferences and members tend to assert that good conditions and salaries or small classes are good for education as well as for teachers. The Union scored its most significant victory when it persuaded Edward Short, Secretary of State and one of its own members, to cease to allow unqualified teachers to teach in schools. In urging the removal of untrained teachers the Union maintained that it was improving standards, though this major victory was not accompanied by any agreement that would safeguard standards in the schools, which were now to be staffed solely by qualified teachers. The Union argued, however, that the elimination of the untrained would make ancillary teachers more acceptable in the schools, a move attempted by Sir David Eccles in the 1950s and successfully opposed. The removal of the unqualified was long pressed for in conference motions. Parliamentary Questions had been placed throughout the sixties and the change came, of course, at a good time, when the Department was about to reduce the output of the teacher training system.

The Union has advanced views well in line with the progressive consensus. On educational matters it has been fully in line with the liberal assumptions of British education. In its evidence to every consultative committee and central council it has protested the need for informality in schools, for curriculum related to children's interests, for the emancipation of schools from the artificial pressures imposed by external examinations or the demands of employers; and was thus party to the creation of the flexible arrangements for the Certificate of Secondary Education. It has therefore found common cause with the teacher training system, HM Inspectors of Schools and the doctrines enunciated by successive committees and Central Advisory Councils, although its liberalism will always inevitably be tempered by the range of its membership.

Secondly, it has argued for the integrative nature of the educational system; that primary, secondary, further and higher education should have no artificial barriers making it difficult for children to transfer from one stage to another, or between different types of, for example, secondary schools. And this argument, of course, reinforces its arguments, favourable to the majority of its members, for the assimilation of primary school teacher salaries and conditions with those of secondary schools teachers, or for the assimilation of conditions of teachers in further education with those in universities.

The Union has been strongly expansionist. It has argued for more and better school buildings, for more and better-paid teachers. Here, indeed, it has not followed the precedent of the older established professions which have kept numbers low so that status and rewards will be high. There is some ambivalence among union members about the drive towards a profession of half a million.

On such issues as universal secondary education the NUT maintains it has kept up a 'bombardment' – for the Union believes in the educability of all children. Its attitude towards comprehensive schools was first a belief in multilateral schools until 1945 (as in its evidence to the Hadow Committee). Until the mid-1960s, the Union had to reckon with its own grammar school membership. The grammar school advisory committee was both elitist and powerful, but was disbanded in 1965. Many of its members first followed the progressive Conservative hope in thinking that secondary modern schools would successfully provide GCE courses and enjoy parity of esteem with the grammar schools. But members who saw how well the secondary modern schools could develop became frustrated, because the next stage of development was inhibited by the existence of grammar schools which creamed off pupils [7]. The Union, however, could only swing behind the comprehensive policy wholeheartedly when it thought that its membership regarded them as both right and inevitable. This it first did in its evidence to the Plowden Committee in 1965.

The NUT is in favour of local rather than central government control as can be seen from the comments on the Maud Report and on the 1970 and 1971 White Papers on local government. But, perhaps paradoxically, it gave evidence in favour of a strong, central HM Inspectorate, because it enabled the schools to get relief, where necessary, from over-parochial influences [8].

While it has pressed for parental involvement in governing bodies, its members are cautious about possible threats to professional control, particularly when this might lead to unqualified intervention in the schools.

The NUT is thus a strong, powerful and well organised group which has long been a major element in developing consensual policies. In the 1960s it found itself challenged by the militant competition of the NAS, by its own Rank and File Movement, and by the general upheaval in salary differentials which upset many continuous and consensual assumptions in society at large.

Putting on the Pressure

How does an interest group such as the NUT make its impact? First, as Coates has documented, there are the conventional means. Its conferences are well reported, it has a large press office, and its pronouncements are part of the normal and major currency of educational journalism. It has continuous contact with the DES though, significantly enough for a professional organisation, not with HMIs. For the most part this is not at ministerial level, although the union's executive committee probably meets the Secretary of State four times a year. They always meet him or her after the annual conference to present the conference's resolutions.

There are regular and more frequent contacts with DES officials who, according to a senior NUT official, contact the NUT as often as they are contacted by it. Most discussion is on educational issues but might also include such matters as consultation with the Union on the study of absenteeism launched in 1973 as well as salary or superannuation issues. DES circulars and other promulgations are sent in draft although, since 1970, the Union complains,[1] more have been 'for information' than used to be the case or than the NUT likes. Often the meetings are on technical but important points. For example, the executive believes that school leaving dates should be altered to 1 June. Detailed discussions took place between two officials from the DES and three representatives of the NUT [9]. Part of the discussion consisted of the Union asking DES officials to advise the Secretary of State to initiate formal consultation with all interested parties, evidently an important step in getting policy moving. In an early meeting the officials had agreed to consult within the DES and with other government departments on the possible implications of changing the school leaving date. 'If there were no difficulties the Union would seek a meeting with the Secretary of State in October or November, but if serious technical or legal difficulties emerged a further meeting for officials would be arranged.' This illustrates the conventions by which the Union puts on pressure.

Their other point of pressure is with the local authorities who own and control the schools. There are frequent meetings with officials and leading members of the local authority associations. All such meetings are fully recorded by the NUT. Such issues as the conditions of service for teachers are raised. In many matters the local authorities share the view of the NUT rather than the DES. They do not appear to the NUT to be simply another local dimension of government. The NUT joins local government in making representations on the numbers for which classrooms are built. Agreement with the local authority associations was reached on the splitting of the London allowance and salaries. On some issues at least education officers identify with the teachers interests – where, of course, most of their origins lie.

The NUT shares local authority anxieties about the Bains

---

[1] This point was recorded before the change of government in 1974.

Report, which seemed to propose an erosion of the powers of the education committees, to which the local NUT organisations have access.

The NUT also has relationships with the other interest groups. They are strongest with the formally established ones. NUT officials believe that such bodies as CASE have a declining role, that ACE is too 'middle class' to be effective, but even the largely NUT supported Campaign for Educational Advance has lost its fire. In their opinion, the more specialist pressure groups such as the National Children's Bureau or the Campaign for Comprehensive Education stand a greater chance of having an impact.

The NUT and Parliament

The NUT has long been strong in Parliament. In 1895, two members became MPs. In 1964, with Labour's return to power, there were thirty-seven NUT members of whom all but one were Labour. There were in 1974 perhaps ninety former teachers in the House of Commons. In 1970, the Union had former members in the following ministerial and parliamentary positions: the Speaker of the House of Commons (Dr Horace King), the Leader of the House of Commons (Mr Fred Peart), the Foreign Secretary (Mr Michael Stewart), the Secretary of State for Education (Mr Edward Short) and the Secretary of State for Wales (Mr George Thomas). Other non-cabinet ministers such as Miss Alice Bacon were also members. In 1973 as many as thirty MPs attended meetings with the NUT.

The Union sponsored four MPs in 1973.[1] They were Edward Short, John Jennings (a Conservative MP), Barry Jones and George Thomas. Each of them received £400 a year, the payment of travel and expenses to Union meetings and an expert briefing service. But other MPs as well, and particularly a shadow minister of education, can expect to receive detailed briefings on issues on which they seek help, or on Bills or other matters being debated within the House. One of them at least [10] saw all its papers, including those coming to the NUT through its membership of official committees. Union officials are in the House of Commons or in the House of Lords before and during a debate. It can be assumed that the Union's relationship with members is valuable to it. Indeed, one Union official in talking of an MP said that, since the MP's performances in the House were poor, it would 'never use him again'.

In 1973, the NUT particularly briefed MPs on three Bills – Child

---

[1] The union is now reviewing its scheme for sponsoring MPs.

Employment, Work Experience, Education and Training – as they went through the House.

There are two particular instruments, apart from briefing for debates, that the Union uses in the parliamentary scene. The first is inspired Parliamentary Questions. Parliamentary Questions tend to follow rather than lead departmental policy (*see* Chapter 9) and, on the whole, the NUT's use of Parliamentary Questions reflects this except on questions of teacher pay and superannuation, where 550 out of a total of 8,000 were asked on this subject during our period – some of them, but not all, inspired by the NUT, but all as policy was being formulated.

The NUT gives evidence to Select Committees. We cannot, again, be certain as to the impact on policy because we cannot even be sure that Select Committees have an impact.

Impact

The NUT is a classic interest group which advances both the causes of its members and of the education service at large. It has all the apparatus and structure of a legitimised pressure group. Its committees and its official structure parallel those of the decision-making structure in the DES with which it must relate.

Its impact on decision-making is uncertain and difficult to ascertain. The pressure is certainly effective when the world at large is ready for changes or when it has a compliant Secretary of State, such as Edward Short, who made training compulsory for all teachers, and followed directly, and without considering the pressure put by others, including the DES's own Central Advisory Council, on corporal punishment in schools. For the most part, however, the pressures it asserts are general rather than specific although it consciously tries to build up a climate for change in its general activity [11].

The NUT effectively undertakes the role of an interest group in aggregating the demands of members, articulating them, and in presenting them at the points of pressure. Its most aggressive actions have related to pay and superannuation.

How far has it affected policy? Here we can only list the areas where the NUT maintains [12] that it has had an impact and perhaps identify one or two areas where others, too, recognise the impact.

The NUT claims that it successfully pressed the DES to recognise the importance of primary education. Its pamphlet *Fair Pay for Primary Schools* was extensively quoted in a House of Commons debate well before the Plowden Committee was convened. The NUT displayed the merits of primary education at the Olympia exhibition of 1959 and in such films as *I Want to Go to School*, which was produced in 1960. It helped build up the climate of opinion about the overcrowding of schools through the building survey of 1962 which showed that conditions in primary schools were poorer than in any others, and this triggered the DES to make its own survey.

The Union gave evidence to the Plowden Committee on selection and on comprehensive education. This was the first occasion on which the NUT came out in favour of the abolition of selection. Previously it had supported no more than substantial experiments in comprehensive education and this decision, it maintains, helped Labour ministers to come out decisively in favour in 1964 because they knew they would not have to fight the main teachers' body. Indeed, it then was able to put pressure on the Secretary of State, Edward Short, through two MPs, Stan Newens and Christopher Price, to make the policy tougher. Headquarters' staff had always been open in favouring comprehensive education. By the time Mrs Thatcher withdrew Circular 10/65 the NUT was in a position to put out a statement immediately.

The NUT also put up pressure through local authorities which were considering schemes for the end of selection. Working parties with such local authorities as Manchester, Birmingham and Bromley were established.

The NUT helped build up pressure against Mrs Margaret Thatcher's refusal to approve comprehensive schemes and thus created a climate of conflict which helped test the decisions made by the Minister.

NUT pressure indirectly caused the DES to abandon an exercise on the cost-effectiveness of education for the sixteen to nineteen year olds.

Again, the NUT conference and leadership, unlike the National Association of Schoolmasters, strongly supported the raising of the school leaving age and backed successive secretaries of state in this; it criticised Patrick Gordon Walker for agreeing to its delay under treasury pressure in 1968. Its influence on this issue at least assured ministers of majority teacher backing.

The NUT claims to have frustrated at least part of the James Report on teacher education even before the report was published, because it acted on well documented leaks of some of the proposals. It has 1,500 members in colleges and university departments of

education, and has close links with the teacher education associations. Before giving evidence to James, it set up an *ad hoc* committee and wrote to 600 local associations (with which it communi-
cates every week) to ask what practising teachers thought might be
wrong with teacher training. Normally there is about a 10 per cent
return to such enquiries but some 50 per cent of the associations
replied in this case. Material collated in *The Reform of Teacher
Education* (May 1971) was the product of five working parties
which met mainly at weekends.

The NUT is not, of course, single minded on all issues. Traditionally, the NUT has believed in all-through secondary education to be
provided in schools for the eleven to nineteen year olds. Part of the
leadership of the NUT is particularly worried about transfers at
sixteen to sixth-form colleges or further education colleges because
they believe that the poorer children are unlikely to make the
transition. And so *Into the 1970s* contains a compromise formula.
Where there is division in the ranks, the NUT has less influence.
Thus views on streaming in primary schools are indeterminate,
particularly since a pronouncement on such a purely educational
issue might conflict with its policy of maintaining the autonomy of
the schools. For the same reason it opposes the banning by local
authorities of corporal punishment.

The NUT claims that the DES has found it easier to get support
for more in-service training because of NUT support. On teacher
supply questions the NUT is still pressing for a larger teaching force
and in so doing it challenges individual local authorities as well as
the Department. This pressure, it claims, has made local authorities
more prepared to budget for the full quota of teachers allowed them
by the DES, there being no compulsion on them to reach any
particular standard. The DES is concerned only with the total output and with general rationing schemes to ensure that no local
authority takes more than its share. The mechanism of the rate
support grant compels nothing.

The NUT briefed the Opposition on, and led the campaign
against, the Teachers' Superannuation Act of 1956. In the same
field, the NUT takes credit for frustrating Sir David Eccles's scheme
to bring in teachers' aides. It maintains that he wanted them to take
on teachers' duties and not simply to be ancillaries to teachers. The
Union felt that it was backed later by the NFER's study of the
teacher's day [13].

The leaders find it difficult to keep the whole membership in line
and feel that their claim is strongest when unified as in the 1969 to

1970 interim pay award negotiations, or in attacking the issue of superannuation contributions [14]. It is not too cynical to note that both of these are concerned with the income of individual teachers rather than any major issue of policy. No teacher will disagree that he is underpaid and should get more; there might well be disagreement about, for example, the place or style of comprehensive education, or the status of teachers in the schools, and, certainly, there are differences of opinion about the management of individual schools in terms of the relationship between the head and the staff.

The Union has increasingly concerned itself with matters affecting the working of schools; the right of teachers to be consulted and to participate in the running of the schools, and their right to be consulted by the heads and to share in decision-making. A working party produced a report which was modified by the executive. Finally, the Union rightly takes credit for killing the Curriculum Study Group and for the creation of the Schools Council [15].

In general the NUT has impact, though one recent member of staff believes the Union weakens itself by taking umbrage on status issues with other unions, by internal bickering, and by rushing into print with sweeping statements. Reports of attitudes towards the work of the Schools Council are that there is a healthy resistance to educational fads but insufficient devotion to sustained enquiry and developmental work. The development of broader aims and more eclectic attitudes and methods in education is not reckoned to be a forte. This does not deprive the NUT of negotiation power and force. On the contrary, it is by that token less placatory and more militant. But it might deprive the Union of a more general appeal to progressive educational opinion.

One former minister regarded it as 'most persistent' [16]. He also believed that it was more interested in advancing education than its own narrow interests. Officials acknowledged its influence on salaries, the aborting of the teachers' council and on the emergence of the Schools Council from the Curriculum Study Group, which the unions helped kill. It has impact, obviously, on all questions of teachers' conditions as with the recalculation of superannuation needs (the 'non-fund') where an attempt to give relief to local authorities rather than teachers was successfully resisted.

But the NUT must be prisoner of its own success. Because it is the most powerful of the unions, anxious to get both improvement and equilibrium, it must be part of the main educational consensus. The consensus must be broken up from time to time and its leaders regard some of the policies adopted between 1970 and 1974 on a change of government as a clear breakdown of that consensus – cuts in finance, in school buildings and in the general pace of educational advance.

As seen by the press, the NUT has been a major force in education. Most major changes affecting the schools were urged by the NUT before they were implemented; the raising of the school leaving age would never have happened without it. It put up pressures for nursery education. Only where larger social values are involved so that consensus is less certain is it less committed. The process has been described as 'drip, drip, drip'. It is the Union which has pushed resource allocation towards primary rather than secondary schools. It is the Union which has created a compression of the salary structure. It is the Union which has made movement in curriculum conservative if in the progressive mode.

But opinion is that the Union is no longer as major an influence as it was. It has lost some public respect partly because the 'professional' stance put forward by Sir Ronald Gould has been affected by the sharper trade union approach of Max Morris and others. The 1969 strike also showed it was as much a trade union as a professional association. And this it confirmed by following the National Association of Schoolmasters into the TUC. By contrast, the National Association of Schoolmasters has been able to make the running as being more aggressive. The NUT has clung to an old optimistic idealism – described by one journalist as 'panglossian'.

Where there is a conflict between teachers and a more general educational interest, the NUT tends to be split. It is relatively united on educational values and the institutional values which back up the present structure, with its provision for teacher status and authority. Inevitably, its attitudes are less certain on the wider social and economic policies, and the impact it will have on more continuous educational assumptions is strong.

THE NATIONAL ASSOCIATION OF SCHOOLMASTERS

The contrast between the NUT and the NAS is remarkable. The NUT is now over one hundred years old whereas the NAS itself states that it largely built up its support from ex-servicemen after the 1914–18 war. The NUT maintains the need for a single teachers' association in which education will be seen as a 'seamless garment' and in which there will be equality of treatment between teachers at all levels. The NAS, however, long resisted equal pay for women teachers. This is not explained by abstract principles but because of

the need to retain well-qualified men in the schools, whose salaries
were depressed because the teaching profession predominantly consisted of unmarried women.

It was admitted to the Burnham Committee only in 1961, and
then because of a glaring tactical error by Lord Hailsham who
insisted on exclusion because he would be 'reluctant to admit a
body to salary negotiations whose declared objective was to oppose
established government policy'. Lord Hailsham was thus confirming
a general assumption about educational interest groups – they are
expected to assimilate themselves to at least some of the consensuses sought by government.

But the officials of the NAS [17] make it plain that the differences go well beyond what is now only one important issue out of
many. The NUT is a trade union, professional body and a promotional body with political and educational attitudes towards the
educational service. The NAS is single-mindedly a trade union. It
does not believe that it can be, in the words of its General Secretary,
'the educational conscience of the nation'. That is what the politicians are for. Nor does it believe that it should be the guardian of
professional standards. Instead an educational or teachers' council
should be established, which can take on a role equivalent to that of
the General Medical Council (which should not itself take on the
functions of the British Medical Association). Only the lawyers, it
maintains, manage to get away with what is a confusion of role
between their trade union and their professional validating body.

Its attitude towards the tactics of advancement for teachers is
radically different from that of its colleague associations. Its
membership shot up from just over 22,000 in 1960 to 31,000 in 1961
because it brought teachers out on strike. Its membership in 1973
was 60,230 and it now has the majority of male schoolteachers in its
membership. This was not so in the 1950s when successive ministers
refused it membership of the Burnham Committee because it was
the principal representative of no distinctive group of teachers. It
broke the traditions of the Burnham Committee by reporting back
to its members on the committee's proceedings. Apparently, the
Association did not realise that it was breaking protocol in doing
this although it was assumed by the other partners in the negotiations that it was done for publicity reasons. Certainly it enjoys
taking credit for unconventionality.

What is the distinctive aspect of its policy? It is undoubtedly
what it claims to be, a predominantly militant trade union. Thus,
the General Secretary displays a hard-headed understanding of

negotiation and militant tactics – 'it is far easier to get members out in the autumn than in the summer period. This is why the DES always tries to pull its fast ones during the summer term' [18]. Terry Casey maintains the importance of putting pressure on a narrow front and making sure that 'one can get one's members out once one has got them in'. Teachers' strikes were held in 1961 in centres selected partly because they were in areas where television news centres were located. The NAS tries only to support a strong case. Once a point has been won on a clear and strong issue, they find it possible to be successful on the more marginal ones.

Its organisation is simple. The Association has an executive committee and a senior staff of four. As with the AEC, the impact of the chief permanent official, Terry Casey, is obvious and powerful. He must carry his executive with him, but he maintains the importance of being able to give them strong and clear advice which, in the main, they ought to be able to accept. The energy and general competence of Casey and his team are not in doubt, even among his opponents.

Relationships with other members of the educational system vary greatly. Once admitted to Burnham and the first rows about the revelation of the proceedings overcome, the NAS increasingly acquired the characteristics of other interest groups. In describing relationships with the DES, Casey repeated virtually the same words as Sir William Alexander (interviewed a few hours before) in saying that individual officials would never be attacked – only the minister and the policies which the official represented. Relationships with individual officials are good, and became better once the Association was admitted to Burnham and the Schools Council.

It is, indeed, part of the general network of educational bodies now. It is associated with some forty bodies as well as the courts of universities and all CSE examining boards. There is no important body from which it is excluded even if the list includes such exotica as the education committee of the British-India Steam Navigation Company (P & O).

On some matters, indeed, the NAS became closer to the DES than had the NUT. For example, it supported a teachers' council and Toby Weaver, then the Deputy Secretary working on the report on the teachers' council, shared Casey's disappointment that the NUT would not allow it to go forward. It has access to the Secretary of State in the same way as do other associations, and in 1973 was vigorously trying to gain advantages in teachers' pensions, particularly in terms of members whose war service was not recognised. To the Secretary of State the NAS argued that this would give them no more than was given to some of the civil servants present in the room with them. The NAS also 'made a comparative study' which, as their officials put it, showed that former members of the Gestapo or the SS, who were now teachers in Germany, had their war service counted, while British bomber pilots did not. This formed the message of an NAS poster. In dealing with local authorities on cases of wrongful dismissal or conditions the NAS can be tough once sure of the case. With the DES, the NAS puts up strong pressure but has reached accommodatory working relationships. The same is true of relationships with the local authority associations, although it does not claim there to be warm working relationships with them. On virtually every issue there is conflict with the NUT although personal relationships between officers can be reasonably cordial. It has acquired a 'trustful basis' of relationships with civil servants.

The NAS has the image of a right-wing, even *poujadiste* and male dominated, organisation. (Casey, in fact, is a member of the Labour Party and does not know the political affiliations of his close colleagues.) The attitude towards equal pay has become more sophisticated inasmuch as it is now concerned with differentiation in salary so as to place a higher premium on long and continuing service, whether male or female, and allowances for family responsibilities. The NAS was not in favour of raising the school leaving age in 1972 but only when it became possible to secure adequate staffing and buildings. The NAS argues for changes in the present law of religious education so as to make it the same as any other subject of the curriculum – an option which teachers should be allowed to exercise as a professional choice.

Yet behind these growing changes in style, so that the NAS can be both militant in arguing a case and consensual in relationhsips with the decision-makers, there remain doctrines which differentiate it from the other teacher associations which are, in general, liberal in their approaches towards educational problems. The NAS is more resolute on the right of teachers to use corporal punishment although it too, asserts that it should be a matter of last resort. Heads should be able to exclude uncontrollable pupils from the schools. 'Indiscipline is getting in the way of the head and teachers' real job.' When asked how a local authority will then exercise its mandatory duty to provide a place for a pupil in school, the NAS retorts: 'that is why a chief education officer is paid £8,000 a year and a head only £4,000 a year'. In 1972 the NAS was in conflict with the National Council for Civil Liberties on schoolchildren's rights [19]. But it also maintains idiosyncratic attitudes on educational doctrines such as the importance of male pupils being taught by male teachers. Here the NAS surely parts company from not only the NUT with its majority of women members, but virtually every other group of educationalists as well.

In pursuing trade union and other functions, the NAS has acquired the usual mechanisms. Until recently one Liberal MP, John Pardoe, was 'sponsored' and received £400 a year. It became technically difficult for the NAS to sustain this practice since it has no political funds from which such a political payment could be made. But he, together with other MPs with whom it relates, Fergus Montgomery (Conservative) and Brian O'Malley (Labour), all received briefing and other facilities. The NAS, of course, briefed such MPs as Charles Fletcher-Cooke in the early 1960s when he led an attack on Sir David Eccles's refusal to admit the NAS to the Burnham Committee. Sir Wavell Wakefield knew Terry Casey (who used to teach in his constituency, St Marylebone) and approached Eccles, who has confirmed that the approach influenced him [20]. MPs are briefed before debates, but Casey and his colleagues do not regard them as a prime way in which policy is moved.

Of all of the interest groups, the NAS is the best example of how legitimisation can be secured by a resolute enough body. By taking industrial action for the first time in post-war educational history it broke the consensual and gentlemanly style in which the DES had traditionally conducted relationships among the 'partners' [21] or 'trimumvirate' [22] in the education service. It has refused to accept the metaphor of partnership. Instead it has looked towards methods of pressure, applied consistently, according to increasingly well-known and understood rules; but it is nonetheless willing to come out into the open and assert a point of view and the interest of its members without inhibition when it feels it to be necessary.

THE ASSOCIATION OF ASSISTANT MISTRESSES

We arbitrarily selected the Association of Assistant Mistresses as being a teachers' association in strong contrast with the NAS. It shares membership of the Joint Four with the Association of Assistant Masters, the Incorporated Association of Headmasters, and the Head Mistresses' Association.

It was founded in 1884 as an extension of the Head Mistresses'

Association and was primarily concerned with the standardisation of conditions for its members. Its Secretary, Sheila Wood, believes that the Association is concerned with the improvement of education generally as well as with the improvement of teachers' conditions [23]. She believes, however, that the Association has placed a high priority on improvements of curriculum and organisation, and on educational issues generally.

The Association in recent years has grown at the rate of about three hundred members a year. There is a big turnover of membership because of marriage. About eight years ago as many as two to three thousand joined, at a time when more women began to join unions. Also the NUT's decision to join the TUC diverted some members towards it. There are between thirty-two and thirty-three thousand members.

The Secretary has worked for the Association since 1960. The long term of office held by leading members of the Association gives them more influence because they know issues, and because they are able to perceive what is possible. The Joint Four secondary associations are a minority but, because they do not have a constant turnover of presidents, are always listened to. The AAM has always assumed that it is important not to try too much at a time but to look for continuity and for a pragmatic testing of possibilities rather than for conflict.

It attitude towards some of the main issues is moderate and unemphatic. Since the 1940s, the Association has been in favour of multilateral schools. It is not now against comprehensive education but believes that reorganisation has not been adequately thought through and is piecemeal, that local authorities have not thought it out in terms of the children involved, and that the balance between different elements of the curriculum is not yet right. Nor as yet is the ethos of the schools clarified between different traditions and expectations. It is concerned that resources are never enough for change and that teachers are given no opportunity to prepare for the new task. It is firm that sixth-form colleges are not really a runner. The Association believes the sixteens to nineteens have a better deal in schools than in further education colleges. The first year of the sixth form comes at a transitional age when the concepts of a family group and parental care are important.

Teachers might like sixth-form colleges and there is no reason why several types of provision should not be established. There should be options for everybody to be in school until they are eighteen or nineteen, and the Association was unhappy about the

Exeter proposal to convert all post-sixteen places into sixth-form colleges. It tried to stop it, but failed, and had made representations to the LEA and the DES.

The Association feels there is no problem about members' rights to participate in decision-making in the schools. It was not in favour, as were the NUT, of a stated machinery for this.

The education committee has concerned itself with such issues as curriculum and homework. Conference may not want to come to a consensus on some issues and there is no attempt to strain for a general policy when this is not absolutely necessary or desired.

It held a ballot on whether to go on strike four years ago, but the NUT had, in any case, achieved the point in dispute by their strike, and so it could avoid action of its own. It was in favour of a teachers' general council.

The AAM for the most part is gradualist, concerned with conditions of service, and takes a fairly detached view of the major issues of education as they affect social matters. It perhaps responds to social changes more than it affects them. Its leadership believes that change is secured by negotiation and a grasp of tactics rather than by dramatic action.

TEACHER ASSOCIATION BEHAVIOUR

This chapter has been connected with the *influence* of the interest groups. Fortunately, there has been an excellent study of their *behaviour*. R. D. Coates [24] has shown how the traditional forms of pressure still persist. Another authority, R. D. Manzer [25], places them firmly within a comfortable consensual network of relationships enjoyed by a triumvirate of DES, local authority and teacher associations. Formal and informal relationships with the DES are strong. Parliament is used and local associations put on pressure through backbenchers. The press has been expertly brought into teacher associations' concerns as the educational journalists proliferated in the 1960s. Such a campaign as the Year of Education in 1963, led by Fred Jarvis of the NUT, could assume that government both could and would listen to demands for continued expansion on the grounds that education was self-evidently good and that the public would support it. The old tradition of close-knit relations still remains. But, as Coates describes, the traditional methods and points of address were widened in the 1960s. The attempts at professional unity and the attempt to form a teachers' general council were traditional teacher politics. But the new militant tactics, triggered off by NAS strikes, the attempts to form alliances outside education which culminated in the NAS, ATTI and NUT becoming members of the TUC by 1971, and the formation of the Rank and File in the NUT, were all movements outside the old framework of consensus. By joining the TUC the associations looked outside the educational system towards general incomes policy.

There are two general explanations of these changes. Coates maintains that because the DES lost some of its power to speak for government, the teacher groups inevitably moved into the wider power network which, at the top, could have access to the powerful economic departments. This is not so secure a point as it seems, because the relationship between the DES and the Treasury has changed more in form than in substance. The Treasury has always dominated not only financial decision-making but, until 1968, the organisation and senior promotions of the civil service. The power of the central departments has become more visible, but it has always been there. This may not invalidate Coates's point of course, because if the change of power is perceived to have happened it could affect behaviour whether it actually happened or not.

The stronger assumption is that teachers' feelings about their place in society have changed as have those of all the hitherto submissive professional groups. They have a livelier sense of their position as salary earners: their leaders now hob-nob with the general trade union leaders. They find themselves facing a wider set of issues derived from changes in social and economic values. Teachers are subject to social punditry as the intelligentsia has moved into education. Teacher associations have moved from policies that are institutionally continuous to far more disjunctive and tempestuous issues of social distribution and control. They still remain believers in the continuities but these general movements put different pressures on them which in turn affect their own methods of putting on pressure.

Chapter 8

The Changing Pattern

1 NEW GROUPS IN THE 1960s AND 1970s

In the 1960s forces largely external to the main schools system changed and developed as new values and policies emerged. Interest groups proliferated. In 1950, apart from the traditionally accepted interest groups, there were a few small bodies such as the National Association of Parent–Teacher Associations, the Nursery Schools' Association and the National Association of Labour Teachers (later the National Association of Socialist Teachers). But since then there has been a procession of newcomers: the Confederation for the Advancement of State Education, the Advisory Centre for Education, the Society of Teachers Opposed to Physical Punishment, the National Association of Governors and Managers, the Council for the Advancement of Academic Freedom, the Comprehensive Schools Association, the Black Paper Movement and many others besides.

And these groups, often concerned with representing the changing aspirations of parents or the intelligentsia, both liberal and conservative, have been accompanied by stronger inputs from the press, the research community and the private foundations. Only, perhaps, the denominations have declined in importance as interest groups as their claims have been accepted by government, and controversy about their place in the system has become more quiescent.

Classification of the new interest groups is not easy because they all lack specified authority. Are all promotional, however, in the sense that they are concerned with advancing good causes rather than the sectional interest of their members? They all can be subject to the process of legitimisation exemplified by the cases of the National Association of Schoolmasters and National Union of

Students and, most important functionally, they differ in their national and local impacts. For the most part, these interest groups have impact on individual matters or local issues rather than on national policies, although they can advance causes which take a hold nationally. Thus comprehensive education began as a local development, and the local interest groups have worked hard either to promote or oppose it, and with some effect. Whilst their campaigns contribute towards the development of national policies for comprehensive education, they focus their attention on the local authority. Again, the fact that they have no authority, in the sense that they are not formally and regularly consulted, does not dismiss their importance in the policy-making process. Within the processes of educational policy-making, putting on pressure may well involve no more than keeping an agenda alive, and that is what, for example, the pre-school education pressure groups did over the long years of waiting for a favourable political climate. The arguments are lodged over time, and the moment comes when a minister, working within a particular political context, takes heed.

The new interest groups have been well written-up elsewhere [1] and so we have selected some of the most relevant ones for particular discussion:

PARENTAL GROUPS

Confederation for the Advancement of State Education

Of the parental groups, one of the more important is the Confederation for the Advancement of State Education. This was started in 1960 and now consists of 105 loosely formed local associations, 88 national members, and 42 colleges and institutes of education with institutional affiiliation. It probably has about ten thousand members. '... it arose out of a protest by parents dissatisfied with the provision of space and equipment in a local primary school' in Cambridge [2]. Publicity in the press about the activities of the Cambridge group encouraged the formation of groups in other areas so that in 1962 the first joint committee was formed, and in 1963 the first annual conference took place. The local groups vary in size from a small group of friends to five hundred people. Some of its local groups have impact. Where it has succeeded most local associations are now consulted by chief education officers on the parents' point of view. It has published local case studies which have brought direct pressure to bear on, for example, Essex councillors just before a local election. In some cases, but this is rare, its members have stood for election either as councillors or as members of local political parties, mainly Labour. It has governors and managers among its members. Its National Honorary Secretary surmises that education has become increasingly important in local elections although surprisingly unimportant in central government elections [3].

It now has a clear policy on most, but not all, of its interests. It did not feel that it could aggregate parents' opinions sufficiently to be clear on comprehensive education policy until the 1965 national conference. It explicitly opposes an extension of denominational education, and is in favour of co-educational schools and the promotion of the place of parents in educational decision-making. There are some internal uncertainties about the role of managers and governors. Some of its members who also belong to the National Association of Governors and Managers argue for strong roles by lay managers in the appointment of teachers and in the creation of curriculum [4]. CASE is somewhat more cautious on such issues and some of its members wish to respect more firmly the role of teachers in determining curriculum from a professional point of view. CASE puts out pamphlets which state clearly its objectives. For example, it has argued for more nursery classes, an end to over-sized classes, the abolition of selection, adequate preparation for raising the school leaving age, dealing with all kinds of handicapped children, improving industrial training, and for parents to be full partners to the teachers and administrators. 'There should be detailed information available about every school, choice of schools, parent–teachers' associations where the majority of parents want one, and parents and teachers represented on school governors' [5].

It argues for an educational ombudsman, to which both political parties are now committed. It quotes the Ministry's Chief Information Officer as saying that CASE 'accepts that it cannot claim to represent parents – ninety-nine per cent of whom do not belong – but does claim to represent the rights of parents to be represented' [6].

It does not act as a classical pressure group. Whilst it meets leading politicians and administrators, it has never put up a question for an MP to ask. It works where it can make an impact: for example, it responded to the Schools Council's request for views in its enquiry into the curriculum for the thirteens to sixteens.

The central confederation does not interfere in individual school matters but is more concerned with advising parents on how to make an impact locally.

Its relationships with the NUT are, perhaps surprisingly, good. In some areas, for example, there are joint meetings for which the NUT will pay the cost; the confederation is very poor and welcomes that kind of co-operation. It has little to do with the NAS. It joins, however, the three main teacher associations and the Advisory Centre for Education on the Home and School Council (which published the document produced by Essex CASE on *How to Become a Manager*), where such issues as teacher control do not secure easy agreement. Contacts with local authority associations are thin. Resolutions are sent to them but 'nothing much seems to happen' [7]. Relationships with individual MPs might be good and are always affable with ministers. The Confederation tries hard to be impartial on major issues and emphasises that it is free from all political and religious ties. Its general aim is 'to secure improvement in the quality and scope of the education provided by central government and local education authorities' [8]. Inevitably it is concerned with the development of comprehensive education, especially since Circular 10/70, and has become more critical of what is actually happening in comprehensives, the parents' place in the devising of curriculum and the restraint of the denominational interest in school matters. The Plowden Committee's Chapter IV, 'A Policy for Parents', was influenced by well put-together evidence from the Confederation for the Advancement of State Education, which also had a member on the Committee.

CASE puts out a great deal of information to parents, including its publication *Parents and Schools*. In this it joins the Advisory Centre for Education which is a full-time service organisation publishing *Where?* a magazine for parents.

Advisory Centre for Education

The Advisory Centre for Education is somewhat different because it has a permanent staff and its own influential paper, *Where?* and it is registered as an educational charity. It was founded by the creative sociologist Michael Young in 1960 as an 'attempt to repeat the achievements of the consumers' association' in education. Although it has perennial financial difficulties it attracts publicity for its findings, has helped form middle-class opinion towards the progressive consensus, has fought for stronger roles for parents, and has certainly helped change general opinion on such issues as streaming or comprehensive education. From the beginning ACE created new ideas, often taken up and used by journalists [9].

In a report on its first ten years [10] its Director, Brian Jackson, could record that a hundred thousand questions had been answered between 1960 and 1970 and that it has acted as a pacemaker for local authorities. It made information more widely available to parents by setting up 'educational shops', often in large department stores, and usually run by parents.

ACE has taken a strong stand on comprehensives. In 1965, in the first supplement to *Where?* it published *A Blueprint for Comprehensive Education*. By 1968 ACE felt that unstreaming in comprehensive schools was possible but not taking place. Since that period ACE has been disillusioned with the extent to which comprehensive education has not been used to its full potential in creating new educational patterns.

ACE supports parents by providing information about schools and current movements in educational ideas, so that parents are able to discuss curriculum development with teachers from a basis of knowledge.

ACE maintains that parents have a right to know about and have contact with the school, which should lead to greater advantages for their children. It argues for reasonable consultation and personal involvement with the school.

Nevertheless, as its then Director regretfully admitted, it represents mostly middle-class grammar school and public school parents. Some of them believe in the grammar school system, others in a mixture of grammar and comprehensive schools and others in comprehensives alone. But he also referred to ACE as a 'maverick', 'idea spinning, risk taking ... unafraid of existing power, pressure and yesterday's ideas' [11].

Nursery Schools' Association

The interaction between the interest groups concerned with pre-school education and the political parties illustrates some important points. The Nursery Schools' Association, for example, has long attracted able people to its cause, among them Lady Allen of Hartwood and Eirene White. It put up documentation in the early 1960s [12] about the bad effects of high rise flats on children's development and has, of course, campaigned for years for an expansion of nursery education. The Plowden Committee took full note of these points, which are now accepted policy. The NSA demonstrates how the informal interest groups do best by keeping matters on the educational agenda until some circumstance, a favourable minister or a public scandal, brings the policy to the fore.

In, however, the hands of the Conservatives a second point of view became equally favoured. The Pre-School Playgroups Association effectively kept going the viewpoint of the voluntary helper who differed from the professionals on the importance of qualified teacher supervision, which was assumed in the Plowden Report. The Conservative Party and its network of women's organisations were more sympathetic to voluntary organisations and such MPs as John Hill, Dick Hornby and Janet Foulkes pressed the issue on Margaret Thatcher who always paid a great deal of attention to backbench Conservative opinion [13]. This must have had an effect on the provisions of the 1972 White Paper which emphasised the role of the voluntary nurseries and pre-school playgroups.

So far we have referred to the growth of parental interest groups. But teachers, too, have created groups to promote particular issues. For example, the Society of Teachers Opposed to Physical Punishment consists of teachers, but admits others as associated members. The Plowden Report recommended the abolition of physical punishment in primary schools. STOPP seemed to have begun at about the same time, mainly as a splinter group of liberal teachers, although the Secretary of State of the time, Edward Short, refused to make the abolition of physical punishment mandatory in schools for maladjusted children. Nevertheless, the pressure put up by STOPP has been continuous and probably affected the ILEA in its decision to abolish it.

What impact can parents have when acting as a group? One former cabinet minister believed that parents find it virtually impossible to maintain a continuous pressure group. They might be vocal on particular and local issues but they are not able to press causes continuously as can the teachers' associations. Because they are run by part-timers they have to work hard to have a say at national level. All a body such as CASE can do is to set down general rubrics which local associations might follow rather than assume that there is a single parental view. It is when an issue becomes sharp at the local level, as in the parental opposition to comprehensive schemes in Enfield, that they are at their most powerful. Otherwise, the building up of concepts of parents' rights to representation and information, rather than fighting on global issues, is the counsel that at least one friendly observer has given them [14].

THE DENOMINATIONS: THE CATHOLIC EDUCATION COUNCIL

The denominations have declined in power as other and less disciplined groups and sentiments have entered the arena. The Roman Catholic Church used to be a major source of pressure on government. But the present role of the Catholic Education Council shows how educational issues can change in relationship to more general social and political changes.

A developing theme in this study has been the wide range of styles, purposes and statuses of the main interest groups. Thus, we have seen that some interest groups are, in effect, part of management. Such bodies as the AEC or AMC take up a role in relationship to the DES not far different from that of the DES to the Treasury. Others, again, present an overtly membership-interest point of view and here the National Association of Schoolmasters is the most obvious example. Others, again, are concerned with pressing a particular viewpoint or ideology on a single issue or a group of related issues.

One would have thought that such a body as the Catholic Education Council would be an amalgam of all of these interests. But it is, instead, a minority group which has become party to a continuing and relatively undisturbed consensus. Its concerns are mainly to express the viewpoint of the Roman Catholic community on how their denominational educational facilities can be expanded and to ensure that they get their due under the 1944 settlement. No major conflicts arise between it and the DES or the local authorities. It deliberately keeps out of such political controversies as the merits of comprehensivisation, if only because its membership is bound to contain the full range of views on such matters. Instead, it aims to follow what is the developing view of local authorities and government and to make sure that it participates fully in the results of such policies. [15].

It is governed by a Council of seventy members. Thirty-eight members are nominated by the nineteen dioceses. Others come from main interest groups from within the Catholic community such as the Federation of Catholic Teachers, the different orders of nuns, or the Association of Catholic Colleges. The Council meets twice a year, as does its executive committee. There is a meeting of three commissioners from each of the nineteen dioceses. The CEC itself has no executive authority over its constituent dioceses, which are each accountable to their own bishop for educational matters. It is concerned with presenting what is, in effect, the general Catholic view on national education issues and on giving advice to the diocesan authorities. Ultimately, it may be that an issue will be taken up by a meeting of all bishops who, increasingly, can sustain collective views as against those of any individual bishop or diocese, but such possibilities are implicit rather than mandatory and are not easily visible to the external observer.

The central organisation consists of a Secretary, Richard Cunningham, with a small headquarters staff. The council gets legal, financial, building and other advice from well-experienced part-time consultants. Cunningham himself was an administrator in the DES, where he was employed in two of the main branches, schools branch and teachers branch, the policies of which affect his present work. He also spent quite a deal of time in the Minister's private office.

In discussing the sort of pressure it might put up, Richard Cunningham explains that the main battles were fought and won before the 1944 Act was passed. Since then there have been questions of emphasis rather than of major principle – the extension of some categories of grant from 50 to 75 per cent, for example. The right of Catholic parents to choose the schools of their choice has become less ardent an issue as Catholic-maintained provision has grown. He will certainly take up issues with the DES or a local authority when some question of defining the size of a building to be expanded at public expense, or when a parent does not get the school of his choice, comes up. Much of this discussion will take place at assistant secretary or principal level in the Department. It is rare now that he, or the Chairman of the Council, take things up with an under-secretary, let alone a minister.

Such an influence as this is continuous and undramatic, but none-theless important. For example, Anthony Crosland in drafting Circular 10/65 said how useful he found discussions with the main associations. In fact, however, some of the paragraphs of the Circular were rewritten upon the basis of comments submitted by the Catholic Education Council on a much earlier draft.

Roman Catholic MPs, notably Simon Mahon and James Dunn, are members of the Council, and the CEC will brief them on any legislation in which Catholics have an interest. None of them is sponsored. But since there has been no major issue between the

Catholic Education Council and government, one looks in vain for controversial interplay on the floor of the House. The 1967 Education Act which increased grants to the denominational schools was, in fact, debated on a Friday afternoon, and one senses on reading the speeches that the debate was perhaps needlessly prolonged by the intervention of a large number of Catholic MPs, mainly from nothern constituencies, who felt it necessary to add their testimonials to the benefits it would bring.

Relationships with the teachers' associations and the local authorities are amicable, although there was no co-operation over the NAS strike at the Sacred Heart School, Teesside. Such questions as the grievance procedures being worked out by the teachers' and local authority associations are referred to the CEC for comment. The CEC can be seen to be running a system within a system and, in this capacity, is certainly an interest group, but one whose edges have been smoothed by the acceptance of most of the points that the denominations fought before the 1944 settlement. It is, perhaps, a good example of how dissent is transformed into collaboration by the ceding of points of principle. For this contrast to be fully drawn it would be necessary to go back to the turn of the century, when religious controversy was a main issue in the development of the public education services.

The denominational interest groups and particularly the Catholic succeeded in getting the dual system accepted. The 1967 Education Act increased grant provision for denominational schools. There was a bipartisan view that the better the conditions in the school the less divisive the system would be: 'there would be less opportunity for priestcraft' as one politician put it [16]. Edward Boyle had consulted Michael Stewart, then leading for Labour, on the 1962 Act, and Stewart had then persuaded his colleagues in the parliamentary committee. Chuter Ede, a strong Nonconformist, had said that MPs tended to speak against issues with the demoninations until just before election time [17]. From the point of view of the Labour Party, the Catholic opposition was acceptable for it was not, in principle, against comprehensive schools but was more concerned with denominational control than with academic differentiation.

In any event, there is a relaxed attitude towards the denominational issue now. Few are openly interested in the abolition of sectarian schools although CASE does not want to see them further expanded (see page 127). The issue facing voluntary aided schools, some of which are not denominational, particularly in London, is whether they should participate in the ending of selectivity and, if so, on what conditions.

About one-fifth of children are in church schools. The Roman Catholics tend to concentrate on secondary and the Anglicans on primary schools. For about twenty years a joint policy committee of Anglicans, Roman Catholics and free churchmen have met to talk about such matters of common interest as the rate of grant. The General Secretary of the National Society administers it and the Bishop of London is in the chair. It is now many years since a religious question has arisen in the education field.

The changes of attitudes towards the denominations illustrate how power relationships change over time.

2   THE INTELLIGENTSIA

Although the press, the research community and the private foundations do not directly participate in policy determination, they have a clear right to comment on and influence policy. No minister would find it possible to exclude them, though politicians' attitudes, particularly towards the press, are ambivalent.

THE PRESS

Educational journalism since the 1950s has grown greatly. Early in the sixties there were only three full-time educational journalists excluding those of *The Times Educational Supplement* and *Education*. There are now perhaps fifty, some of whom work for the educational press and others as educational correspondents in the general press. They have their own group which meets regularly and which has as its guests those most powerful and fashionable in educational matters.

The impact of the press has been both strong and difficult to chart. Since the early 1960s it has backed the liberal and expansionist consensus and in doing so has probably expressed what most people wanted. One former minister described it as 'the most conformist' of any of the educational groups [18]. In the opinion of some observers it is now becoming less important in affecting or reinforcing popular attitudes towards education. It is suffering from the declining fortunes and general pessimism of the service it has been supporting, and from the slowing down of expansion. Within these limitations it remains strong. All the education interest groups seek to get press coverage. The NUT, NUS and NAS keep it informed of their more public events: strikes and demonstrations as well as conferences. The NUT executive agreed to increase the money spent on press and public relations rather than finance research into teachers' salaries. The NUT has close relationships, built up particularly in Fred Jarvis's time, and has employed journalists to produce some of its pamphlets.

One senior DES administrator pointed out that there are as many full-time educational journalists as there are administrators in the DES, all testing and publicising educational issues. They benefit from the fact that there is hardly a household which is not touched by education or has a vested interest in its expansion: for example, half a million certificates of one kind or another go into people's homes each year. Each year eight hundred thousand children have to choose their secondary school and a smaller, but still large, number make choices in higher education.

Yet most observers feel that the press does not always centre on the main issues. One former minister observed that the only good education articles in the *New Statesman* are on universities [19]. Another minister thought journalists began as hostile and 'needed feeding' – with both information and drink [20]. Leading politicians have close relationships with them, however. A shadow minister described them as 'good but neurotic', met them every three months and lunched with one or other journalist most weeks. It is important to politicians that speeches go to members of the Education Group of the Press Association [21].

Relationships between the press and the DES are strong and, as with all government department now, the DES reacts to newspaper reports. Each day a comprehensive file of cuttings is assembled and seen by ministers and top officials. When Eccles was first Minister there was only one press officer and he was without particular experience in the world of the media. Now there are one chief and five other press officers. Again this is true of all government departments.

The importance of the press is obvious though some interviewees were laconic about it. Michael Stewart thought the *TES* essentially reactionary, the *Guardian* more benign. The influence of such papers as the *Daily Mail* was minimal as they were 'forever changing their minds'. One journalist thought that the educational press had been liberal and expansionist because it was dominated by the liberal establishment particularly at the sub-university level and for the same reason it had to be expansionist.

Many observers, some hostile, have noted the left-wing orientation of the eduational press. The proportion of right-wingers has been variously stated as being between two and ten out of fifty. This orientation is now slightly changing as Max Wilkinson of the *Daily Mail*, John Izbicki of the *Daily Telegraph* and a few others, who represent a less liberal and optimistic point of view, become a more accepted part of the educational press.

The move towards the right in the press was reinforced by the appointment of Mrs Thatcher. Before 1970 Rhodes Boyson, the NAS and the Campaign for the Defence of Academic Standards were, in the opinion of one Conservative journalist, 'merely ludicrous'. But then Mrs Thatcher as Secretary of State began to say things similar to them, if in the lower key appropriate to a minister. Before Mrs Thatcher came hardly anyone was prepared to talk about the reading difficulties experienced in schools. The right-wing journalists then took heart, and some journalists would claim that it was they who created the Bullock Committee on Reading Standards in the School.

The press has influenced opinion in key areas. For example, it poured out stories of the expansion of the universities and the polytechnics. The present vogue for polytechnics must owe something to the favourable reports on them in the serious Sunday press.

It has also helped opinion about higher education go sour by its reports of troubles in universities and polytechnics. Student leaders have become national figures overnight as a result of press reports. The press plays a part, too, in making academics known to the public; and it has had an indirect effect on social science activity by giving space to some subjects as against others, and by making decisions on which books to review, who will review them and by what criteria.

Almost all correspondents were in favour of comprehensive schools so that when the Conservatives were returned, for example, and tried to dilute the previous administration's plans for comprehensive schools, the local press in Newcastle helped make them change their minds. Even the right-wing papers were against the eleven-plus exam although still, perhaps, in favour of grammar schools. For example, the *Daily Express* favoured Reg Prentice's declaration that Labour will go ahead with comprehensive schools.

The press has changed the emphasis in the ways in which it has covered educational issues. *The Times*, for example, in 1960, mainly reported on higher education, particularly Oxford and Cambridge.

This continued until 1967 although gradually the number of topics dealt with increased, especially with the advent in 1965 of the 'education correspondents's diary' which appeared once a week and covered a more varied and detailed analysis of educational topics. In 1967, an educational correspondent was appointed. From then onwards the whole area of education was covered, although few leading articles were devoted to it. In 1967, 184 articles were devoted to educational matters compared with 70 in 1960. This level has been sustained and topics such as government reports on education, student unrest in 1967 and 1968 and comprehensives, starting with the Enfield case, are given detailed analysis. By 1974 a political correspondent was writing regular attacks on comprehensive education. The *Guardian* has expanded in a similar way, until in 1972 a two-page educational supplement appeared once a week. This is concerned with the whole range of educational subjects and special emphasis on new developments in education, such as new curriculum developments and research in the various sectors of education, is given.

In recent years, too, there have been two major changes of structure and coverage, which allows for more 'straight' reporting as well as judgement-forming, in educational journalism. First, the Press Association now has a full-time education correspondent. This enables coverage of news to be more comprehensive, so that somewhat more technical matters can reach newspaper offices without them having to rely exclusively on their own reporters and writers [22]. Secondly, the local press's interest in education has grown. Newspapers in, for example, Croydon, Sheffield, Leeds, Cardiff, Manchester and Birmingham have full-time education correspondents who are an important part of the local educational scene.

At the same time, the serious press has enjoyed a large increase in educational advertising which has presumably encouraged it to stimulate its educational readership by increasing coverage of education.

The role of the press will always be ambiguous. It has had a benign influence from the point of view of those who want to see educational interest sustained and advanced. Yet there is, inevitably, some danger in assuming that journalists' interest in educational matters guarantees an accurate articulation and aggregation of popular feelings. Edward Boyle complained that journalists make the news [23]. They certainly make educational public figures, some of whom are guaranteed immediate and extensive reportage, no matter what their institutional or other status.

RESEARCH AND DEVELOPMENT

Before 1960 there were four main sources of educational research: the NFER, a largely local-authority financed and 'semi-official' body; departments of education in universities and area training organisations; the colleges of education; and some large local authorities which had their own research departments. Social scientists, in addition to psychologists, began to come on the scene in the 1950s with the publication of Floud, Halsey and Martin's study of educational opportunity [24] and Vaizey's *The Costs of Education*, which was the first attempt by a British economist to state the inputs to and benefits from education.

In the 1960s interest became both wider and stronger and the products can be summarised by such names as Michael Young, John Vaizey, A. H. Halsey, J. W. B. Douglas, Basil Bernstein, and Mia Kellmer Pringle and Ron Davie's National Child Development Study. At the same time there was a considerable growth of public funding. A DES research fund began in 1962 with about £100,000 a year and grew to £467,000 by 1974–5. This was accompanied by major institutional charges – the creation of the Schools Council with its research and development budget in 1965 and the creation of the SSRC and its education board in 1967. At the same time private foundations, particularly the Nuffield Foundation, became more active. An educational research community began to build up. The first conference of the British Educational Research Association, which met in Brimingham in 1974, was able to assemble a meeting of nearly two hundred researchers.

The political scientist can never be clear about the impact of research and its organisation on policy. No adequate studies of research effectiveness have been made and much of the writing simply has to assume that there is a relationship which 'ought' to be better.

As we write there is, as far as the outside observer can tell, no systematic arrangement whereby policy needs are scanned totally in relationship to an overall research policy, as is the case in health [25] or defence or economic policy or agriculture. There is no chief scientists in the DES and that Department has defended the situation by maintaining that professional advice from HM Inspectorate is available [26].

Nevertheless, changes have been considerable. The Schools Council, for example, has funded projects since it was founded. It used to receive £100,000 from the DES to spend as it thought fit and the equivalent sum is now part of its general financial allocation. The DES has funded a large number of projects and amongst the projects which have benefited from this finding are those of Basil Bernstein. The Plowden Report was based on several researches which backed up or tested its conclusions.

In 1967 the SSRC Education Board began work. Peter Jay, one of the Treasury officers then concerned with education, had thought that departments should not be 'patrons' but should only finance projects concerned with policy, whilst the research councils should be concerned with more general research encouragement. In 1967–8 the Education Research Board of the SSRC began to send 'policy' research to the DES, while the DES would refer more fundamental research to the SSRC.

The DES works closely with the SSRC. Halsey's EPA researches received money from both the Council and the DES. The NCDS has moved from departmental to Council and back to departmental support. The SSRC and the Department use each other as part of a referee system, and, within the SSRC, projects are referred between the Education Research Board and the sociology and psychology committees.

Since then the Department has tried to use research to monitor such developments as the expansion of nursery education and programmes to reduce adult illiteracy.

The Department has links with the Schools Council through the schools branch. It also has links with CERI of OECD, though often weak or even desultory. There have been informal contacts with the Nuffield Foundation, particularly over curriculum development in higher education and school curriculum (see pages 144–6).

From the point of view of some DES officials there are imbalances in research interests. Higher education is fashionable, almost certainly because of the particular interest shown in it earlier on by Toby Weaver and Edward Boyle. Higher education was so much tied up with other fields of policy that the schools were not regarded as so interesting. Higher education opportunities became the main criterion of progress. There was thus a wrong tilt in research and development programmes which needed to be redressed [27], although the DES found it difficult to encourage such changes, perhaps because of its own uncertainties. Also officials feel that there is no applied research group prepared to concentrate on key policy problems.

Problems also arise because of the associations' constraints over certain types of research. The NUT has certainly used its influence to veto projects which seem to affect its members' interests.

Ministers tend to be interested sporadically in research programmes. Within the Department, the Secretary of State receives a report annually from the research branch, but does not vet individual projects unless they are politically sensitive. Even hostile ministers tend to become converted towards research after a while, as witness Edward Short's speech to the NFER in 1970.

The National Foundation for Educational Research

The National Foundation for Educational Research is financed largely by a local authority grant, though the DES has always given it a small grant. It receives money for research projects commissioned by the DES, local authorities, the Department of Health and Social Security and the SSRC.

The NFER is a service-orientated organisation. It services the needs of its own members and all projects are triggered off by their needs. Its stated objectives include: 'to contribute a stream of information to the educational decision makers'. Local authorities need reviews of the findings of research in certain areas and recommendations resulting from them. The Director visits the regions of the Association of Education Committees and regularly meets with teachers' associations to nose out their needs. The NFER responds, for example, to meeting the demand for more research on further and higher education by setting up an advisory group on this sector. It was one of the main producers of selection tests for entry to secondary education. It was responsible, with HM Inspectorate, for the famous national surveys of reading. It has to compete for grants in much the same way as other bodies and has perhaps twenty projects running at any one time.

The board of management consists of representatives of local authorities, teachers' associations, colleges of education and the DES. The board of management and its finance and general purposes committees make decisions on all major projects and their input into decision-making is active and lively. In recent years the non-researchers on the board have become more confident in their ability to question research purposes and are no longer intimidated by the technology of research design [28].

Much of the NFER's influence is implicit and indirect. Thus the selection system was effectively serviced and, to that extent, reinforced by its tests. The Bullock enquiry into reading standards was triggered off by its 1972 reading survey. The NFER has had impacts on comprehensive education and the education of immigrants by its research. It has now begun its first development project on materials for immigrants. The Foundation is getting to work on research into the pre-school expansion programme. Its research on battered babies has drawn public attention to the problem, although the research is not necessarily followed up. It publishes a regular newsletter about its projects.

The NFER's relationships with its sponsors are inevitably ambivalent. Its sponsors' demands are pre-emptive and research discretion is unavoidably reduced. Thus the DES's creation of research on pre-school education and its associated DES management group, together with the recent emphasis on research related to effectiveness, tend to occupy a great deal of the NFER's concern.

The NFER and other sources of research cannot directly relate their efforts to policy formation. No Act obviously results from their efforts but the climate of opinion is changed by research which filters through to policy-making. Thus the NFER's work on the eleven-plus produced changes in the content of the test and eventually to a strong assertion that teacher assessment leads to better prediction. They also provided ammunition for those who did not like the eleven-plus. Some researches are obviously likely to influence policy-makers. A survey of the teaching of French in primary schools over the last ten years may well persuade practitioners to drop the teaching of this subject in such schools.

The National Children's Bureau

The National Children's Bureau is also concerned with policy-relevant research.

The Bureau combines the functions of a research organisation and pressure group. It conducts major and responsible research such as its National Child Development Study, and has many other studies commissioned and paid for by the Department of Education and Science, the Department of Health and the Home Office. But it also launches campaigns so that something might be done about what its research has discovered. For example, it created study groups under David Donnison to consider the implications of the findings of its National Child Development Study [29]. It has no particular political stance and it helps local authorities set up study groups on issues within its sphere of interest although it tends to relate to the 'progressive' assumptions of the education service.

A survey of the policies listed in Chart II would reveal many issues which have been affected by research findings. The development of comprehensive education, the changing curriculum, the build-up of more egalitarian educational patterns in higher and school education – all are part of a changing frame of reference partly, at least, fashioned by researchers. It is outside our scope to consider how far this has resulted from spontaneous work or projects systematically commissioned by the authority system.

The Schools Council

The Schools Council is important not only for the work that it does but also for the way in which it relates to the role of the main educational interests.

It was founded in 1965 after Sir David Eccles's attempt to found a Curriculum Study Group had been defeated by teacher association opposition. Manzer [30] has recounted in convincing detail how and why the teachers' associations, and, to a lesser extent, some of the local authority associations, combined to destroy this 'commando-like unit' which was to lead the Ministry of Education into what Eccles called 'the secret garden of the curriculum'. It might be added here that the present author was the first ministry official to be allocated to the Curriculum Study Group and that Eccles's description of it as having commando-like characteristics was both comically inaccurate and damaging. It was far from the intention of the officials who first proposed it – and they included Derek Morrell, Toby Weaver and Ralph Fletcher – to establish a unit that could prescribe. The intention was to ensure that decisions made by the Ministry of Education were better informed by educational considerations and that the education service at large would have an opportunity of relating better to the national decision-making process.

In the event, however, the interest groups won and officials themselves reluctantly decided that since a central government department could not be relied upon to be participative and progressive for long, it would be better to build up an autonomous entity outside the Department [31]. The result was the Schools Council for the Curriculum and Examinations established as a result of a working party under the chairmanship of Sir John Lockwood, which took on the examination development and monitoring role of the Secondary School Examinations Council but added related curriculum development work.

The Schools Council's stated achievements are large. It has produced many research and development projects in the main curriculum areas and also in the fields of compensatory education, gifted children, health education, special education, school, home and community, and school organisation and resources. It has also put about half of its research and development effort into its traditional field of interest, school examinations. The main associations strongly support the work of the Schools Council and they have been protective of attempts by the DES, when Margaret Thatcher was Secretary of State, to cut budgets.

There are three joint secretaries and the leadership both at official and political level has varied. Two masters of Oxford colleges, a former President of the NUT and a former President of the Society of Education Officers have been chairmen. The joint secretaries have been DES administrators, HMIs, local authority administrators and advisers and practising teachers.

Several important criticisms have been made of the Schools Council. First, it is maintained that it is too captive to its members' interests and, particularly, to those of the teachers' associations [32]. There are forty-five teacher members on the eighty strong governing council, of whom most come from the member interests. The five local authority associations have ten members between them. Of the programme committee's eighteen members, ten come from teachers' organisations, four of them from the NUT. So a relationship is imputed between the recognised teachers' associations and educational development, but it is generally admitted that the teachers' associations may not always be able to aggregate the best thinking about educational development.

Yet there is no other obvious way in which teachers' feelings will be brought into the Schools Council. Nor is there a clear point of entry for 'other' interests in education, notably those of the social scientists, parent bodies and other consumer groups.

The second type of criticism has been about the educational assumptions underlying the Schools Council's work. It has been criticised for not making an all-out attack on examinations. It has also been criticised by radical members of the London Institute of Education for perpetuating traditional assumptions about education for early leavers or sixth-formers. M. F. D. Young in particular [33] claims that the Schools Council reinforces a curriculum differentiated by ability and social class and related to aims of social control.

A further criticism [34] is that the Council lacks a coherent overall policy for the curriculum and that its projects reveal a 'diffusion strategy', 'a centre-periphery' model which is no longer tenable with the decline of 'the stable state'. 'It is too slow to respond to change, too centripetal and too dependent on central direction to provide the dynamism for self-transforming change at the periphery.' It is attacked for making only a token move towards creating a local structure instead of its present twelve regional officers.

The Schools Council is undoubtedly a triumph of the established teachers' associations. The Schools Council claims that it does not prescribe developments or their take-up in the schools. Nonetheless, the Council is one of the largest forces with resources for development work and the associations have a strong voice in determining what it does. In so doing, however, it perpetuates assumptions about institutional autonomy.

It has been fairly successful at keeping at bay dissident voices from within the educational system, particularly those deriving their assumptions from the sociology of knowledge, or from the 'outside' interest groups in education. It may well be, however, that the arrangements allow for a dynamic of change. If the teachers' associations represent official teacher opinion whilst project leaders are concerned with change and development, the tension built up between those who propose and carry out projects and those who sanction them may be a way in which change can take place.

PRIVATE FOUNDATIONS

The Nuffield Foundation
If the Schools Council is a coalition of many official and legitimised interest groups, the Nuffield Foundation exerts influence on curriculum which is not related to a specified role within the education service. So do other foundations such as the Gulbenkian which has supported studies of educational administration.

Its interest in school curriculum begin in the early 1960s [35], when it took up an initiative from the then two science teachers' associations, the Science Masters' Association and the Association of Women Science Teachers, which became combined as the Association for Science Education with the aim of improving O-level physics, chemistry and biology syllabuses.

Lord Todd, the Chairman of the Council for Scientific Policy, was a trustee. He backed the then Director, R. Farrer-Brown, in moves towards curriculum development. The Foundation began looking at the work of the American curriculum developers – particularly the Physical Science Studies Committee based at the Massachusetts Institute of Technology – and then worked out a new curriculum development strategy and put pressure to bear on changing examinations.

The Foundation identified people to lead the teams and in doing so unashamedly followed through various networks in the science establishment. Cambridge and London professors joined with the Institute of Physics, the Royal Institute of Chemistry and other professional associations in selecting team leaders. A total of a quarter of a million pounds was put aside for the initial development costs.

From this start in science there was speedy expansion of interest into the teaching of primary school French and mathematics. The Foundation made direct approaches to the Minister, Permanent Secretary and Senior Chief Inspector who at the same time had decided to set up the Curriculum Study Group. When the functions of the group were transferred to the Schools Council, connections with the Schools Council became strong. The Schools Council made arrangements for the Foundation to use trial schools for the primary French project and also advised on the in-service training of the teacher aspects of the project. When the Schools Council was ready to take over fully the Nuffield Foundation withdrew.

The Nuffield Foundation has an ambitious view of the process in which it was involved. It began by being concerned with the interpretation of what the curriculum implied in terms of subject content, different forms of examinations and so on. But its officials increasingly became interested in underlying aspects of the education process – the values in the curriculum and ways of changing teachers' attitudes. After a few years various new curriculum materials had been published, but implementation differed between schools. So the emphasis began to centre on implementation.

The Foundation's teams found themselves involved in the move towards comprehensive education and creating O-level programmes suitable for all types of schools. In the early stages, they were sensitive to the need to ensure that the experiments were kept private until they were sure of their ground, so that they should not be written off too early. This led to correspondence in *The Times Educational Supplement* on why secrecy had been maintained. The trial schools had to be protected from outside criticism, but opinion changed as the Foundation found that schools were interested and tolerant of the experiments.

Other conflicts that had to be faced were the ways in which education researchers complained that money was going into

K

development rather than into curriculum research. HMIs were supportive although some attempted to remain 'neutral'. Few LEAs refused to sponsor trial schools. For the maths and French projects the DES sent out letter to LEAs. Fifty to sixty said they were interested. Most elements in the programme derived from teacher dissatisfaction with the curriculum and met a need already present in some areas. Examining boards were annoyed because they were not formally approached until after the first year when Nuffield had something to show them. But there were then meetings with the principal examiners, and agreement was reached to put on experimental exams with one board as agent for the others, with any candidate being able to take a paper of that board.

The Foundation has not attempted a total critique of the educational process or attempted to change it. It has always relied on a desire for change from within. Now approximately half the schools that teach science are using Nuffield Science Programmes and it is proportionately much larger than the similar programme in the USA. But it is difficult to assess because of the different ways in which the programme is being implemented. In the end, professional associations, LEAs and teachers' unions did not regard Nuffield as impinging on their interests.

Nuffield's position outside the system gave it freedom to manoeuvre. The science lobby is very well organised through the Royal Society and professional associations. The larger employers like ICI helped to establish what they needed in science teaching and they helped with subsidiary grants and training films.

The interests developing around education in the 1960s were various and often important and strong. Those discussed here give clues to the ways in which educational policies had to respond to wider social assumptions and criticisms of parents, of the participative movement, of the educational research community, of the more widely based social science intelligentsia, of a press which developed momentum simply not visible in other areas of the social services, and of the interested voluntary groups and private foundations. As education became more value-volatile, so did the constituency to which it must respond. It also responded under the wider influences of the education institutions themselves.

Part III

PARLIAMENT

Chapter 9

Parliament and Education

The educational interest groups put pressure on government either through direct negotiations or by creating an environment in which consensus is authorised or tested. We now turn to the role of Parliament and, in particular, the House of Commons and its institutions.

It is accepted that MPs are not decision-makers but review the decisions of those who make policy – the ministers and departments [1]. So the main concern here is with the influence MPs have as reviewers or critics of government decision-making. This distinction does not occlude the fact that those who criticise and review policy themselves participate in policy-making. For there is 'non-decision-making' [2] as well as decision-making, and the input of hostility or questioning or general support to what is decided affects what happens. This chapter considers the cohort of MPs who were particularly active during the period in order to see how far they helped to create the changes in educational policy from the time when Sir David Eccles took office as Minister to the time when Mrs Margaret Thatcher left the DES.

Before turning to this task we ought to make firm the supposition that MPs are not decision-makers by glancing at the very different pattern of governance presented by the American scene. Aaron Wildavsky's classic study [3] of the politics of the budgetary process, for example, illustrates how those who create and execute federal programmes regard congressional intervention as an intimate part of the sanctioning process. A bureau within, say, the Department of Health, Education and Welfare puts up an annual budget to its departmental officers, who, on gaining the agreement of the Commissioner for Education and the Secretary to the Department, a member of the Cabinet, then clear it with the Office of Budgets and Programmes (OBP). The OBP then acts much the same way as the Treasury. It criticises the logic and reasonableness of the proposal in terms of general government inclinations about the level of expenditure to be sanctioned in a particular fiscal year. Internally, one suspects, the processes are much the same as ours since the Plowden Committee in 1961 [4] proposed the creation of a Public Expenditure Survey Committee of senior officials which would make provisional plans some four or five years ahead [5]. Other government mechanisms such as programme analysis review, too, are similar in both countries in their effect on government's controls over patterns of expenditure.

The official and preliminary procedures, then, do not greatly differ between the two countries. It is their fate from then onwards which differs so strongly. In Britain, estimates are considered by the Commons and are debated. But the debates are non-specific. In theory the Estimates, or later the Expenditure, Committee subjects them to close review, but this never really happens because members take the opportunity instead to test officials on the way in which monies might be spent on policies already determined. At a far later stage the Public Accounts Committee, aided by the Comptroller and Auditor General, scrutinises efficiency and probity *ex post facto*. And that scrutiny is random rather than systematic.

The congressional system is different. All departmental votes are submitted to exhaustive examination by the OBP which, it is complained, in, for example, the research and development programmes in the Office of Education, indulges in 'second guessing' about them [6]. But they then go through an ordeal quite unknown to the British civil servant, though certainly part of the annual life cycle of the local authority official. Budgets have to be approved by the substantive committee of the House of Representatives and by the Appropriations Sub-Committees of both the Representatives and the Senate. It is not a generalised process as in Britain, but a make-or-break procedure. Each budget has to be defended annually. Bureau chiefs appear 'on the hill' and are required to justify their estimates in great detail. The Committee goes into private session when it makes decisions about budgets that can only be overturned by the whole House or by a presidential freeze or budget. Senators and Representatives thus have a direct place in decision-making.

There are two important points here. Congressional scrutiny directly determines the fate of federal programmes and does not fall short of substantive amendment. Secondly, as Wildavsky so elegantly shows, the process of approval develops social networks and behavioural patterns between programme-makers and congressmen which are quite unknown here. Bureaux plan their tactics in securing congressional approval even to the point of having mock congressional hearings at which they practise their testimony. They consult individual congressmen about their predelictions, often related, of course, to constituency interests, and seek their advice about what would be acceptable to a committee. And the power of committees is enormous. One Chairman, in the author's hearing [7], used the expression 'the committee had its will of the bureau' as if it was a process of rape rather than of parliamentary activity.

The contrast with MPs is striking. They have no real authority over departmental votes and can do no more than give ministers a rough time. Giving ministers a rough time might, however, affect ministerial attitudes and policy. It is that point which we evaluate here.

In seeking to evaluate this point, several sources were examined: Parliamentary Questions and debates over the thirteen years of our period, the reports of the Estimates, and Expenditure Committees, and the Public Accounts Committee, which are so well recorded for the student. We interviewed the present and former MPs listed in the Acknowledgements to this book. What is said in these pages is a stratification of information from these sources. But we also tested what MPs told us about their roles by interviews with leaders of the main interest groups as well as with some DES officials and some of the more pertinacious observers among the educational press.

It is well to remember the general environment within which Parliament reflected attitudes towards education. In 1955 education was not a prestige department. Indeed, Churchill on his return to office in 1951 did not include the Minister in the Cabinet. In the early 1950s capital expenditure was limited to the bare essentials necessary to ensure that every child had a place in a school. It was with David Eccles in the mid-1950s that the pace quickened. The education service became the provider of one of the main consumer durables for which customers were voting with their feet.

The first improvement of education came about with Eccles's reorganisation of rural schools. Then the Government, even before it set up the Robbins Committee in 1960, conceded that the main imperative for higher education planning was student demand. In the late 1960s there was a reaction against higher education and particularly the special case of the universities.

By any standards, these were sufficiently major developments of policy for the parliamentary process to be involved. It makes it relevant to ask whether the Government responded to demands and, if so, whether they were made explicitly and cogently. And, if so, whether the parliamentary process contributed to the expression of demands.

Two main witnesses, Edward Boyle and Anthony Crosland [8], did not think that parliamentary activity was an index to the importance placed on the subject by government, or even by MPs. Crosland asked: 'But how do you judge [the importance placed on the subject]? By the number of Parliamentary Questions? The number of debates?' He pointed out that parliamentary activity would be heavily influenced by which departments happened to have major Bills going through the House, 'which Education did not while I was there'. Attendance at debates is not a good index of the degree of interest. 'Few debates in the House of Commons are [well attended] unless there is a good political row going on.' Parliament 'spends most time on things that are going wrong or things that are acutely party-controversial, and education didn't fall into these categories at the time'. Crosland went on to explain that with the changing social composition of the parliamentary parties – more ex-college lecturers and fewer ex-primary school teachers – there was a change in the balance of interest. 'The debate on overseas students' fees was infinitely more crowded and animated than any debate on primary schools.' He doubted if 'this is wholly a good sign', or presumably because the future of primary education is the more important subject.

Boyle remarked that education 'isn't the department which has enhanced one's career in politics'. But of the role of MPs, Edward Boyle said that Parliament is a rather more important partner to the education service than it always gets credit for being. Although both parliamentary debates and winding up speeches are poorly attended (compared with twenty years back), some speeches 'accurately registered the change in the norm of thinking on this during the last four or five years'. The 1922 Committee and the party committees also have an impact.

'Some forty or fifty MPs, in all parties added together, follow education and take an active part in debate. It's very much level pegging these days between the two sides, much more so than fifteen years ago, and, whether they like to admit it or not, they have more in common with one another than with the rest of the House of

Commons. They do understand the inwardness, they talk the same kind of language. ... It is not difficult to detect the general sort of state of doctrine on most educational subjects.'

This assumption that education is a bipartisan subject would not, of course, be accepted by anybody now although it might have been credible in the early 1960s. 'In the early fifties, if you had a particular issue like church schools, the Roman Catholic lobby might encourage members to speak, but the number of MPs who really follow education now and have informed views of it is not so few.'

So much for the testimony of two ministers. We now turn to an analysis of the main instruments of parliamentary process: the Parliamentary Questions, debates and committees.

PARLIAMENTARY QUESTIONS

Parliamentary Questions are a ritualised part of the democratic process and to get some notion of their range and impact we have analysed all the questions asked on education between 1960 and 1973,[1] and attempt to relate the flow and intensities of Parliamentary Questions to the policy movements depicted in Chart I and Chapter 2.

We first briefly describe the historical setting and some of the procedures [9] surrounding Parliamentary Questions before going on to ask whether they are an important instrument for the MP who wishes to challenge or cause changes in educational policy.

In 1850 only 200 questions were asked. By the 1890s this had increased to between 4,000 and 5,000 annually. There are now about 24,000. At the same time the ratio of supplementary to main questions has increased. The increase in the use of Question Time during this century has been rapid, although the allocated time for questions has not changed radically.

Notice of questions must be given between forty-eight hours and a fortnight beforehand, so that a minister can be given time to prepare an answer. The cost of answering oral and written questions in 1970 was £14 and £10 respectively. The total annual cost is £300,000 [10]. The member has the right to ask one or more supplementary questions arising out of the minister's answer to an

---

[1] The analysis applies to questions asked of the Minister or Secretary of State for Education, or to the Prime Minister, on education in England and Wales. Our analysis does not include Scottish education, science, sport or art, or universities before their transfer from the Treasury to the DES in 1963.

oral question. Other members may also put supplementary questions, but the Speaker will prevent the proceedings from developing into an impromptu debate. Members may also put down questions for written answer. In this case the question and answer will be reported in *Hansard*.

About a quarter of the total are answered orally because the rota system limits the numbers of days upon which a minister need appear. It puts each minister at the head of the list on certain days, his position moving up one each week until he reaches the top. This may mean the question is answered when it is no longer topical. Questions may not express an opinion and the questioner is held responsible for accuracy, which may involve him in a great deal of research and time. A question may not deal with issues of policy which are too large for treatment in one answer.

In spite of the priority and publicity given to questions, all the MPs whom we asked agreed that there are limitations on their use in influencing government decisions directly, or even for helping to find out how a particular policy was made.

There are no equivalent restrictions on answers and many ministers have been able to establish their reputations, or damage them, during Question Time. As one of the interviewees put it, the power is with the minister during Question Time.

Parliamentary Questions can seek information or press or question a decision of a government department. Neville Johnson [11] has established categories of questions useful to the discussion of their role in education. Some are constituency questions. These enable the MP to establish that he is conscientious in pursuing such questions as those concerned with school buildings for his constituents. They constitute a large proportion of the questions asked in education. Others are more politically controversial, especially when the Government is being criticised or unwilling to commit itself. Comprehensive schools in the mid-1960s (*see* page 223) and the restriction on free school milk by Mrs Thatcher in 1971 are obvious examples. But relatively few of these are asked (*see* Chart VI). Others arise from connections with interest groups. For example, the MPs sponsored by the NUT or related strongly to the AUT (*see* Chapters 7 and 10) can put questions on teachers' or university staff's superannuation [12]. There are also Parliamentary Questions stimulated by the media. Obviously these are a category which overlap with the other three. But they are less apparent in education than they are in, say, defence of foreign policy or Home Office affairs. Parliamentary Questions can form part of a campaign run by either an individual member or by a group of MPs as when the NUS encouraged members of all parties to campaign against the increase in fees or overseas students in 1968 [13]. The abolition of independent schools, the expansion of medical education and the provision of more school dentists are further examples.

Another analysis by Chester and Bowring [14] relates the Parliamentary Question as a means of publicity for a particular MP or issue to its use for local constituency matters, including education. Parliamentary Questions have advance notice so that journalists can spot questions likely to hit the newspaper headlines. If they 'smell' a story, they can get further information from a minister or a member. Parliamentary Questions are asked at a time convenient for evening or early morning daily editions. They provide 'copy' in a more convenient form than debates. And, particularly relevant to education, many Parliamentary Questions are of local or specialist concern, if not of national interest, and will therefore interest local or specialist newspapers.

The MPs interviewed seem to differ as to whether Parliamentary Questions had any effect on policy. The evidence of former ministers of education is important since it is they on whom the impact was intended to be made. Edward Boyle and Anthony Crosland hardly mentioned them [15]. In our interviews, Edward Short [16] thought they monitored the way in which policy is carried out and that ministers in fact take great note of them; Dennis Howell also felt this. Michael Stewart felt that they were more effective on particular issues than on general ones. His comments relate well to the type of questions actually asked as in our content analysis of Parliamentary Questions (*see* Charts VI and VII). Lord Eccles doubted that Parliamentary Questions had any effect on government policy at all. Timothy Raison thought they tested the DES well and affected official behaviour and his arguments are related later in this chapter.

Variations in MPs' opinions on this issue might reflect their individual styles. John Jennings thought they were useless except as a last resort and that it was far better to see the minister. Gilbert Longden thought that they were mainly related to constituency matters, although issues about individual teachers' pay or students' grants could not usefully be raised but were better dealt with through a letter to a minister which must, after all, be answered by the minister or a junior minister. Eric Deakins thought that though they were usually related to constituency matters, some had policy

Chart VI: *How Main Topics in Education were Dealt with by Parliamentary Questions (1964–71)*

Topics	1964	1965	1966	1967	1968	1969	1970	1971
Overseas student fees	0	0	0[a]	0	45	2	1	1
Educational immigrants and race relations	2	9[a]	3[a]	6[a]	14[a]	0	6	6
Public schools	0	12	4	5	13	2	4[a]	
Abolition of eleven-plus	1	0	2	1	0	0	2	1
Comprehensive schools	9	37[a]	45	53	66	49	14[a]	33
Binary system and polytechnics	6	3	9[a]	9	6	8	14	7
Raising of school leaving age	0	0	5	11	9[a]	2	7	14[a]
Nursery education	0	7	10	4	11	10	18	22
Special education	3	1	5	1	8[a]	18[b]	11[a]	29[a,c]
Further education	6	8	2	1	5	8	1	7
Open University	0	4	5[a]	7	11	2[a]	7	2
Business studies	1	2	2	2	0	1	0	0
Youth service	0	3	9	1[a]	8	5[a]	5	1
Teachers' pay and conditions	11[a]	29[a]	24	43[a]	17	58	37[a]	85[b]
Teachers' education structure	1	0	0	1	0	1[a]	0[a]	4[a]
Secondary school exams	3	4	1	5	0	1	2	
Student unrest	0	1	0	0	15[a]	21	1	7
Student participation	0	0	0	1	1[a]	4[a]	2	0
Schools Council	3[a]	1	0	2	3	1	0	2
Corporal punishment	0	0	0	8	6[a]	4	4	0
School milk charges	0	0	0	3	2[a]	3	5[a]	22[a]
School meal charges	0	0	1	8	16	5	2	5
EPAs and urban priority areas	0	0	0	1[a]	10[a]	3[a]	3[a]	14
Industrial training	0[a]	2	0	0	2	4	2	0
Primary education	3	9	5	7	13[a]	20	14	31
Medical education	5	14[a]	14	4	9[a]	11	4	1

[a] Coinciding with the dates of major legislation or DES circulars.
[b] A large number of questions placed on the same day.
[c] The majority placed by Jack Ashley.
Source: *Hansard*.

Chart VII: *The Number of Parliamentary Questions Referring Directly to Government Reports (1964–71)*

Reports	1964	1965	1966	1967	1968	1969	1970	1971
Henniker-Heaton	3[a]	0	1	0	1	0	0	0
Dainton	–	–	1[a]	1	5	1	0	0
Gittins	0	0	0	0	9[a]	1	1	0
Plowden	5	1	2	13[a]	10	4	0	0
Robbins	8	2	7	4	2	5	10	4
James	–	–	–	–	–	–	3	5[a]
Newsom	8	4	1	0	1	0	0	0
Albemarle	1	1	1	1	0	0	0	0

[a] Date of publication of report.

Note: All other reports (*see* Chart I) were either mentioned once only or not at all.

Source: *Hansard.*

importance. Thus questions had put pressure on the Government on London teachers' allowances in 1973 although this was, in effect, a 'super-constituency' issue. There was Conservative pressure on their ministers to increase aid to direct grant schools in 1970 which did not succeed. But he thought that there was a limit to the effectiveness of Parliamentary Questions. No Conservative minister would change attitudes on, for example, comprehensive schools. Kenneth Marks thought Parliamentary Questions might speed up rather than change policies if they were combined with adequate access to ministers. But this applied only to members of the government party. Edwin Wainwright felt that Parliamentary Questions, especially supplementary ones, compelled a minister at least to supply information.

One commentator [17] sums up that the answers given by ministers are 'of a very general nature and provide very little in the way of explanation for the behaviour of individuals'. The Order Paper for a typical day records no clear or immediate purposes of a large number of them.

Our own analysis of Parliamentary Questions from 1960 to 1973 was of two kinds. First we aggregated the numbers of questions on each main subject during the whole period. From this it is plain that there is no obvious, significant correspondence between policy generation, as represented by the events identified in association with the thirty-five policies listed in Chart II, and the 8,000 Parliamentary Questions asked during the period. But this is only a crude quantitative comparison. More important, on each of the main issues of the time, as identified by a ministerial statement or circular as listed in Charts I and II, there was no significant grouping of questions, no true reflection of change in intensity of parliamentary interest. Questions rarely preceded change and therefore could have hardly created it, and the subjects barely coincided. At most they reflected some changes in intensity of interest.

In, for example, 1960 – to take a year at random – the Labour Party did not use Parliamentary Questions to assert policies for comprehensive schools. It did not use them to assert the need for an expansion of higher education although this issue came up in the debate on the Crowther Report [18]. In that year, MPs mainly used them to advance the well-being of their constituencies. Some questions might have greater potential than others. For example, throughout much of 1960, Stephen Swingler asked question after question about the opportunities for pupils in secondary modern schools to take GCE courses. This might have been a probing that intended to lead to attacks on the divisive secondary school system although the follow-through is not obvious, and, in the event, no concerted attack came. Or a question can border on other subjects. A group, including Will Griffiths and Sydney Silverman, both of whom normally kept clear of education, got the scent of something engagingly political when it was discovered that security officers approached heads of schools for information about the political affiliation of former pupils. There was a flurry of questions.

In 1968 comprehensive schools and fees for overseas students appeared to be two key issues in education. But this interest in comprehensive schools did not emerge in Parliamentary Questions as a national issue and questioners were not confined to Labour MPs. Indeed, out of the sixty-six Parliamentary Questions forty-three were concerned with local comprehensive school plans, buildings and lack of amenities. The year in which students in higher education raised important issues was 1968, yet comparatively few questions were asked about them. Instead many MPs were more concerned with the plight of overseas students whose fees had been increased, and R. Davies and Joan Vickers repeatedly asked questions concerning this issue.

Chart VI shows the numbers of Parliamentary Questions asked annually about twenty-six key policy areas between 1964 and 1971. In only nine out of twenty-six of the policy areas shown does there seem to have been some correspondence between policy statements and Parliamentary Questions asked. In the majority of them, however, no such correspondence can be remarked. But even where some correspondence can be seen, the change in activity was often unremarkable. For example, the Public Schools Commission produced its first report in 1968. The number of Parliamentary Questions on public schools increased from five to thirteen out of an annual total of all Parliamentary Questions of about 24,000 between 1967 and 1968; the number on the binary system increased from three to nine between 1965 and 1966.

They were, in fact, quite small flickerings of quite small dials.

Yet most Parliamentary Questions helped generate the political environment within which ministers and officials made decisions. The agenda for most educational policy is incremental and cumulative rather than dramatic. But we can only rely on scanty evidence to see what might happen. The evidence conflicts but it is interesting to note that former ministers Stewart, Short and Raison felt that they had more impact than did MPs.

If the effect is incremental it is also largely internal to the DES. For on education alone there were during our period an average of 630 questions a year, which meant that the DES had to spend time and manpower in assuring itself that it could stand up to parliamentary scrutiny of these issues. All these issues came under the eye of a minister. A minister cannot deal with more than half a dozen cases in any one day, but Parliamentary Questions are seen by at least one and probably more ministers. The file comes up through the department with a draft answer prepared by a principal. It then goes through the whole official hierarchy, which is thus able to see what the arguments are, within a particular division, on a particular issue, at that point in time. It is a good way in which the quality of work of officials can be tested by their own hierarchy and by ministers. It is an important positive element in what is essentially management by exception, within a broad-based hierarchy working on the assumption that almost everything is going all right unless it is proved to the contrary. One former Minister, Timothy Raison, rated them more highly after than before being in office. They tested the Department and made clear which policies and decisions could or could not be defended even though the power on the day was always with those who answered Parliamentary Questions, for the Speaker is keen to keep Parliamentary Questions on the move.

Parliamentary Questions thus have effects which do not obviously show themselves at the political level of educational policy-making. Ministers are forced to take notice. The great men of our age – Eccles, Boyle or Crosland – were constantly reminded that outside toilets and even earth closets existed in British rural schools in the 1950s and early 1960s. Ministers could see how well different parts of the DES stood up to the challenge to justify itself quickly on any bit of educational policy. Officials not only provide substantive answers, but also invent potential supplementary questions and answers to them. This helps sharpen the appreciation of officials for the political hammering through which ministers must go if they are to defend the policies which they may have little opportunity to examine at first hand. Parliamentary Questions make ministers healthily vulnerable. If they are not quick on their feet, if they cannot see trouble coming, the Parliamentary Question exposes them. For these few minutes every six or seven weeks they are on their own. They are not protected by highly competent officials who are able to run up an answer to any attack, no matter how awkward, at a few hours' notice. Parliamentary Questions can, then, 'monitor' the ways in which policies are carried out.

Parliamentary Questions relate to the fact that an MP has a series of roles to play. He has a duty to the nation as a whole, he is a member for his constituency with a primary duty to represent its interests, he is usually a member of a political party owing loyalty to the party, and he is under pressure from a miscellany of interest groups and the general public. This means that he is forced to respond in different ways, that is, as either a party member or a representative or a publicist. In this respect, Parliamentary Questions are not far different from other forms of expression available to MPs or the way in which they may express themselves through their own party committees.

Questions may allow an MP to conduct a campaign in a way allowed by no other House of Commons procedure, although the only MP to mention this was James Boyden who campaigned with other MPs to get regulations changed for correspondence colleges, but campaigns of this kind seem to occur rarely in education in spite of the fact that many MPs come from the teaching profession and four are sponsored by the NUT. Fletcher-Cooke and Wavell Wakefield on the admission of the NAS to Burnham, Hector Hughes on swimming education, Pavitt on school dentists – the list is not long nor impressive. Questions may be particularly useful to individual MPs as the loyalty of the party supporter is not at issue, and they are not part of a set piece staged by the party leaders. They seem to reflect the views and wishes of the individual member, rather than the government or the party as a whole. So questions are a continuous if unsystematic way in which the smaller issues are expressed and become aggregated. But this does not explain why so many educational Parliamentary Questions are on minor issues or concerned with obtaining statistical information – in fact approximately one-third are concerned with minor and constituency issues and one-third with statistical questions – and do not initiate many new arguments or ideas compared with Parliamentary Questions on, say, defence or foreign affairs. Perhaps education consists of many small issues in a way not true of other subjects.

Parliamentary Questions also have special uses. It has been known for a government department to ask a group to put down a question so that it can give out certain information. Government departments, including the DES, use inspired questions when they want to make announcements of a certain kind. For example, the establishment of the Plowden Committee was announced in this way. Interest groups use Parliamentary Questions often simply to get information. The questions from the interest groups' point of view can be seen as 'a weapon against inaction rather than against action'. Many groups argue that a minister who is not convinced by argument is not going to be influenced by a Parliamentary Question, so that the use of Question Time varies from group to group. The groups that make use of Question Time, such as the NUS and ATCDE, enlist the support of an MP on some issue. Others, such as the NUT, sponsor an MP or enlist his help by giving him an honorary title, as for example, the AMC does. This MP is more likely to approach the minister informally or by deputation. Occasionally a group may initiate a debate, but normally it will merely intervene either by a question or letter to make clear its point of view.

Parliamentary Questions have some relationship with letters to ministers. They can be asked as a last resort after a member has failed to persuade a minister by correspondence [19]. But essentially, as Barker's analysis shows [20], the use of them varies according to the individual style, the attitudes towards publicity, the intensity of the issue and the importance of the interest group in question as perceived by both individual members and ministers.

In spite of the fact that there are committees on educational subjects in both parties, there does not seem to be a specific group in any party that puts forward Parliamentary Questions on education. On average, throughout our period, 220 individual MPs placed questions on education (*see* Chart VIII). Only ten MPs managed to sustain an interest in Question Time for four or more consecutive years on education and these four MPs concentrated on national

L

Chart VIII: *The Number of Individual MPs Asking Parliamentary Questions from 1960 to 1973*

1960	184
1961	190
1962	200
1963	180
1964	199
1965	252
1966	224
1967	228
1968	223
1969	212
1970	240
1971	279
1972	275
1973	272

Source: *Hansard.*

issues, although these may be concerned with one area of education, for example, higher education. Ninety-two MPs sustained an interest in education of between one year and three years. This is often because they became absorbed with a local issue or a minor issue; for example, one Labour MP in 1964 asked how many children in Colne depended on outside earth closets. In 1965 Cyril Osborne asked several questions on why foreign potatoes were used in school meals in Lincolnshire.

The pattern has not changed with time though the turnover of MPs concerned with education remained considerable throughout this period. In interviews with MPs, none referred to specific help received from their party on educational issues, but approximately 30 per cent of them have been connected with education either as teachers or lecturers. MPs must spend a lot of time researching for each question. This may be another reason why so many Parliamentary Questions deal with constituency and minor issues and tend to react to rather than initiate policy.

Each year the questions are evenly split between both parties. Liberals ask few questions in proportion to their numbers; for example, in 1968 they asked seven. The great majority of MPs that do ask questions concerning education are backbenchers. They are not a precise instrument applied systematically by the party leadership.

DEBATES

Parliamentary Questions have dramatic interest because they are essentially adversarial. Even the least well-known backbencher can be sure that a minister, if only a junior minister, will answer him face to face and in the House at a time when a large number of members are present. But they are episodic and momentary, and the next question is called within a minute or so. So other forms of parliamentary encounter might demonstrate perhaps more systematic ways in which parliamentary activity may affect policy.

How far do debates reflect the development of sentiment in the whole society, and what impact do they have on government decisions? There are only a few examples that help answer this question. It is reputed that Lord James's attack in the House of Lords on the Robbins Committee's proposal that there should be a separate ministry of higher education was a decisive intervention, although there is always strong Treasury or Civil Service Department pressure within government for larger and co-ordinative departments, and it might have happened anyway. An Early Day Motion found support amongst enough MPs to put pressure for changes in government policy on teachers' pensions in 1973; the Chief Whip was reported to have warned ministers of the strength of feeling [21]. For the most part, however, it can be assumed that both debates and Parliamentary Questions offer undefined and imprecisely applied pressure on governments rather than help determine policies. Indeed, many of the larger debates are initiated by the Government, since it is they who have control over parliamentary time.

A study of the indices of Hansard for 1960 to 1973 showed some difference between the pattern of Parliamentary Questions and the subjects of debates. Every major government announcement as made through a White Paper or other form of ministerial announcement was debated. So were the more important reports of government committees – Newsom, Robbins, Plowden, James, for example – and the reports of select committees. And, of course, educational legislation was debated through the formal procedure of three readings in both Houses.

But it is possible to ask much the same questions as about Parliamentary Questions. Did MPs initiate or react to policy generation from the DES or other sources? The DES initiated all debates other than adjournment, private members' and supply day debates, and the adjournment debates covered much the same type of issue as the bulk of Parliamentary Questions constituency claims for school buildings, teacher shortages and so on. Chart IX lists all the educational debates in the House of Commons in 1960, 1964, 1968 and 1970 to illustrate the issues discussed in Parliament.

If we take 1960 as a typical year, some of the minor debates – on the Avigdor Jewish secondary school and on the Cornish building programme, for example – show the MP as a constituency advocate pressing a case on an unwilling minister. In the event, pressure by MPs did not succeed. It is unlikely that any building programme issue raised by an MP throughout the whole of our period affected the allocation of building programmes.

But even local issues, when presented strongly, can be related to larger policies and constitute generalised pressure on government. We can take Norman Dodds's adjournment debate on the Kent school building programme as an example. He helped to put pressure on a junior minister, Kenneth Thompson, who soon ceased to be a junior minister at all. He was attacked as 'sarcastic, complacent, misleading and anxious to absolve his Department from all responsibility', which did not, said Dodds, referring to an exchange in an earlier encounter, realise the gravity of dental disease among children. Warming to his theme. Dodds made a strong attack on the fact that schools were still housed in old buildings in spite of the promises of the White Paper 'Secondary Education for All – A New Drive' (December 1958), which had promised three hundred million pounds of building investment in five years to bring an end to all-age schools.

Dodds's speech echoed the arguments about education as they were being deployed at the beginning of the 1960s. He began with a retort to Harold Macmillan's famous statement:

'We have been told that we have never had it so good. It may be that there are more TV aerials, more cars, more hire purchase and more refrigerators, but when we see what other countries are spending on education, is it not vital if we are to survive in the competitive world and to pay for all the things that we need, that we should invest more in education?'

Here was the unchallenged creed of education as investment. It was one which the Crowther Report had stated eloquently and which Eccles was to repeat later in the year.

In the same adjournment debate a Conservative MP, Richard Hornby, thought there was now too much emphasis on secondary

Chart IX: *Subjects of Debates in 1960*

Initiator	Subject
Norman Dodds	Kent school building programme (adjournment debate).
Sir David Eccles	Statement on the Government's acceptance of the Albermarle Report on the youth service.
Barnett Janner	Debate on the Albermarle Report on the youth service.
Ray Gunter	The building of a school in Southwark (adjournment debate).
Barbara Castle	Rebuilding of a technical and grammar school in Blackburn (adjournment debate).
Sir David Eccles	Crowther Report (debate).
Charles Fletcher-Cooke	Ministry's refusal to accept the National Association of Schoolmasters into membership of Burnham Committee (debate).
Anthony Greenwood	Primary education (debate).
	The closure of a Jewish voluntary aided school in London (adjournment debate).
Sir Frank Markham	The design of school buildings (adjournment debate).
Will Griffith	Political enquiries about schoolchildren (adjournment debate).
Phillip Goodhard	School text books (adjournment debate).
Eirene White	Reference in the Queen's Speech on 1 November 1970 to education. An amendment proposed.
William Hayman	School building programme in Cornwall (adjournment debate).
	Library Bill – authors' rights (debate).

Subjects of Debates in 1964

Initiator	Subject
Frederick Willey	Consolidated Fund Bill (2nd Reading) (education) (debate).
James Boyden	Training colleges (library) (adjournment debate).
Quintin Hogg	University grants (statement).
Christopher Chataway	Public Libraries and Museums Bill (2nd Reading) (debate).
Richard Crossman	Supply: Committee-Education (debate).
Patrick Gordon Walker	School building programme, Smethwick (adjournment debate).
G. W. Reynolds	School, Islington (sanitary conditions) (adjournment debate).
Quintin Hogg	Secretary of State for Education and Science Order (debate).
Sir Niell Cooper-Key	University and College Estates Bill (2nd Reading) (debate).
Clifford Kenyon	Grammar school places (Surrey) (adjournment debate).
Quintin Hogg	Universities and colleges of advanced technology (staff remuneration) (statement).
Sir James Pitman	Initial training alphabet (debate).
Raymond Gower	Education (status of secondary schools) (debate).
James Boyden	Adult education (adjournment debate).
Sir Charles Taylor	Education (debate).
Sir Richard Thompson	Teacher training college, Croydon (adjournment debate).
Sir Edward Boyle	Public Libraries and Museums Bill (Report) (debate).
T. L. Iremonger	School building programme, Ilford (adjournment debate).
Quintin Hogg	Education Bill (2nd Reading) (debate).
Patrick Wall	Education (East Riding) (adjournment debate).
Frederick Willey	Education Bill (in the Standing Committee).
Dr Jeremy Bray	Scientific and technological education (debate).
James Boyden	Further education (day release) (debate).
John Wells	Education (Mid-Kent) (adjournment debate).
William Yates	Dawley (university) (debate).

Initiator	Subject
James Scott-Hopkins	Education (Cornwall) (adjournment debate).
Lord Balniel	Education (Mid-Hertfordshire) (adjournment debate).
Sir Richard Thompson	The case of Mrs Braganza (teaching qualifications) (adjournment debate).
Michael Stewart	Remuneration of Teachers Bill (2nd Reading) (debate).
Alan Hopkins	Grammar schools (adjournment debate).
John Hunt	Recreation and leisure facilities (adjournment debate).
Col Sir Harwood Harrison	School transport (rural areas) (adjournment debate).
Michael Stewart	Science and Technology Bill (debate).
Reginald Prentice	Remuneration of Teachers Bill (Report in Standing Committee debate).

Subjects of Debates in 1968

Initiator	Subject
Government	Education Bill (referred to 2nd Reading Committee).
Sir Edward Boyle	Education (debate).
Denis Coe	Secondary schools (co-educational) (adjournment debate).
Renee Short	Education Bill (as amended in Standing Committee) (debate).
Dr Hugh Gray	The Case of Mrs Mary Wareham (Maltese teaching qualifications) (adjournment debate).
Kenneth Lewis	University students (adjournment debate).
Norman Miscampbell	Nursery schools (debate).
Sir Edward Boyle	Student grants (adjournment debate).
Shirley Williams	Student grants (statement).
Joan Lestor	Development of playgroups (1st Reading of Private Members Bill).
William Deedes	Schools (dangerous drugs) (debate).
John Hunt	Schools (computer programming) (adjournment debate).
Alice Bacon	Education Bill (3rd Reading) (debate).
Sydney Bidwell	Secondary education (Ealing) (adjournment debate).
Peter Kirk	School, Great Dunmow (adjournment debate).
James Callaghan	Urban programmes (government aid) (debate).
Julian Ridsdale	Education (finance) (debate).
Edward Short	School meals (statement).
John Boyd-Carpenter	Schools, Kingston-upon-Thames (building works) (adjournment debate).
Edwin Brooks	Education (autistic children) (adjournment debate).
John Peel	Secondary school building (Leicester) (adjournment debate).
Alan Davidson	School building programme (Accrington) (adjournment debate).

Subjects of Debates in 1970

Initiator	Subject
David Lane	Teachers' salaries (debate).
J. Dickens	Educational grant (the case of Mrs J. M. Basnett) (adjournment debate).
Edward Short	Education Bill (2nd Reading) (debate).
Edward Short	Teachers' pay (statement).
Neil Marten	Schoolteacher (the case of Mrs Green) (adjournment debate).
M. Jopling	Schools, Wath and Kirklington (closure) (adjournment debate).
Frederick Willey	Janice Gamble (physically handicapped child) (adjournment debate).
Sir Arthur Vere Harvey	Mosley Primary School, Congleton (adjournment debate).
Sir Cyril Black	Convicted teachers (employment) (adjournment debate).
Margaret Thatcher	Education Bill (debate).
A. G. F. Hall-Davis	Education (the case of William Higgin) (adjournment debate).
Edward Short	Queen's Speech – Education (debate).
William van Straubenzee	Education (Handicapped Children) Bill – 2nd Reading (debate).
Fred Mulley	Castle School, Sheffield (adjournment debate).
Sir David Renton	Education (Handicapped Children) Bill (debate).
Laurence Pavitt	The education of autistic children (adjournment debate).
Paul B. Rose	Autistic children (adjournment debate).
William Rodger	Teeside (university provision) (adjournment debate).
Tam Dalyell	Medical Inspection (Evidence of Drug Taking) (School Pupils) (Private Members' Bill).
David Clark	Secondary education, Saddleworth (adjournment debate).
Selwyn Gummer	Secondary education, West Lewisham (adjournment debate).

Source: *Hansard.*

education and that it was time to give more resources for primary schools. Here might be one of the minor impulses leading to the creation of the Plowden Committee in 1963.

On 3 February Sir David Eccles accepted in principle all the recommendations of the Albermarle Report which was to provide for the training of youth leaders, the provision of better buildings for the youth service and create a Youth Service Development Council. Anthony Greenwood leading for the Opposition accepted all the Minister's decisions because they 'followed Labour policy'. Questions were raised about specific grants to local authorities, about the adequacy of the building programme and about the relationships between the development of the youth service and the proposals in the Crowther Report for raising the school leaving age. But here, again, the working of pressure groups on government might be detected as there had been attacks on the Ministry of Education for its complacency in treating the youth service.

Richard Hornby's demands that more should be given to primary schools was repeated by Ray Gunter, again in an adjournment debate, on 25 February. Again government policy was defended as essentially providing roofs over heads in secondary schools as the population bulge moved in.

A more obvious example of interest groups at work occurred on 14 April when Charles Fletcher-Cooke pressed on the Government the claims of the National Association of Schoolmasters for representation on the Burnham Committee. He referred to the famous tactical mistake committed by Lord Hailsham as Minister of Education when he wrote, in 1957, that 'I would be very loath to allow the Burnham Committee to be used as a vehicle for undermining this policy'. The policy referred to was for equal pay for women teachers, which was resisted by the NAS. For the Minister to say that representation should be 'by types of school' was unfair to those who did not feel they were adequately represented by the NUT. At least one local authority wanted to admit the NAS to the education committee, but the NUT refused to attend the committee for three years as a result. Horace King, a Labour MP, was against admission because the NAS has two aims: that boys should be taught by men and that pay should be unequal. Eccles's reply was on familiar lines. The NUT at that time represented 201,000 teachers of whom 185,000 were in primary, secondary modern and all-age schools. But 60,000 of its members were men and they represented 75 per cent of all men in primary and secondary modern schools. This was three times the total membership of the NAS which thus had no claim to represent any single group of teachers.[1] Finally, the NAS was admitted to Burnham and has since become a very powerful interest group.

These examples show well what could happen as a result of debates in one year. The NAS case demonstrates that ministers listen to their own backbenchers. But the actual pressure came from outside the Commons chamber. No education debate has led to a vote that has had any effect since the Churchill Government was defeated in 1943 by a demand for equal pay. And the war-time coalition government had the amendment deleted the next day [22].

ADJOURNMENT DEBATES

Both the subject range and time given to adjournment debates and Parliamentary Questions are similar. Thirty members compete for the right to initiate the five half-hour debates a week and this means that the subject of the adjournment debate might lose its topicality. Thus debates tend to be concerned with constituency interest. They occupy a relatively large proportion of the time spent on parliamentary activity by the DES and its minister: in 1966 to 1967 there were sixteen on education and science out of a total of 175 (9·2 per cent) [23].

They can give rise to conflict between government and opposition but, conventionally, backbenchers rather than the Shadow Cabinet raise matters on the adjournment debates from constituency complaints or from a member's specialist interest in the subject. The member has to undertake a considerable amount of research before raising the matter on the adjournment.

He might contact or be contacted by interest groups, and MPs are certainly briefed by educational groups, research organisations, private firms or individuals in order to obtain the facts, figures and opinions which are presented in the debate. 'This enables useful information to be obtained and examined without making too heavy demands on the time of the House or on Ministers and their officials' [24].

The backbencher is more dominant in an adjournment debate than during Question Time. For example, in 1966 to 1967, only one out of 175 adjournment debates was not moved by a backbench member and, again, the debates were almost equally divided bet-

[1] This issue is well discussed in R. D. Coates (See ref. [6], Chapter 3).

ween the two main parties. Like Parliamentary Questions, the adjournment debates are reactive and either press the Government to reverse previous policies, or ask for assistance from the Government for certain local or regional cases, or demand statements from the Government either of an explanatory nature or relating to the past or to what progress has been made, or request the Government to widen its activities. It is an opportunity for enabling back-benchers to assert themselves and affect the climate of opinion, but their direct impact is again uncertain.

SELECT COMMITTEES

The Expenditure Committee and the Public Accounts Committee are those which have concerned themselves with education. So far, the Committee on the Parliamentary Commissioner has not reported on any educational matter. Occasionally the Committee on Statutory Instruments will take up a DES issue but this is rare. Chart X contains a list of Select Committee reports on education from 1960 to 1974.

The Committee on Expenditure developed from the Committee on Estimates in 1960, and subjects for study have been selected

Chart X: *Select Committees: 1960–74*

Public Accounts Committee 1960–1974

1　Session 1961–2; Third Report: *Universities and Colleges, etc., Great Britain* (paragraphs on grants to universities; non-recurrent grants).
2　Session 1966–7; Special Report: *Parliament and Control of University Expenditure.*
3　Session 1966–7 (Part II); Third, Fourth and Fifth Reports (*section on DES Expenditure*).
4　Session 1969–70; First, Second and Third Reports (section on *University Expenditure*).
5　Session 1969–70; First, Second and Third Reports (section on *Universities and Colleges, Great Britain*).
6　Session 1970–1; First, Second and Third Reports (section on *Bath University of Technology: Disposal of Property*).
7　Session 1971–2; Third Report (sections on the *UGC and Accounting Records*).
8　Session 1972–3; Eighth Report (sections on *Grants to Universities, Colleges, etc., Grants to the Open University, Control of Issue of Grants in Aid by the DES*).

Estimates Committee 1960–1974

1 Session 1960–1; Eighth Report: *School Building.*
2 Session 1961–2; Second Special Report: *School Building.*
3 Session 1962–3; First Report: *Dental Services* (section on *School Dental Services*).
4 Session 1964–5; Third Report: *Variations in Estimate.*
5 Session 1964–5; Fifth Report: *Grants to Universities and Colleges.*
6 Session 1966–7; Fourth Report: *Government Statistics Service.*
7 Session 1970–1; *Education and Arts Sub-Committee.*
8 Session 1970–1; Second Report: *Education and Arts Sub-Committee.*
9 Session 1970–1; Eighth Report: *Relationship of Expenditure to Needs* (section on *Nursery Education*).
10 Session 1972–3; *Education and Arts Sub-Committee: Further and Higher Education* (Volumes I–III and Report).
11 Session 1972–3; Fifth Report: *The White Paper: Public Expenditure to 1976–7,* cmnd 5/78.
12 Session 1973–4; Third Report: *Education and Arts Sub-Committee: Postgraduate Education* (Volumes I and II and Report).
13 Session 1973–4; *Education and Arts Sub-Committee: Further Developments in Higher and Further Education.*

Select Committees 1960–1974

1 Session 1967–8; *Her Majesty's Inspectorate (England and Wales)* (Part I and II, and observations by the DES on the recommendations in Part I).
2 Session 1967–8; *Education and Science.*
3 Session 1968–9; Fourth Special Report: *Education and Science.*
4 Session 1968–9; *Student Relations* (Volumes I–VII).
5 Session 1968–9; *Race Relations and Immigration. The Problems of Coloured School Leavers* (Volumes I–IV).
6 Session 1969–70; *Teacher Training (The Open University).*
7 Session 1969–70; *Teacher Training* (Volumes I–V and documents).
8 Session 1970–1; *The Problems of Coloured School Leavers* (observations on the Select Committee on Race Relations and Immigration).
9 Session 1970–1; *Science and Technology Research Councils.*
10 Session 1971–2; First Report: *Science and Technology Research and Development.*
11 Session 1971–2; *Science and Technology Research and Development.*
12 Session 1971–2; First Special Report: *Race Relations and Immigration Statistics of Immigrant School Pupils.*
13 Session 1972–3; *Race Relations and Immigration Education* (Volume I and Report).

(This chart does not include Committees concerned with Scotland, sport or the arts.)

somewhat fortuituously for its Sub-Committee on Science, Education and Arts. One MP whom we consulted had been present for discussions on further and higher education and grants to postgraduate students; indeed, post-school education has had a large share of committee time in recent years. Most members have educational backgrounds, though this does not necessarily make them more credible on the Committee. The memberships of the Select Committees on educational subjects have been described to us as consisting of out-of-date technical college lecturers.

One of the more important parliamentary institutions is the Select Committee, although the PAC has more traditional weight. Neither can compare with the US Congressional Committees, because neither has authority to amend or propose budgets. Select Committees are important, nevertheless, for many reasons. First, they require the DES and the Treasury to state, both in writing and in exchange of dialogue, how they implement policies which can then be held up for scrutiny by the Select Committee. Secondly, they reveal to the outsider a great deal about the way in which MPs perceive the change in educational policies and values. Thirdly, they not only require the departments to show their hands, but also make the interest groups do so. They come to give both written and oral evidence and thus open up their biases and pressures in a revealing way. This is not to say that this information is then well used. We will argue in our final chapter that too much useful information is disregarded by MPs and in outside critiques.

Not all observers or MPs see them as particularly important to education. A former chairman regarded them as mainly a device to keep the left-wingers occupied. He thought that no one took any notice of them and that very little legislation resulted. Another Conservative MP thought they needed to be taken seriously and that they did influence secretaries of state, particularly when their reports were debated in the House. It was generally agreed, however, that they were in difficulty because not enough MPs could be found for them and because they were inadequately serviced by the secretariat. One MP thought that Select Committees had little effect so that members who joined them were those with little to do and who wanted to make their mark. Their maximum role, in his view, was of publicising issues rather than of helping to determine them.

Other MPs took less astringent views. One MP thought that Select Committees did encourage government to act (even if it eventually went its own way) and, in any event, did influence public opinion. For example the DES, in replying to the 1973 Select

Committee proposals which attacked the binary system and proposed joint machinery for the two parts, virtually ignored its report. The Government tended to accept only the minor suggestions. More important than what the Select Committee proposed, one MP felt [25], were the vested interests of the UGC and the local authorities. But at least it was something that the issue had been exposed and the Government forced to consider a reply for publication. One MP summed them up as follows: 'Members do not pay much attention to Select Committees as there is an element that feels it is more important to make a rhetorical speech in the Chamber. . . .' He thought that an aggregate of local feelings could cause change. 'Many MPs respond much more passionately to constituents and the personal impact can have a greater political impact' [26].

One former minister, in office when the report on the education of immigrants [27] was made, thought that the DES paid a lot of attention to it. DES officials believed the chairman, William Deedes, to be hostile to the Department. Margaret Thatcher acted strongly to meet the Committee's wishes, although it is observable that her Labour successor has continued the same policy. Select Committees are, however, seen to be far more important in the areas of economics, trade and industry than in the social services [28].

Again it is difficult to specify precisely what the impact of the Select Committees, and of the parallel Public Accounts Committee, has been. But the following generalisations might be made. First, in some cases there have been direct effects of the Select Committee probing; for example, the Select Committee on Estimates, very early in our period, attacked the Ministry of Education for what it thought to be a complacent view of the future of the youth service. In particular, it has been surmised that the somewhat negative attitude of one of the officials in giving evidence convinced MPs that the Ministry was both uncommitted and cynical. As a result [29] Sir David Eccles set up the Albermarle Committee [30] which led directly to an expansion of the youth services and the provision of the first adequate training courses for them.

A second example was the important report of the Public Accounts Committee on university expenditure in 1966 [31]. The universities, the UGC, the DES, the AUT and other bodies were examined closely as to why the universities should not surrender themselves to public audit as do other receivers of public funds. Both the detailed scrutiny as recorded in the transactions and the report of the Committee must have greatly strengthened Anthony

Crosland's hand in requiring the universities to submit to audit. At this time universities were still regarded as largely untouchable and had only recently left the ambit of the Treasury for the control of the DES.

Thirdly, the Select Committee's investigation of HM Inspectorate [32] might have had long-range effects. For one thing the status of the senior chief inspector was more clearly defined into that of a deputy secretary within the Department following its recommendations. More important, according to the senior chief inspector writing in the *TES* in April 1974 [33] HMIs became more closely involved in policy-formation within the DES as members of policy planning teams. This is certainly a development since the evidence given by a former senior chief inspector, Sir Cyril English, to the Select Committee. Whether or not there is a clear casual relationship between the Select Committee's work and this or other developments it is difficult to say. We can only surmise that it at least helped to tighten up the DES's own appraisal of relationships. Even the Committee report on students [34] was thought by one MP 'to bring things into focus'.

If, however, we take the broad definition of the main parliamentary function as expressed by Edward Boyle, that MPs 'register the norm of public opinion', the Select Committees are surely important. They expose the workings of the system to public view.

They brought out into the open the DES's methods of financial control in an exhaustive study of the way in which decisions are made between the Treasury and the DES and the local authority associations [35]. They entered into an area where some would think only absurdity could result – a scrutiny of student unrest – and thus they could experience the problems faced by all university administrators and teachers in making a rational judgement on what is essentially an irrational movement [36]. A Select Committee study of nursery education needs exposed what seemed to be uncertainty in the DES before the major move forward came in the White Paper of 1972 in expanding nursery education [37].

Two main changes would be needed to make them more effective. First, they need adequate advisory services which are able to do research for them. Secondly, they need real power. Their functions are deliberative rather than executive. No minister appears before them. They certainly open up the workings of administration but no official, ultimately, has to justify himself to them – only to his own minister. And it is not at all clear to us that the rich data that they produce are adequately used by MPs, who are the only full-time guardians of the public interest at the national level.

PARLIAMENTARY PARTIES AND MPS

So far we have discussed the main parliamentary institutions. But they might well be no more than the formal institutions which to some extent conceal the real processes of policy-making underneath. It has already been seen that Labour MPs were weak in advancing fundamental Labour policies, so it might be that much policy manufacture takes place off stage. And, the fact that Edward Boyle and Eccles were often outside the mainstream of Conservative policy might also indicate that opinions were forming underneath which were not articulated through parliamentary institutions.

The Labour Party
Throughout the 1950s and much of the 1960s the Labour Party was ambivalent in its educational policy. One strand was inherited from its Liberal and Fabian antecedents which broadly expressed the need for creating a meritocracy to work for the best interests of the nation. This attitude became policy when the municipalities became Labour controlled [38]. Other themes related to the improvement of free elementary education and free secondary education for those who could benefit from it. Both of these fed the soft concept of equality which saw opportunity for all as the main consideration. By the 1960s Labour was uncertain as to whether it wanted more grammar school places or none at all, an issue no more clearly determined by Harold Wilson's double-think dictum of 'grammar schools for all'. It was only in the early 1960s that the party came out definitely in favour of comprehensive schools, after a long period in which the official leadership and the party conferences were apart from each other. It also came out in favour of mass higher education, as in a report of a Labour Party committee which sat under Lord Taylor in the early 1960s. This belief hardly showed itself in debates or in Parliamentary Questions until Michael Stewart became Secretary of State in October 1964.

The Labour Party has been confused about educational policy. For example, Michael Stewart recounts how, when he was Parliamentary Under Secretary for War in the 1945 to 1950 Labour Government, Emanuel Shinwell would never accept that army education was important. Aneurin Bevan was never particularly

M

urgent about the need for educational opportunities. This attitude has changed now as more teachers from all areas of education become Labour MPs and as working-class parents find educational opportunities less alien to their own background.

There is an education group in the parliamentary party but it has, according to two senior witnesses, little influence on policy. Few MPs take part in its work. Its membership varies from time to time and there is little continuity. It is consulted or perhaps informed on large policies, but not actively. Education is not in any case considered as politically controversial as housing or taxation. A few enthusiasts work to influence other members in becoming interested. One MP [39] thought that membership of a Transport House working party more influential than the party education group or than the role of the MP altogether.

Debates in the House are preceded by a meeting of the Parliamentary Labour Party convened by the education group. Perhaps two or three dozen members attend. The Shadow Cabinet and Education Sub-Committee of the National Executive Committee of the Labour Party are formally concerned with policies, but in fact it is the Opposition leader who has to create them. Thus it may be that the Shadow Minister is not in the Shadow Cabinet and does not share the Education Sub-Committee's tactical priorities. For example, Roy Hattersley drafted the eight lines in the 1974 Party Manifesto dedicated to education. But because he was not in the Shadow Cabinet he could escape the detailed scrutiny of some of his other shadow colleagues.

He would show speeches to those who helped him shadow on education such as Joan Lestor, Robert Moyle and Eric Armstrong, who would see perhaps the second draft of his speech. A third draft might go to Harry Pitt, the head of research at Transport House, or to Edward Short or even to Harold Wilson. His proposals to withdraw subsidies to public schools were shown to Harold Wilson. Edward Short would see them both as Deputy Leader and as former Secretary of State with a strong interest in education. The parallels with the ministerial and parliamentary systems are obvious: the leaders lead and the rest catch up as best they can.

The Conservative Party

The Conservative Parliamentary Education Committee is a subcommittee of the 1922 Committee. It meets every week at six o'clock during the parliamentary session and its executive meets one hour before the main committee meeting. The 1922 Committee might take up particularly important issues, but otherwise the Parliamentary Education Committee sees ministers direct. Its members, and a former chairman and secretary (Gilbert Longden), claim that it has an effect [40]. It contributed to Florence Horsborough's removal because of the Teachers' Superannuation Bill in 1955. It commented on policies of comprehensive education, on the James Report – Lord James had visited them – and on the Russell Report.

Before a minister appears before the Committee, the Committee's opinions are conveyed through the chairman to him. The Chief Whip is always also informed. The chairman of the Parliamentary Education Committee meets interest group leaders such as the President of the NUT.

Gilbert Longden was also Honorary Secretary to the Conservative National Advisory Committee on Education which included Conservative teachers and local authority representatives. Central Office provides a secretariat but the chairman and officers are teachers. It also meets once a quarter and passes on its conclusions to the Minister.

THE ROLE OF OPPOSITION

The impact of parliamentary processes and of the parliamentary party committees on ministerial decisions affects the role of the Opposition, which can be no stronger than Parliament itself. One Labour frontbencher maintained that the Opposition could not markedly influence government. Its main duties were to become the next government, prepare itself for government and only lastly to deflect government from its purposes. There was no point in perpetually chiding Conservative ministers for not being socialist. It was also important to get one's own party committed to policies before elections so as to ensure that resource alibis could not be used once they were in power. Moreover, the interest groups could not be certain about the usefulness of trying to influence through the Opposition since they would simultaneously be trying to influence government directly. The Opposition would be a last resort. 'If the Opposition shows too much interest then that is the kiss of death' was a sentiment expressed more than once in interviews [41]. And it would be a foolhardy lobbyist who would assume that the Opposition was about to get into office. Who could have accurately forecast the 1964, 1970 or February 1974 election results?

Opposition leadership may be affected from the party network as well as through Parliament. Roy Hattersley, for example, wrote to Labour authorities to say that they should not be too quick to close colleges of education in case the Labour Government decided to re-expand higher education; a piece of advice not borne out by Labour policies once the party took power. Relationships between the Parliamentary Labour Party and local authorities have grown. The local leaders in Birmingham, Manchester and Sheffield were consulted on speeches by Roy Hattersley, who would also attend Labour meetings before the main meetings of the AEC, CCA and AMC. Frank Hutton of Manchester, for example, had advised on Hattersley's major speech on building costs in education. Relationships with the Labour-led ILEA were not so close.

This leads to an important point about educational decision-making generally. Many leading policies have been initiated or resisted with most vigour locally. Comprehensive education is the best example of this. The central parties have perhaps been slow to make connections with local parties and to capitalise on their experience. Local parties do consult the central party leaders, as did London on the appointment of its leader when the Conservatives came to power [42], and Southampton, when the local Conservatives consulted Boyle, Richard Hornby and Charles Morrison on the extent to which it should resist comprehensivisation [43].

INDIVIDUAL RELATIONS WITH MINISTERS

MPs have privileged access to ministers. Not only can they ask Parliamentary Questions and expect an answer, but can also expect to exchange letters which are signed by ministers. Private offices normally send most letters addressed to ministers from the general public to the policy division concerned which answers them without further reference unless the issue seems to be important. Letters which demand a special answer because the writer is particularly important may get a reply from a parliamentary private secretary. But all letters from MPs, important or trivial, are replied to personally by a minister. And this means, in effect, that the issues raised fall under the minister's eye. It is thus one of the implicit review procedures, and MPs participate in it.

We have recorded that one MP [44] told us that there was no real point in putting down Parliamentary Questions and that they and adjournment debates were simply a somewhat feeble last resort. It was far better to see a minister, who could not refuse to see an MP and would try hard to appear helpful if only to cut down the possibility of a further meeting in a busy life. He indeed claimed to have influenced a minister's mind on a local comprehensive issue by these means, a somewhat irregular procedure if true.

Former ministers agreed, however, that MPs influenced them. The fall of Horsborough was mentioned by at least three MP respondents [45]. The acceptance of the NAS as part of the Burnham system was also especially pressed on David Eccles by two Tory MPs. After the February 1974 election, both parties seemed to some [46] to become firmer in holding ministers and shadow leaders to pre-election policies. And the more liberal Conservative Opposition seemed to be under fire from its back-benchers after a speech to the NUT at Easter 1974. In any event, there was a change of Shadow Minister soon after.

What does this add up to? Parliamentary Questions and debates do not closely relate to the development of the policies listed in Chart II. They do not anticipate policies and provide no systematic critique of them. Select Committees reflect policy preoccupations more accurately and are more systematic in exposing the administration of policies. But none of these instruments gives Parliament substantive authority. And there is also the problem that, as one MP put it, 'few MPs know how government works'.

We have seen that ministers and MPs have different views on the impact of parliamentary scrutiny, but that ministers more than MPs take it seriously. Officials with whom we have discussed the impact also differ. One regarded the parliamentary process as a very real constraint, especially when the issue attracted the interest of a specialist and knowledgeable group. Others thought that MPs made more impact through direct meetings. But those meetings with ministers are, of course, part and parcel of the parliamentary process and may be an occasion for the MP to extend or withdraw the threat of a parliamentary challenge. Another, in a fine piece of official *de haut en bas*, thought that Select Committees led to 'an imperfect understanding of the facts', but that the Public Accounts Committee meetings which are held in private have a much more formidable atmosphere, where officials feel they are in the dock in a way not felt in the more amiable atmosphere of the Select Committees.

One teachers' leader quoted examples of lobbying that had succeeded [47], though Coates suggests that contacts with Parliament waned as contacts with the Education Department increased. And Coates describes how the NUT created a parliamentary committee in 1962 which, however, only regularised present practices. The NUT and NAS make vigorous use of the lobbying of local MPs on most of their campaigns. In the NUT's campaign to prevent ministerial imposition of salary scales in 1963, they briefed their sponsored MPs. Sir Ronald Gould met leading Labour spokesmen and addressed 100 Conservative backbenchers. The President of the NUT announced he would stand against the Minister at the next general election. But the teachers' campaign failed and, in Coates's view, typified the increasing weakness of traditional methods of putting on pressure.

There was a reflective judgement from another teachers' leader: 'If one wants to influence MPs, then local members should lobby their own. Lobbying the chief ones is a waste of time' [48].

The most that can be said is that parliamentary mechanisms provide part of the environment in which policy is made and help, in part, to aggregate local feelings and project them on to a national screen. In performing these functions they raise questions about how local feelings and developments *are* aggregated and what the connection is between the development of local practice and policies and national policy generation. These issues will be discussed further in Chapter 12.

Part IV

CASE STUDIES

In the next two chapters the development of higher education and policies for comprehensive secondary schools are used as case studies of the way in which change processes may take place. The interest groups particularly concerned with the two issues are also described.

Chapter 10

The Case of Higher Education

Changes in higher education have been more dramatic and important than in perhaps any other area of education since the war. The
universities, which seemed exclusive and permanently viable
institutions in 1960, increased in number, expanded in size, and
were brought under stronger public control and social challenge.
Many of the uncertainties that beset British society in the second
half of the 1960s were projected on to the new campuses. Egalitarianism, the left wing challenge to institutional authority, the first
waves of public uncertainty about educational expenditure and the
shock waves of economic trouble all successively hit higher
education.

1 THE PUBLIC SECTOR

The changes in the non-university or public sector were the more
substantial, if less dramatic. From the Percy Report of 1945 until
the White Paper on the polytechnics in 1965, change, expansion,
stratification, a broadening of purposes and the development of
status, all came to further education.

From the point of view of our values classification stated in
Chapter 3, the case of higher education, in both its main sectors, is
illuminating.

The main objectives of expanding the non-university sector from
1956 onwards, when Sir David Eccles's White Paper set the framework for expansion, were economic and social. The constraints

within which the changes took place were institutional rather than educational. And because there was no stable ethic of further education to which the planners had to defer, as there was and is in the schools, the social, economic and institutional values revealed themselves in non-continuous, innovative and volatile policies.

The reader will see from Chart II how continusously and comprehensively further education progressed until a clear, highly stratified and ambitious sector, led by its thirty university-status polytechnics and covering every other level of post-school education as well as degree level, now provides a network of educational provision for any citizen who cares to avail himself of it from the age of sixteen into retirement.

The cause of the further education sector was promoted by the Ministry and Department of Education and Science and by its own interest groups.

On the DES role, the structure of educational government is relevant. The DES does not control the schools. They are owned, maintained and administered by the local authorities. Curriculum and internal organisation are a matter for the schools and for their local authorities. Institutional statuses in the school sector are not determined by the DES, which simply disposes of institutional destinies under the terms of Section 13 of the Education Act, 1944, in response to local authority plans which might be modified for general social reasons, for example, comprehensivisation, or in response to parental and ratepayer protests. In principle, the local authority creates its school system and the DES does no more than to monitor it.

Further education is different. No polytechnic can be created without the Secretary of State's designation. No advanced course can run without the approval of the Regional Advisory Council and the DES's staff inspector for that region. The examinations are run, at the national diploma and certificate levels, by joint committees consisting of professional institutions working with HMIs. Many circulars from the DES are concerned with the development of particular subject areas or with the organisation of the further education institutional structure.

The reasons for centralised development are plain. Further education, particularly in the sciences and technologies, is expensive. It usually has consequences well outside the area of the providing local authority and, indeed, many of the polytechnics are now national institutions. But there are other reasons which cannot be documented. HM Inspectorate is more powerful, clear in its objectives and accepted by the system as a determining force within the further education sector, than within the schools. Two recent chief inspectors who later became senior chief inspectors led an able team of perhaps a hundred. They advocated further education's point of view in the DES and did the detailed work in order to secure further education's place. Eccles gave further education a fair wind.

The system, then, had its own powerful advocates, and the institutional framework is now strong. It is perhaps for this reason that the further education interest groups are less obvious in their impact than their counterparts in other areas. The expansion and increase in status of further education have been well in line with the demands pressed by the Association of Teachers in Technical Institutions (ATTI) It does not go out of the way to court publicity through close relations with the press.

These advocates represent the case with skill and force but the issues are regarded as more national, and belonging to government, than those in other areas. It is also relevant that the two most important, the ATTI and the Association of Teachers in Colleges and Departments of Education (ATCDE), have experienced large fluctuations in their fortunes since the early 1960s.

THE ASSOCIATION OF TEACHERS IN TECHNICAL INSTITUTIONS

The ATTI's aims and objects are 'to protect and promote the interests of members and to regulate the conditions of employment and relations between them and employers'. More altruistically, the Association intends to 'advance further and higher education generally and professionalism and vocational education in particular' [1].

Its membership rose from 23,300 in 1968 to over 48,000 in 1974. It covers virtually the whole of the non-university sector except for colleges of education. As they merge with polytechnics and other institutions they, too, may come into membership and discussions are now, in fact, taking place [2].

The large increases in membership directly reflect the post-war increase in scale and range of further education work. It first benefited from the increase in national courses leading to diplomas and certificates and also from the increase in general and non-national courses. As the CNAA degree courses developed largely in the polytechnics, the numbers taking HNDs and HNCs began to decline. The Association is now somewhat anxious about the downturn in demand for courses in science and technical subjects.

The ATTI is concerned with the expansion of, and better conditions for, the further education sector but its main concerns have been with the relationship between its colleges and other sectors. The development of the polytechnics owes much to the ATTI's way of thinking. Anthony Crosland has referred to his consultations with it before the Woolwich speech which quoted an ATTI submission [3]. The Association is now less certain about the binary policy. It wants there to be a higher education commission [4] but believes that the DES so jealously guards its own power that it will continue to resist.

Its response to the 1972 White Paper [5], apart from expressing fears that economic rather than social criteria were being advanced, also claimed that there was no coherent policy for post-school education, that a single council should have a regional structure, and that there should be immediate compulsory day release for the sixteens to nineteens and a crash programme of development for the colleges.

A second main concern has been to loosen up the arrangements for the sixteens to nineteens so that co-operation between institutions and a free choice for students can be developed. It feels that pupils want to come to further education colleges particularly in south-east England. Twenty-five per cent of O- and A-levels are taken in further education colleges. Common regulations began to be drafted in 1971 and 1972 when a new education act was being thought of.

It has also been concerned about the influences of the 1964 Industrial Training Act on part-time education 'and the DES has done virtually nothing about it' [6].

The ATTI is part of a somewhat different and broader network than the other unions. It presses on the TUC the importance of general education as against craft training. Its recruitment and salaries policies look not only to the schools and the universities but also to industry.

The Association has not had an easy time in coping with a self-confident DES. And it now has competition from the directors of polytechnics as well as from other unions. Its fortunes fluctuate with changes in further education although as a group it has not suffered the anxieties facing another higher education group, the ATCDE.

THE ASSOCIATION OF TEACHERS IN COLLEGES AND DEPARTMENTS OF EDUCATION

The ATCDE [7] is an example of an association whose fortunes have fluctuated directly in response to government policy. It is one of the smallest interest groups, though as teacher education expanded its membership grew from less than 1,000 to 7,000 between 1950 and 1974.

The Association represents both teaching staff and principals (who are part of the management system) in a sector which still has a particularly large number of voluntary colleges. It was only in 1974 that the first non-principal chairman took office. The executive committee used to be made up largely of principals

Most of the day-to-day work is concerned with individual members' problems. But the Secretary, Stanley Hewitt, has played a prominent and shrewd part in negotiation on the broader issues of college government and on the vexed question of the future of the colleges. It is through no fault of his that the colleges now seem unable to resist DES intentions to absorb them into polytechnics and other further education institutions. In the last resort the DES can decide. The ATCDE played an important role in establishing the agreed procedures resulting from the Weaver Report which led to the sharing of principals' authority, particularly over promotions, with academic boards. The ATCDE was involved in the preparation of the 1968 Act which provided for agreed disciplining procedures, including committees with student membership. Other changes have not improved relations with the local authorities, which no longer provide clerks to governing bodies and whose pleas for approval of courses by the Regional Advisory Councils were not successful.

The Association does not concern itself with teacher education curriculum but with the framework within which curriculum is created. It had a hand in formulating the McNair Report proposals of 1944. It has an authoritative journal specialising in teacher education. It argues for institutional freedom but also for sufficient uniformity to allow easy transfer of staff. It pressed for the three-year course and for the implementation of the BEd degree. It has worked with the NUT on the vexed question of the nature of the probationary year.

Since the publication of the James Report, occasional formal meetings have given way to frequent and informal meetings with DES officials, mainly at the Under-Secretary level but, surprisingly, less frequently with HMIs. This may be because structure, control and government are now the important issues.

It considers itself as a source of information to the Department on teacher supply matters. It negotiates on such matters as the safeguarding of staff made redundant as the teacher education system shrinks. The DES consults it on draft circular or other letters to the colleges.

Relationships with university teacher trainers are amicable on such matters as their reaction to the James Report.

The teacher training system is under pressure from many groups who think 'if one could only get at the training systems all would be well'. The ATCDE has had demands for perhaps 100 representative members on external bodies including the Schools Council, the BBC and the ITA. The colleges are vulnerable, too, to demands relating from changes in curriculum factions.

The ATCDE has no links with MPs but relates to the party which is in government. It occasionally has contact with the shadow spokesman but this could be the 'kiss of death'. Roy Hattersley and William Moyle used to ring it up for help with information.

The ATCDE is at present concerned with survival but in the past it has developed under the General Secretary as a group with a reputation for effectiveness because it worked at the facts and made a case clearly.

It is somewhat detached from educational controversy and it is perhaps inevitable that a group of teachers whose institutions depend wholly on government supply policies should not be able to defend itself against such rapid and large-scale changes as the wholesale expansion of their colleges in the 1960s and the virtual extinction of them in the 1970s.

THE POLYTECHNICS

The polytechnics are a major policy and institutional artefact of the last ten years. Within this period thirty polytechnics, some of them as big as the average university, and able to give a wide range of qualifications, have been established. Their development has been associated with the creation of a new charter institution, the Council for National Academic Awards, and a new power structure which has affected the whole landscape of higher education.

They are, in terms of the values described in Chapter 3, ambiguous. They carry forward the technical college tradition of public service and economic utility as well as individual opportunity and usefulness to the local community. They also carry with them the elitist and 'scholarly' values of the universities although many of their leaders are disposed to challenge this tradition. Their concern for teaching has been paralleled with a concern for research, much of it indistinguishable from that proposed by the universities, and particularly the newer universities which used to be technical colleges. They have strong degrees of freedom, and teaching staff have grown in participative power within the institutions, yet they are run by local authorities and their relationships with both individual local authorities and the associations are various.

Leading polytechnic protagonists maintain that government is too prone to map out university provision and to leave the polytechnics as a 'balancing factor' which can be brought in to meet the remainder of student and other demand. They believe that they still do not have a fair share of resources [8]. Yet the polytechnics are firm supporters of the binary system. When the system was first created in the 1965 White Paper there were objections which they did not share. It was maintained that the binary system would suffer the fate of the bipartite system in secondary education in which modern schools were deemed to have parity of esteem with grammar schools, and which never happened. Far better, it was argued, and was implicit in the Labour Party's Taylor Committee Report, to have a large number of universities which would each find their own level, and which would ensure that all of them came into a far more responsive approach to public needs. The proponents of a unitary system do not, therefore, share the DES's and the polytechnics' fear that they will move into becoming 'a new wave of CATs', but rather propose that removing distinctions will solve the problems of differentiation.

The polytechnics feel now that they are beginning to fail in not recruiting a large number of part-time students and non-degree students in certain local communities.

Committee of Directors of Polytechnics

The Committee was set up in 1970 before all the polytechnics had been established. It was encouraged by DES officials but discouraged by the local authorities who felt that it was not going to serve a useful purpose in return for its cost. In fact, it employs only one officer, two assistants and a secretary, and relies on the Polytechnic of Central London for accommodation. It is therefore paid for out of pooled resources. Sir Norman Lindop succeeded Sir Alan

Richmond, its first chairman, in February 1972, and held the post for two years.

There are now five standing committees for the main business. It meets the Committee of Vice-Chancellors and Principals twice a year informally. On a personal level the vice-chancellors are helpful and approachable but, it is felt, they tend to think that 'the polytechnics are aspirant universities and react as anyone would react to competition'.

School bodies consult the Committee about entrance procedure and qualifications. Because the NUS regards the local authorities as the decision-makers because they pay student grants and appoint directors, the Committee is not ineffective when dealing with student problems.

The polytechnics, which are the creation of DES officials strongly backed by HMIs, with somewhat ambiguous support from the local authorities, are beginning to form a structure of their own. The Committee of Directors may not have the full range of consultative relationships as does the CVCP. But a chairman has received the first knighthood given to a director. One director is on the University Grants Committee and another is on the Science Research Council, where they are concerned to promote such causes as those of the part-time research student and fair shares for the polytechnics. They get what some universities regard as a disproportionate amount of favourable publicity in the weekend papers and in the educational journals. And undoubtedly, as institutions, the best of them are making their way to full parity with many of the universities, particularly the new ones.

The tensions that lie ahead will be of major interest to the student of politics. As polytechnics become stronger, their relationships with their parent local authorities and the local authority associations are not likely to become easier. Their relationships with the rank and file of further education, as represented by the ATTI, are not completely congenial. Perhaps they will show the same characteristics as did the leaders of the secondary modern schools within the NUT in the 1950s and 1960s. They, too, were strong in promoting the cause of a new form of egalitarian educational institution, but they found the ascribed status to be too limiting and moved forward, through the NUT and elsewhere, to first accepting and then promoting the notion of the common secondary school. In so doing, they had to face grammar school opposition. It might well be that the polytechnic teachers and their directors will find them-

selves in a similar relationship with the vice-chancellors as region-
alisation of higher education and other policies get under way.

2 THE UNIVERSITIES

The non-university sector, then, has been greatly expanded and
stratified since the mid-1950s. The colleges of education are now
being pulled into the zone of the polytechnics and, although the
manner of doing this is deemed brutal, it follows the logic of creating an increasingly integrated higher educational system.

The universities have also undergone startling changes. Here too
there is no certain continuum. From the end of the war until the
early 1970s, social demand and economic argument pointed the way
towards expansion. As we write, however, first a deceleration of
expansion and then proposals for positive reduction in scale, pro-
visioning and status seem certain to emerge from government.

As a case study of policy formation, the universities are both
fascinating and elusive. Pressures to expand were placed on government but are barely identifiable. Changes in social attitudes cogently
pressed on the existing institutional structure and the social assumptions underlying it, but they cannot be defined. The universities,
indeed, illustrate the lack of underlying principles within the policy
generation and confirmation process.

HISTORICAL BACKGROUND

Before the great expansions of the 1960s, universities were for the
most part small and precarious in their funding. Some civic institutions came near to extinction in the 1914–18 war. In the 1950s
decisions on resources were made *ad hoc* by the UGC, although the
terms of reference as amended for it in 1946 required it 'to assist, in
consultation with the universities and other bodies concerned, the
preparation and execution of such plans for the development of the
universities as may from time to time be required in order to ensure
that they are fully adequate to national needs' [9].

A major university such as Birmingham illustrates the changes
which universities have encountered.[1] In 1938–9 Birmingham had

---

[1] We are indebted to Geoffrey Templeman for much of this information as
well as for many shrewd and knowledgeable observations underlying this
chapter.

N

only 1,600 students, including its medical school, and an annual income of £200,000, of which one third each came from fees, endowments and the UGC. The Further Education Training Scheme (FETS) with its special matriculation concessions for returned soldiers brought numbers up to 2,300 in 1947–8. By 1970 it had nearly 7,000 students.

Changes began throughout the university sector immediately after the war. Nottingham received its charter in 1947. Two new university colleges were established at Leicester and Hull in 1945. The University College of North Staffordshire was established. But the Murray Committee [10] believed that both teaching and research were seriously hampered by lack of space. The declared purposes were still classic. The UGC Report, 1947 to 1952 said at the time, and could still say today:

'Society requires much more of the university graduates than a degree or the expert knowledge of a particular field. It also requires the breadth of outlook necessary for those who are to fill positions of responsibility, and a university cannot be said to have risen to the height of its obligations until it has so designed its teaching as to ensure for all of its students who use their opportunities the chance to become, in words spoken by J. S. Mill more than eighty years ago, capable and cultivated human beings.'

These words still represent the ambitions of most university teachers, but could attract derision among many in the student body.

There was, indeed, an increase in teaching staff and the UGC justified this less by relating it to the increase in the number of students, than by its making possible an increase in the growth of knowledge. They worried about growing departmentalism, the need for buildings, the fact that more students were studying at universities more than thirty miles from their homes so that residential amenities and health centres were needed, and the shortage of well qualified teachers. They worried, too, that junior academic staff and non-academic staff should have some sort of representation. By the time of the 1952–7 Report (published in 1958) pressure for more technical education in the universities was being felt. Government departments set up a committee to advise on the education and training of scientists and technicians in nuclear science and technology. The UGC established connections with the Advisory Council for Scientific Policy, the Technical Personnel Committee and other parts of the government funded advisory system. At the same time, the first talk of cost analysis emerged. And, with expansion continuing quite steadily, the university colleges of Southampton, Hull, Exeter and Leicester received charters. In the late 1940s the UGC had predicted a decline in the number of university students after the post-war bulge of ex-service men. But pressures from the schools were already being felt. The number of pupils up to the age of seventeen and over was nearly double that of before the war.

The 1950s were therefore a period of gradual growth and organisational development but were, except towards the end of the decade, as yet untouched by the ideologies of expansion or of universal or even mass higher education. They responded instead to the demands created by increased staying on at school and by the consumer expectations of a growing economy. In this respect, 1952–7 was the first post-war quinquennium. It was then that opinions towards expansion began to be formed, stimulated mainly perhaps by the transatlantic examples of the California, New York State and Florida higher education plans. OECD and Council of Europe thinking, too, helped to establish international fashions towards democratisation of higher education. Seminars funded by the Ford Foundation were being held at the end of the 1950s at which such prominent figures as Noel (later Lord) Annan, Anthony Crosland and Wilfred (later Lord) Brown discussed the coming explosion in demand and the best ways of meeting it. Pressure was felt internally within the DES from the schools. This is evident from Sir David Eccles's speech on the Crowther Report in 1960 [11] as well as from the paragraphs drafted by the Ministry of Education secretariat of the Secondary School Examinations Council on the Use of English Test [12] in which the Council made plain its concern that competition for university admission resulted in pressure on the schools.

The science establishment, too, was urging the case for expansion of its subject within the universities. Some [13], indeed, doubted the inevitable maintenance of demand as stated by Robbins and thought the quantification of demand was bogus. They also thought that, in any event, the polytechnics could take the increase.

These movements of thought, however, led to the Robbins Report of 1963 [14] which, rather than revolutionise concepts of higher education, codified, reinforced and promulgated them. This high status committee confirmed the precept that higher education should meet all qualified school leaver demands. And the massive expansion plans leading to their peak in the 1972 White Paper got under way. Even now as the system goes into reverse the underlying assumptions have not changed: that higher education should be provided because it is socially desirable. Social demand must be met and the needs of the economy fed by the universities and the polytechnics.

By the end of the 1950s, all was already set fair for expansion. Students who took three A–levels increased by 48 per cent between 1951 and 1957. And in the period 1957–62, seven new universities were established, new salary scales were negotiated, and there were developments of special fields of study such as architecture, education, medicine, dentistry, criminology and business studies. The machinery of the UGC began to be extended and tightened up. By the end of the 1950s, a sub-committee on new university institutions was dealing with applications for universities in eighteen different places. A target of 120,000 student places was set for the 1970s. In 1960–1 the UGC planned an increase of 31 per cent by 1966–7 over the 1961 student numbers.

The stage was set for Robbins.

INCREASING GOVERNMENT CONTROL

In 1960 the Government's relationships with universities were still *ad hoc*. Only in 1949 were national scales for academic staff created, and at the same time the Treasury began to fund growth as well as maintenance. It was perhaps ominous that Sir Stafford Cripps made it conditional on fee scales being approved by the Treasury.

From then on relationships became more definite and prescriptive. In 1952–7, for the first time, the UGC asked for institutional predictions and bids for growth. By the time of the 1957–62 quinquennium, the UGC was following government in saying what universities might do to help keep up with USA and USSR plans for science and engineering. All of this was accompanied by a decisive backing of funds for buildings and salaries.

With expansion, the Government began to tighten up its controls. While Michael Stewart, who was the first Labour Secretary of State in 1964, hardly noticed the universities as a problem area of an interest group [15], they had to get used to the transfer of authority from the Treasury to the DES; for the Treasury is notoriously bad at controlling anything directly [16] and the DES has a different style. But then changes occurred quite rapidly. There was a distinct change of tone in the quinquennial letter issued in 1968 which made it plain that universities would get their funds in response to explicit guidelines on the number of students within certain subject categories.

The more important changes in government style occurred in 1967–72 when Sir John Wolfenden completed his period as Chairman of the UGC and, with it, the assumption that chairmen of the UGC would stay in office for ten years or more. The DES took over the Treasury role in funding higher education. The numbers of students recruited became the basis of the universities' claim for resources under Sir Kenneth Berrill. And, increasingly, the UGC created staffing ratios and subject policies which become the basis for the national policy of universities as well as for the public sector of higher education.

This degree of prescription increased throughout the quinquennium until the 1972 allocation letters and the 1972 White Paper were explicit on student numbers, disciplinary emphases, the proportion of postgraduate students, the number of students doing research as opposed to taking taught courses, and the number of part-timers. There is now hardly a category of university expenditure that is not conditioned by UGC prescriptions. Letters of guidance come in droves, revealing how the UGC itself can barely keep up with the chops and changes of government policy. One Vice-Chancellor, Stephen Bragg, quoting Dorothy L. Sayers, wrote to the UGC in 1973 that their latest letter was 'like the thirteenth stroke of a grandfather clock which sheds doubt on all of those which preceed it'.

We have already referred to some of the irritation felt by politicians and the rest of the educational system at the universities. The resistance of the vice-chancellors to the thirteen points put out by Mrs Shirley Williams, as Minister of State responsible for higher education, seemed to prove the universities' reluctance to take the expanded numbers required of them [17]. MPs shared the DES's growing irritation about the ability of universities to get away with it because they were on a sellers' market. They received growing sums from public funds and yet remained unaccountable for their spending, in the interests of academic freedom. Anthony Crosland felt no compunction at making them submit to audit after the Public Accounts Committee had strongly backed up what he intended to do [18]. The key report of the Public Accounts Committee which helped bring the universities to heel was written under the chairmanship of the Conservative MP, John Boyd-Carpenter, and the work was taken up later under the chairmanship of Sir d'Avigdor Goldsmidt in the Select Committee. This sentiment by MPs was reinforced by the student troubles during 1968–70 at the LSE, Essex and Warwick.

The Committee of Vice-Chancellors and Principals was opposed to public audit as were other leading academics [19]. It had also opposed DES rather than treasury control of university expenditure on the grounds that if there were conflict between schools and higher education demand, it would be settled within the Ministry instead of at cabinet level. This was not so much toffee-nosed as naive. It seems most unlikely that any such issue ever goes to the Cabinet, particularly when we recall both David Eccles and Anthony Crosland saying that an educational issue only reached the Cabinet perhaps once in their time as Secretary of State or Minister. Indeed, one vice-chancellor thought that policy is not undertaken by government, but that 'policy is made by the House of Commons when it approves estimates'. The CVCP's arguments against scrutiny by the Comptroller and Auditor General were weak intellectually and weak as a failure to read the attitude of the times. Its attempts to define academic freedom in terms of freedom to spend unobserved were unimpressive. The AUT in its evidence made a far more impressive analysis of the main constituents of academic freedom, and none of its criteria really rested on the extensive financial autonomies stated by the vice-chancellors or by individual senior academics such as Sir William Mansfield Cooper or Max Beloff [20]. Indeed, the vice-chancellors' committee had the grace to admit that it had been unnecessarily worried when it met the Expenditure Committee later in the decade [21]. But, then, it is doubtful whether the full blast of efficiency audit has ever reached the universities. After all, nobody ever thought that their hands would be in the till.

Social and economic values thus dominated the original educational and institutional assumptions. In 1950, the universities were untouchable because it was assumed that they should best be allowed to have their own ideals of excellence and their own ways of contributing to the social good. This would be enough accountability for the public. The Charters of the Privy Council established them, by definition, as equal in the eyes of the state with the government departments from whom they might receive their funds. They were a publicly paid elite. There had always been public restrictions over the universities, but tentatively stated. Thus Sir John Wolfenden is reputed to have said that the function of the UGC was

to act as a septic tank between the Government and the universities
– as if only waste effluence can come from government.

Apart from expansion and growing prescription, the Government
set up a second stream of higher education which could compete
with the universities. If there is any doubt about the British Government's ability to create new forms of institutions in the teeth of
established interests, the creation of the polytechnics is a prime
example.

Other trends could hardly have been suspected. The universities
had become increasingly unionised not only for teachers but also for
all other staff and for students. Even the vice-chancellors' authority
to fix the salaries of individual professors – a major remaining
source of patronage – has now become increasingly subject to AUT
intervention.

There have been changes, too, in university governance and
politics. Small cabals have become more powerful as universities
have increased in size. The dynamics of the system have now
changed [22].

These changes in control accompanied changes in the whole
approach to the universities, and the universities' own expectations.
The love affair between Whitehall and the universities became a
dull marriage, in which timorous demands for freedom and constant
haggling over household budgets became the main subject of the
marital dialogue. The new generation of academics assumed greater
control to be natural and inevitable. Two-thirds of those in post in
1970 were not in university work at all at the beginnings of the
1960s. The somewhat craggy great men who led university departments in the 1930s and 40s and who would resist intrusions on their
freedoms from their own vice-chancellors, let alone the UGC, gave
way to a different style of academic. Academics who were consultants to government and industry, who combined serious journalism
with academic work, who were increasingly in demand to help run
such parts of the public system as the CNAA assessment teams,
were more prone to accept arguments of public purpose in preference to the delights of isolated academic excellence. The new
generation assumed growth to be natural and inevitable. And with
this assumption have come, naturally enough, the national scales
for academic and non-academic staff, nationally stated ratios for
senior staff (40 per cent), and national arrangements for admissions
promoted by the Committee of Vice-Chancellors and Principals
through the UCCA scheme.

And so the spiral of change made its way. Consumer demands

grew and with them ideological commitment to change. Resource
and other feasibility constraints led to a change in relationships
between institutions and the Government as the testing of, and
hostility towards, the universities grew in both Whitehall and
Westminster. This change of relationship was sharpened as universities became mass institutions lacking the glamour of the
prototypal Oxbridge ideal of pre-war, as the international movements of unrest hit the universities in 1968, and as graduate un-
employment and economic uncertainties became stronger in the late
1960s and early 1970s. Against these movements the main interest
groups, the Committee of Vice-Chancellors and the Association of
University Teachers, were virtually helpless. Instead, the harbingers
of the mass movement, the radical intellectuals, the National Union
of Students, the schools and the local authorities, were bound to
make a lot of the running and the Government was bound to assert
its rights to control.

The UGC and Public Control

The UGC is variously described by witnesses as both part of
government and a universities' interest group [23]. Thus it is an
undisputed channel for the transmission of national needs to the
universities, although the DES is the clearing house for this purpose. The UGC finds this a difficult role to fulfil as its evidence to
the Select Committee [24] showed. 'We should like to know what
the social needs really are, and one could perhaps get more guidance'. 'The DES catchment is not wide enough nor are relations with
the other government departments dealing with manpower sufficiently in line.'

When an MP asked the Chairman: 'In other words the UGC is
not a maker of policy?' Wolfenden replied: 'No, I think that policy
emerges.' Two levels of decision-making can be distinguished. The
DES decides the number of students, at what cost and in what
general manpower categories, the universities should provide. These
figures become the planning framework within which the UGC
makes decisions on allocations to individual universities on the
basis of its visitations and other information. Its decisions increasingly determine the future of departments within universities.

How does the UGC relate to the universities? In his evidence to
the Public Accounts Committee Wolfenden said that in the course
of an ordinary day he gets half-a-dozen letters and has three or four
phone conversations with vice-chancellors. The fact that the UGC is
staffed with very senior officials is not reflected in the fact that vice-

chancellors instinctively go to the Chairman rather than the civil servants. This is a situation quite unlike any other in Whitehall where, for example, the education officer for London might well call on a principal in the DES dealing with a matter although, of course, for other issues of general importance he might go to an Under-Secretary or higher.

Membership of the UGC is predominantly that of professors, and no vice-chancellors are recruited to it. The UGC itself changed somewhat in the mid-1960s to take in two technology specialists.

It is, then, a curious mixture of interest group and part of government. It used to act as a collection point for individual university data and for what was then regarded as a free grant to free institutions, rather like Arts Council grants to the Tate Gallery or the Covent Garden Opera. With the post-Robbins expansion and

Chart XI: *Number of University Staff*
(*Academic*)

1938–9	3,994
1946–7	5,500
1951–2	8,952
1956–7	10,485
1961–2	13,104
1970–1	27,975
1971–2	28,871

Source: UGC Reports.

Chart XII: *Total Number of Students – Estimates of Increases*

After the war	90,000 in the immediate post-war years
1956–7	124,000 by the mid-1960s
1961–2	{ 124,000 by the mid-1960s { 170,000–175,000 by the late 1960s and early 1970s
1963–4 (Robbins)	{ 197,000 by 1967–8 { 218,000 by 1973–4
1966–7	220,000–225,000 by 1971–2
1971–2	308,000 by 1975–6
1973	[a] 321,000 by 1976–7

[b] This estimate is now being revised.

Chart XIII: *Total Number of Universities and Institutions Financed by the UGC*

1947–8	16 universities	5 university colleges	2 colleges of technology
1951–2	18 universities	3 university colleges	2 colleges of technology
1957–8	21 universities	1 university college	2 colleges of technology
1960–1	22 universities	1 university college	2 colleges of technology
1961–2	24 universities	1 university college	2 colleges of technology
1962–3	27 universities	1 university college	2 colleges of technology
1963–4	30 universities	1 university college	2 colleges of technology
1964–5	31 universities	10 CATs and Herriot-Watt	1 college of technology
1965–6	37 universities	6 CATs and Herriot-Watt	1 college of technology
1966–7	42 universities	Manchester Institute of Technology and the London and Manchester Business Schools	

Source: UGC Reports.

Chart XIV: *Total Number of Students*

	Men	Women	Total
1935–6	38,650	11,879	50,529
1938–9	38,368	11,634	50,002
1946–7	49,764	18,688	68,452
1951–2	63,970	19,488	83,458
1956–7	67,310	22,556	89,866
1957–8	71,855	23,587	95,442
1961–2	84,425	28,718	113,143
1962–3	87,654	31,350	119,004
1966–7	134,871	49,928	184,799
	Undergraduates	Advanced Students	Total
1938–9	46,908	3,094	50,002
1946–7	64,960	3,492	68,452
1949–50	78,064	7,357	85,421
1953–4	68,436	12,116	80,552
1960–1	89,863	17,836	107,699
1972–3	196,073	44,840	240,913

Source: UGC Reports.

increasing public restlessness about their imputed privileges, and with the first wave of manpower planning in British government, this changed. These changes became accentuated under Sir Kenneth Berrill who both defended the universities in Whitehall and brought them in line with the UGC. The formal terms of reference now include an encouragement to universities 'to be responsive to national needs'.

UNIVERSITY HIGHER EDUCATION INTEREST GROUPS

If the DES and the UGC are the main determinants of university policy, which interest groups press on them? Some are open and fully acknowledged; others are not so overt. For example, the scientific establishment had a strong effect on higher education policy in the 1960s [25]. Such major scientists as Sir Brian Flowers and Sir Frederick Dainton, who were highly respected by their scientific colleagues, were able to articulate opinion within government to an extent that was out of proportion to their grasp of the overall issues in higher education. In a public statement Sir Brian Flowers, then Chairman of the Scientific Advisory Policy, promoted

Chart XV: *Sources of University Income 1938/9–1970/1 (UK)*
(Sources as a percentage of total income)

Year	Total income of universities	Parliamentary grants	Grants from local authorities	Fees	Endowments	Donations and subscriptions	Other sources
1938–9	6,712,067	35·8	9·0	29·8	15·4	2·6	7·4
1946–7	13,043,541	52·7	5·6	23·2	9·3	2·2	7·0
1949–50	22,009,735	63·9	4·6	17·7	5·7	1·7	6·4
1953–4	31,112,024	70·5	3·6	12·0	4·3	1·6	8·0
1955–6	38,894,000	72·7	3·1	10·8	3·8	0·9	8·7[a]
1961–2	74,113,000	76·4	2·1	9·0	2·7	0·9	8·9
1964–5	124,161,715	79·9	1·4	8·1	1·9	0·6	8·1
1967–8	216,204,321	72·9[b]	0·9	7·4	1·7		17·1
1970–1	315,564,060	74·0	0·4	6·8	1·0		17·8

[a] Other sources include payment for research contracts from 1955 to 1956.

[b] There is an apparent drop in 1967–8 because only grants from the DES are distinguished in the statistics. Grants and payments for research from other government departments are included in 'other sources'. Previously all parliamentary grants had been grouped together.

Source: UGC Reports.

such doctrines as 'centres of excellence'. They undoubtedly were part of the pressure for the expansion of technology in higher education.

There was no equivalent group [26] which pressed the case for social science with the Labour administration. Social scientists instead pressed for changes of policy in housing, education or other areas of social concern. It was only later when the methods of social science began to be applied, such as with the use of social indicators, the creation of government units to monitor social policy, and the creation of an explicit organisation within government for 'useful' research, that social scientists built up more power. As numbers expanded, social scientists became identified in the public mind with dissent rather than with expansion related to a more general concept of the public good. Demonstrations were thought of as 'lab experiments'. The social scientists also had difficulties with their own institutions, where they were often regarded as outsiders.

The whole sector has vastly expanded and the universities no longer have any guarantee of financial support and recruitment. Their monopoly of power in research and in furnishing the nation's intelligentsia has been broken. This affects the main interest groups concerned with the universities.

The Committee of Vice-Chancellors and Principals
There are several higher education pressure groups which have yet to redefine their relationship with government and with each other. The Committee of Vice-Chancellors and Principals (CVCP) used to be able to present a university point of view that heeded little to the demands of either manpower policy or to the feelings of the contingent school system, as the arguments in the late 1950s and early 1960s about university entrance requirements and their impact on school curriculum show. Often the antagonisms flared out into the open, as is shown in some of the reports of the Secondary School Examinations Council and the universities' reports to them. The Committee of Vice-Chancellors and Principals has since had to preside over several retreats in its own supremacy. The prescription of student numbers, and balances between different subjects and between teaching and research culminating in the publication of the Rothschild Report (1972); the erosion of teacher and vice-chancellorial status, by student demands for participation which have tended to obscure the differentiation in role of teacher and student: all these changes have affected the role of the vice-chancellors.

Their position as an interest group reflects the changing role of vice-chancellors. At one time they were highly esteemed figures. Their political high point was reached, perhaps, when Harold Wilson invited them to dinner at 10 Downing Street. Many, of course, are men of great distinction and serve in their own right as chairmen of government committees and commissions. But some are perceived now more as managing directors than as leading scholars and major public figures. They are not a clique who meet in the Athenaeum Club. As a collective group they have to take what the Government gives them.

The Committee of Vice-Chancellors is a legitimised interest group though without a statutory relationship with the Government. The relationship derives from the almost total dependence of the universities, to the tune of 92 per cent of their revenue, on government.

The Committee was founded fifty-five years ago and consists of all universities in receipt of UGC grants. London, Oxford and Cambridge have more than one representative. There are fifty-five members of the full committee and they meet once a month in term time. A general purposes committee of fourteen members meets more frequently and there are four standing committees, recruited on rotation, concerned with development, academic matters, staff and student matters, and overseas affairs. Specialist sub-committees are created *ad hoc* to cope with such matters as the rate demands made on universities and VAT, and the Committee issues notes of guidance on these somewhat technical matters.

The Committee is far larger than might be suspected in its working organisation. It has twenty administrators, who have a low public visibility, but who are concerned with important administration and resources issues such as the creation of UCCA. The Committee is the only body which could have persuaded all universities to work with UCCA. It has also created such machinery as a common service unit for university appointments boards.

Its role in national policy-making is essentially reactive and uncertain, particularly since November 1973 when it seemed to the Committee to be the end of 'peace time' for the universities. This is why it appointed, in addition to the Executive Secretary, a Secretary General, Sir Roy Marshall, who is a former vice-chancellor, so that it can become more openly political in its work.

Such issues as increased public control exercise them greatly. The impact of the student grants issue has probably been felt most by vice-chancellors, who have to put up with sit-ins and disruptions.

On this issue the Committee goes to the DES rather than to the University Grants Committee. It has also had to face the unionisation of universities, the activities of auditors, the increased hostility of Parliament, simultaneous allegations that universities are both posh and full of unruly students, and the abiding interest of a vigorous press in university matters. Nothing a vice-chancellor says is likely to be unobserved by such journals as *The Times Higher Education Supplement.*

The changes in the vice-chancellors and their Committee are not simply those of style. They manage large plants for which they are accountable. Student protest and action has made vice-chancellors more sophisticated politically and more concerned with the machinery of university government. They often seem to be lonely in their role. Trade union law and legal problems have been thrust at them, mainly by the activities of the National Union of Students. The Committee is reluctant to speak on behalf of all universities but claims that it can do so and does so when this is necessary. It has to meet an increasing number of requests for responses on issues of government and other matters but does not, however, treat on academic issues which are within the power of individual senates. The Committee gives guidance to universities on such matters as academic tenure and freedom and provides an information service to others. The Committee makes joint studies with the NUS on some procedural issues.

Relationships with the UGC are informal. The chairmen see each other a great deal as do officials. All circular letters are exchanged. The Committee operates with the UGC only on general issues and never on individual institutional ones. Student numbers, superannuation, loan financed residences and rates of grant are the type of issues discussed. The Vice-Chancellors' Committee pays for the Brown-Tress index, which helps the UGC to calculate the supplementation of grants made because of increased costs.

The UGC does not, however, consult the Committee about the membership of the UGC and no vice-chancellor is, in fact, a member of the UGC. It is substantially rumoured, however, that the Chairman of the UGC is consulted about vice-chancellorial appointments.

The Committee has a regular consultative machinery with the AUT, particularly on salaries, although the AUT does not wish to have a negotiation relationship with it.

The Committee sees itself as having a 'midwife' role. It helped to create the committees on salaries and conditions of academic staff.

A member of the Committee of Vice-Chancellors is the Secretary to the Committee on Non-Teaching Staff Salaries, but he receives his authority direct from the vice-chancellors and not through the Committee.

There is a joint committee with headmasters and headmistresses but not one with the NUT. There is a joint committee with the Confederation of British Industry, and occasional meetings with the directors of the polytechnics, particularly at the level of officers of their committee.

Relationships with the DES are through the universities' planning and finance branches, but the Committee tends to stand behind the UGC rather than go directly to the Secretary of State (except on student grants). The Secretary of State is seen formally at the beginning of the quinquennium, but the Committee is also in touch with other government departments such as the Department of Health and even Customs and Excise (on VAT as it affects universities). There is some relationship with shadow ministers, but mainly to give them information rather than get their support on issues.

The Vice-Chancellors' Committee is an example of a sectional interest group which, because it is essentially a managerial body, is not able to challenge the Government effectively even if it had collective policies. On such questions as the Government's insistence that overseas students should pay higher fees than home students, it has remonstrated openly with the Government. It has openly sided with the students on the rate of grants. But, for the most part, it has been, up to now, reluctant to face the Government's attacks on its institutions or to take a common line against students' militancy. One of the problems has been an inability to speak for the universities, which has made its critics refer to it as impotent. The development of new machinery may, of course, change all of that.

The Association of University Teachers

The AUT represents several important aspects of the range of pressure on educational policy-making. First, it is a trade union with no ultimate power. Secondly, it demonstrates the extent to which education has become unionised and formal in all its negotiative machinery. Thirdly, it illustrates how the potency of educational institutions and individuals reduces the effectiveness of collective bargaining.

The General Secretary, Laurie Sapper [27] joined the AUT staff from the Post Office Engineering Union about five years ago. The

AUT was suffering from the 1968 Prices and Incomes Board Report and needed a professional negotiator. This in itself is an indication of the changing *milieu* within which the AUT must now work.

The AUT represents about 26,000 teachers, librarians, administrators and research workers. In the past four years the percentage has increased rapidly within a potential membership of 32,000. Clive Jenkins's Association of Scientific, Technical and Managerial Staffs provides little competition as only 400 of its members are eligible for AUT membership and only at Lancaster, East Anglia and Imperial College are its numbers in double figures. To some extent the ASTMS might have taken up a role similar to that of the NAS *vis-à-vis* the NUT on the grounds that the AUT is too subservient, establishment minded and disinterested in the young lecturers. In fact, the AUT claims to know the limitations imposed by its position and goes not only for more pay, but also for fringe benefits. It is difficult, however, for the AUT to be effective because university teachers are individualistic, and many at best are concerned with their own subjects or their own careers rather than with collective development.

The executive committee is elected by conference. The governing body is a council which meets twice a year and represents all the university associations and branches. There are seventy-six of these from the forty-six universities and the separate London and Welsh colleges. The council has 216 members and representation depends on size. While this takes policy decisions, the executive meets quarterly to deal with special problems. The number of sub-committees has been cut from thirty-two to four concerned with salary, superannuation, education and development, finance and domestic housing matters.

The AUT sees, apart from the trends in universities already recounted here, the recognition of trade union practices as an important recent development. The local branches negotiate on many matters. Even professorial increments are now under scrutiny and with them the last vestige of the vice chancellors' power is being removed. The universities as self-supporting academic communities have disappeared with expansion.

The AUT is on a joint consultative committee with the CVCP. It works easily with the DES, both officials and ministers, although during Mrs Thatcher's period of office the Government seemed to have become tighter and junior ministers became less powerful than in the days of Shirley Williams or Gerry Fowler. The personality of Sir Kenneth Berrill affected the style and results of policy-discussion

o

with the DES because he became an important intermediary between the AUT and the DES.

The AUT meets the UGC formally three times a year. There is an
exchange of information and statistics. It receives memoranda on
the quinquennial allocations and there are discussions on such
matters as library buildings.

The AUT has not found it easy to gain recognition. It can appeal
only to the sense of fair play of the Government. It has no real
sanctions except 'not to behave as gentlemen or to threaten to call
a meeting with the Committee of Vice-Chancellors'.

Joint committees with the NUS have been established and there
are discussions with it, as with the ATTI and the ATCDE. All three
organisations have agreed on a joint document on student assessment. The AUT sided with the students on their grant campaign,
but not with their methods. There are, however, few ways in which
the AUT can influence the NUS, particularly since the latter's
policies are volatile and its leadership ephemeral.

Pay structure is regarded as the most important of the AUT's
concerns. In advancing this and other causes it has frequent contacts with the press, particularly the *THES*, and it tries to keep
regular and informal contacts with MPs, with the shadow spokeman
on education and with a number of MPs such as Marshall and
Clarke who were university teachers. Parliamentary questions are
'planted' as the quickest way of obtaining information. Lobbying on
superannuation takes place through briefing local branches to get
at local MPs in the constituency. This seems to have had an effect
on such matters as FSSU negotiations. The AUT has drawn up a
list of marginal constituencies where there are universities and this
helps to create a lobby. The MPs whom we interviewed, however,
record only occasional approaches by the AUT.

The AUT thus has a difficult role to play. The academics are
mainly interested in their own subject area and are quite content to
have salaries negotiated on their behalf. The employers still trade
on the academics' intangible rewards of status and freedom in the
way that they used to with the teaching profession, whose attitudes
towards relations with employers changed so markedly in the 1960s.

The National Union of Students: A Case Study in Legitimisation
The National Union of Students cuts across many of our interest
group classifications. It is not part of a management system as, in a
limited sense, teachers are. It is both legitimised and, in the technical sense of the term, irresponsible. Its internal government is

essentially ephemeral. The committee is temporary and responsible only to its members. There is no danger that the organisation or ethos will become the mirror image of those it confronts. The NUS reflects changing values and fashions in education and, indeed, in general political thinking more quickly, and less enduringly, than the other associations which are admitted to consultation. This legitimised irresponsibility has become sharpened by the policy of recent leaders to 'politicise' student politics. In this respect, Jack Straw's election as President in 1968 was a turning point in NUS history.

The students' increasing role in policy-making relates to one of the major policy developments of the period – the enormous increase in the number of higher and further education students: three quarters of a million are now enrolled in courses. They represent a quickly changing generation of political attitudes and of life style. They test modes of educational government; they persistently argue for the expansion of the system and its share of total national resources. They offer the strongest challenges to the established order. This does not, of course, necessarily mean that the NUS is the most successful of the interest groups.

The National Union of Students has, perhaps, shown more development in role, structure and effectiveness than any other single interest group in the last ten years. It carries with it the full force of changed attitudes towards higher education as a facility open to all rather than to an elite body, which has led to an enormous increase in both size and range of membership. From being representative of the less prestigious part of an elitist higher education system – it had no hold in Oxford and Cambridge in the 1950s – it now represents the new and large non-elite bulk of higher education's clients.

It has participated in, and been an active force in, creating the decline in the universities' claim to special treatment and in the respectful aura that used to surround university teachers and administrators. Several of our interviewees pointed out how student unrest had helped create a disenchantment with higher education. It has been a powerful ingredient in the politicisation of the student body and in the growth of the politics of confrontation that is now evident throughout public institutions. 'Demands are made rather than arguments lodged', and there is no issue upon which there is not likely to be physical confrontation if the students do not get their way.

The NUS has self-consciously taken on new roles to be consistent with the trends described above. On questions of students' rights, either as individuals who might be suspended or sent down for breaches of discipline or failures in examination, or on questions of university government, it finds legal costs for precedent cases. The case in 1969 against the University of Aston seriously damaged the universities' rights to dismiss students on academic grounds. It joined with the National Council for Civil Liberties to produce *Academic Freedom* [28] and *Student Rights and Duties* [29]. In Jack Straw's presidency (1968–70) in particular, it was established that a contract exists by virtue of what universities publish in their prospectuses and in the students' acceptance of a place.

The growth in status has several manifestations. During Shirley Williams's tenure of office as Minister of State it developed, as far as the DES was concerned, a 'fact-finding' status. It is generally reckoned that many of the NUS's statements on general policy, as that on the James Report, were highly competent. The NUS moved, too, on questions relating to the students' place in the government of higher education institutions. Concordats were written in 1968 with the local authorities, the ATCDE and the vice-chancellors which, for example, gave students the right to participate in university government except on the reserved areas of teacher appointments and examinations. It set up some of the pressures leading to the 1968 Act which caused a revision in the arrangement for the governance of colleges of education and polytechnics.

As militancy increased, so it became more accepted in the decision-making system. The stages of the process are worth remarking [30]. It was necessary to be established as a union which should be seen to have power, and not simply be another pressure group. So it became part of the list of bodies consulted by the DES on some circulars and on more informal matters. It showed it had the facts about higher education right, as provided by its own excellent research and information system. The Union then found itself taken into confidence. Its leaders were told things which should not be published. And they kept confidences. They have always been consulted on grants, but two levels of consultation became obvious: there were the public discussions on grants, and there were 'dirty deals'. So the interim grant awarded in 1970 was, by agreement, announced just in time for the NUS conference. The Union was, in fact, becoming so structured that it would be able to undertake consultations at this level and it became important for the leadership to establish reliability with government, which meant establishing adequate control over policy-making within the Union.

A further stage was when ministers felt it important to be able to say that they had discussed the matter with the NUS when challenged in Parliament. And all this enabled them, in turn, to become more influential with students. Negotiations with the vice-chancellors also became stronger and more formalised. The joint statement on student participation made in 1968 meant that the union was now on a consultative basis with the leaders of the universities.

Recognition by the press as a major interest group became easy to achieve. The press turned up in force for all union events. Union leaders found themselves taken out to lunch by the press. The publicity department has five members who aim to keep things out as well as to get them into the press.

So it was not all through confrontation that the Union made its way. The DES and others took it seriously. It produced cost options for the proposals it promoted and these were accurate, as, for example, in a working party on the abolition of the means test. Its leaders found that they were taking a synoptic view of student finance as against the somewhat compartmentalised official expertise.

The union leadership built up these relationships throughout the period of sit-ins of 1968 when international student militants such as Cohn-Bendit, Dutschke and Tariq Ali were coming to Britain to address student union meetings; these were a threat to the NUS leadership.

But the romantic example of confrontation is not and cannot be, sustained by a regular leadership. Conflict between two concepts, of the reliable Union able to negotiate from knowledge and acceptance, and a student mass able to force its way through demonstration, remains unresolved.

The NUS has contacts with some MPs whom it 'uses' when appropriate. It finds the mechanism for parliamentary enquiry useful. The Select Committee under Fred Willey in 1969 provided a forum through which the student point of view could be stated. Otherwise, however, MPs are only used selectively. There is never a 'mail' drop to MPs. But they are briefed carefully and helpfully in the Union's own interest.

Apart from the sharpening of impact on educational issues and the acquisition of places within the consultative machinery, the NUS has become more generally politicised. That is to say, it now displays left-wing attitudes on general political issues over which, as one student recently complained, ordinary Labour Party views are regarded as reactionary.

It puts up pressure for the expansion of the system – some would say as a way to a larger membership for the Union. It has certainly influenced government on student grants, although some of the more way-out ideas that the students should have wages rather than grants caused some loss of credibility. It is, however, also effective in part because of the limited groups for which it acts. It is concerned primarily with expansion for the eighteen to twenty-two age group and has evinced no public ideas about continuing education for older people.

As with the most educational associations the NUS is a confederation. It has nearly 750 student unions, each of them virtually autonomous. A conference meets twice a year and each union is allowed one delegate for every thousand students. The delegates have mandates from their own unions which can be quite tightly specific. The conference reflects the opinions of the various influential unions. It 'prioritises' motions by ballots. The resolutions passed form the policy of the NUS. The executive is elected.

The executive has an income of £200,000 a year and most of this is taken up in paying staff. Most of it comes from student unions and other affiiliated organisations. Employment costs £120,000 a year. Running costs are £40,000. International delegations cost £8,500, campaigning £8,000; and other costs are for fighting such legal cases and eternal issues of civil rights as that of a girl student thrown out of a college of education because a man was found in her room. Although the case was lost, the DES sent round a circular clarifying the rules.

The President is elected by conference for one or two years and usually comes through a promotion ladder in the union machine. Most presidents have been full-time; and, before being elected, have had part-time office on the executive. Conference has a major constraining power on the executive. The executive has four full-time officers whose positions are powerful, although the presidents are the strongest. Presidents have been able to disregard the executive and conference, but this has now become more difficult. Jack Straw came in when changes were taking place. He had a strong personality and was there, as well, when it was newsworthy to occupy administrative buildings.

The NUS has access to the minister concerned with higher education on grants, and has regular contacts with the head of awards branch or with a deputy secretary when discussing such matters as the James Report or the review of grants. There are both formal and informal meetings. The NUS was consulted as much as anyone else on the James Report and the White Paper. The Union not only acts on education matters but on issues such as the Housing Finance Act, where student housing was an issue.

NUS figures are often used by the DES. When it cannot get information from the DES the Union can go to a sympathetic MP, such as Frank Judd, who will ask a question in the House.

The UGC never used to send the NUS information until the NUS proved that it could get hold of any document generally circulated within ten days. Relationships with Sir Kenneth Berrill were, however, very good. There are formal meetings with the UGC in each quinquennium as well as informal meetings, which are about such issues as student housing and university expansion.

Relations with the CVCP are naturally ambiguous. They make friendly joint statements and also have public arguments. The rent strike has been the most serious issue so far but normally relations are good. Vice-chancellors have no real power, however, in the view of the NUS, and will only talk on behalf of the universities on very broad general issues. They are seen as reactive rather than initiators.

Relationships with the LEAs are good. Letters are sent to them on such matters as discretionary awards or housing and responses are usually quite good. Information taken from questions is often put together in surveys. The NUS normally deals with them through the local authority associations. It sees William Alexander twice a year.

Meetings with the AUT and the ATCDE are frequent. The ATCDE is seen to be in an ambivalent position as it is not always seen as a teaching union but sometimes as representing college authorities. Nevertheless confrontation with it is rare. There is frequent contact with the NUT, the NAS and other teacher organisations. There are 120,000 student teachers, many of whom are associate members of the NUT.

The recent history of higher education thus illustrates the large number of influences that can be brought to bear on educational policy. Economic, social and ideological pressures set in motion a spiral of change which radically altered the whole landscape of a hitherto protected zone. But new institutional patterns quickly built themselves on the sites of battle. Thus the NUS became legitimised and institutionalised. The polytechnics, so eager to demonstrate the superiority of public purpose over elitism, soon acquired characteristics remarkably similar to those of the universities. The next wave of change will find itself beating against an even more complex and entrenched set of institutions than its predecessors.

Chapter 11

Case Study: Comprehensive Secondary Education

Comprehensive secondary education is one of the two largest areas of policy change – the other being higher education – since the 1944 Act. It is an issue that goes well beyond the education service and touches on social stratification and individual statuses, concepts of community and the place of voluntary schools within a public system. It has accordingly become one of the few educational issues of major political importance. It also raises doubts about the importance of the pressure groups.

The development of comprehensive education has already been described in authoritative studies [1] as have the ideological issues underlying its development [2]. There are illuminating case studies of local developments [3] and the first trickle of substantial unpublished research theses. The details need not, therefore, be repeated, but can be subordinated to the main themes of the role of the interest groups, political in leadership, and main institutions in determining the issues.

At the beginning, few wanted to disturb the assumptions that the 1944 Act was adequately egalitarian. 'For nearly twenty years after the 1944 Act, local councils and their officers showed no greater wish to challenge the accepted principles of selection at eleven-plus than did successive ministers of education, both Labour and Conservative' [4]. The central administration put most emphasis on the development of secondary modern schools which would enjoy parity of esteem with the grammar schools. Within the NUT, the largest general purpose teachers' association, there was a strong committee consisting of grammar school headmasters and headmistresses who certainly had no wish to see the present system change. Parkinson [5] has well described how the Labour Government from 1945 to 1951 approved the system whereby the needs of different children could not be met within existing institutions. The National Association of Labour Teachers, under the leadership of W. E. Cove, W. B. Spikes and C. T. Smith, urged the Minister to repudiate Conservative principles and to reshape the education system in accordance with socialist principles which meant multilateral reorganisation. But neither Ellen Wilkinson nor George Tomlinson moved. Successive Labour Party conferences repudiated the Labour ministers' policies. The attack was led from within the Labour Party by the National Association of Labour Teachers which kept up a continuous campaign in the constituencies [6]. The issue was brought to Labour Party conferences by W. E. Cove, Margaret Herbison and Alice Bacon, but to no avail. In 1948 George Tomlinson rejected the Middlesex development plans for comprehensive organisation. His letter to the authority said that the tripartite system was 'logical and usual'.

From the early 1950s changes continued which were ultimately to make it possible for a Labour minister to move towards comprehensive education in the mid-1960s. The changes in psychological and sociological perceptions of educability, and the ability of the system to measure educational potential, have been well recorded elsewhere [7]. The arguments of the psychological school deriving mainly from the writing of Francis Galton and Cyril Burt were strong until the early 1950s. A second phase started in the early 1950s and continued to the end of the 1960s and relied on the environmental school, which tried to show the importance of environmental as opposed to innate intelligence in shaping the child's actual performance in school [8]. Secondary modern heads took development as far as they could and began increasingly to realise how further development was frustrated by creaming off the ablest children to the grammar schools [9]. Parents, at first content with secondary modern schools, increasingly wanted grammar school places for their own children whilst believing that comprehensive education was fairest for all children [10]. The teaching profession generally, and particularly primary school teachers, felt that the pressure of the eleven-plus examinations on the primary schools was harmful. And, within the Labour Party, the shift of opinion was marked by the publication in 1951 of *Secondary Education for All* which committed the party to a policy of comprehensive reorganisation, a commitment reaffirmed in 1959 by a similar statement drafted by Michael Stewart [11].

During all this period, however, there was serious ambiguity within the Labour Party. Thus whilst the National Association of Labour Teachers met executive members such as Jim Griffiths and Alice Bacon, with Michael Young as secretary at one meeting, and whilst a party committee was appointed which produced the 1951, document, there was correspondence in the *New Statesman* in 1951 between Clifford Smith, the Secretary to NALT, and R. H. S. Crossman, who maintained that the Labour Party ought to concentrate on the content of curriculum in education rather than its structure. Whilst the trade unions were well behind comprehensive education for many years and speakers from NALT received great support in the constituencies, in the stratosphere of the party, with such party leaders as Gaitskell and Wilson, no enthusiasm was aroused during the twenty years of Labour opposition. There was hardly a leading speech by a Labour shadow minister in support of comprehensive education during this period.

But this points to a generalisation about education in Great Britain. It is not an issue which attracts major political controversy or support. It is, however, the most important service at the local level. It is therefore to the municipalities and counties that we have to look for the real drive towards comprehensive education. London, Middlesex, Manchester and Birmingham fought successive Conservative administrations on this. Conservative authorities such as Leicestershire, Shropshire, Staffordshire and Oxfordshire under chief education officers who believed in integrating secondary education made substantial advances within the rubric set for them by successive Conservative ministers between 1951 and 1964. They were not, in fact, primarily concerned with the ideological arguments for comprehensive education but with providing a viable secondary education for children who would otherwise be dispersed to schools then thought to be too small to provide an adequate range of subjects.

But we must not underemphasise the confusion felt by supporters about comprehensive education. Thus the National Association of Labour Teachers attacked the Ministry of Education's pamphlet *The Nation's Schools* not because it did not propose comprehensive education but because it said that it would be reasonable to suggest that numbers in the direct grant and public schools might be reduced. 'The above paragraph is a class biased attack on the grammar schools ... and therefore an attack on equality of educational opportunity for the ordinary child.' Immediately before the 1964 election, Harold Wilson assured teachers that the grammar schools would be abolished 'only over his dead body', and as late as 1970 he was representing the comprehensive school as 'a grammar school for all'.

Various case studies have shown how the comprehensive issue was fought through local authorities in Gateshead and Darlington, Southampton and Bath, for example [12]. And even at the local level, uncertainty was pervasive. In Southampton, apparently, although Labour was in control in the crucial years of 1965 and 1966, there was scant interest in education as a service and 'little pressure for comprehensive schools' before Circular 10/65 was issued. Some changes in selection procedures were made in 1958 but the teachers and administrators favoured them. Labour's policy was to accept the selective system and gradually 'wear it away'.

Elsewhere, however, and in Middlesex and London above all, there was a strong ideological commitment to comprehensive education even though it meant the unwinding of arrangements which involved well established voluntary aided grammar schools, and the appallingly heavy burdens of old buildings on separate sites which might constitute the new schools. The Labour Party in London persisted in its policies in spite of successive ministers' refusal to allow it to close grammar schools. And in appointing leading head-mistresses at both Kidbrooke and Mayfield, and by putting relentless pressure on the Ministry, it made comprehensive schools thinkable and acceptable.

Had Labour not come to power in 1964, there would have been a gradual extension of comprehensive education until the point would have been reached when a substantial minority of children would have remained in 'good' grammar schools, which the DES would have refused to allow to be closed. By 1964, what was the stage reached?

Chart XVI shows the development of comprehensive education over our period. It also shows the massive acceleration that took place following the impetus given by Circular 10/65. According to Circular 4/74 issued on 16 April 1974, in January 1973 38 per cent of all secondary schools in England and Wales, housing 48·4 per cent of the pupils, were already designated comprehensive. Of the 163 authorities existing up to 31 March 1974, 72 had received approval to reorganise totally on comprehensive lines, 76 had reorganised in part, and only 15 had received no approval to reorganise. Of the 104 authorities in existence from 1 April 1974, only one has not reorganised any of the county schools in its area.

When Labour took office in 1964, it caused the major spurt for-

Chart XVI: *Development of Comprehensive Secondary Education*

Secondary Schools	1961	1962	1963	1964	1965	1966	1967	1968	1969	1970	1971	1972
Modern	3,872	3,899	3,906	3,906	3,727	3,642	3,494	3,200	2,954	2,691	2,464	2,218
Grammar	1,284	1,287	1,295	1,298	1,285	1,273	1,236	1,155	1,098	1,038	970	893
Technical	228	220	204	186	172	150	141	121	109	82	67	58
Comprehensive	138	152	175	195	262	387	507	745	962	1,145	1,373	1,591
Bilateral and multilateral	62	63	66	69	—	—	—	—	—	—	—	—
Middle deemed secondary										105	147	186
All other schools	263	269	245	246	417	346	351	355	331	324	274	210
Total	5,847	5,890	5,891	5,894	5,863	5,798	5,729	5,576	5,454	5,385	5,295	5,212

Source: Ministry of Education and DES Statistics of Education (1961–72), HMSO.

ward as it will, again, in its present administration. But these
changes are part of a complex spiral of change. Comprehensive
education began as an ideal within the teaching profession, mainly
activated by socialist thought. It gained the credibility which would
otherwise have been lacking because of the particular needs of such
rural areas as Staffordshire, Leicestershire, Anglesey and Oxfordshire. It did not gain the active support of the main radical party
except in formal terms in the 1951 and 1959 statements. Only in
1964 when Labour was returned to the Ministry of Education with
a former teacher, Michael Stewart, as Minister was the critical
decision taken. Even at that point the major educational interest
groups remained passive. The NUT had too wide a span of opinions
within its membership to decisively come out against selection until
it gave evidence to the Plowden Committee in 1965. From then onwards it was able to unify opinions and become stalwart in favour
of comprehensive education. Local authority associations were
primarily concerned with the extent to which a drive towards comprehensive education reflected on the relationships between central
and local government. So they were anxious to be involved in
decision-making and in the formulation of Circular 10/65, and
resistant to the somewhat arbitrary methods employed by Margaret
Thatcher in issuing Circular 10/70 without consultation. The issue
as such did not seem to concern them. Individual local authorities
each went through their particular agonies over the subject and the
principal studies show a wide range of interrelationships from
which few generalisations can be drawn. Thus, as we have remarked, a Labour majority in Southampton was unenthusiastic. In
Bath a chief education officer was hostile but once convinced that
there was no point in prevaricating became very strongly in favour
of comprehensive education [13]. In some authorities the committee was widely consultative of teacher and parental interests, as
in London throughout an elaborate series of consultative documents
[14] where, indeed, the consultation process aroused pressure
groups, a process apparently expected and hoped for by those who
consulted them [15]. Elsewhere, small and more or less oligarchic
groups of councillors either resisted change or were strongly in
favour of it.

So we must attribute changes to four different groups. First, there
were the radical teachers. Secondly, radical teacher opinion joined
forces with Labour councils which were prepared and eventually
determined to devise the models of change and to make them work
in the 1940s and 1950s. Thirdly, the experiences of local authorities

were aggregated into Labour Party policy which was put into effect
only when a Labour majority took office. And, fourthly, those
Labour authorities and the Labour Government were legitimised in
what they did by the flow of sociological and psychological writing
in favour of the demolition of selection and the creation of all-in
schools.

But the fascination of the comprehensive school case study lies
not only in the ascendancy of comprehensive policies in the late
1960s but also in what happened in the early 1970s. For any
exponent of a heroic theory of politics will find plenty of support
here. Anthony Crosland's Circular 10/65 asserted the policy and it
would have been reinforced by law had Edward Short's Bill not
been lost by the absence of a few Labour MPs during a critical
committee stage. Mrs Thatcher came into office and within three
days had issued Circular 10/70 restoring freedom to local
authorities who did not want to make a move. In April 1974, Reg
Prentice issued Circular 4/74 which withdrew Circular 10/70. In
the meantime, however, the argument had moved into other and
unexpected directions. Labour's plans aroused opposition from the
voluntary schools in London and elsewhere. They also aroused
opposition from more surprising quarters. Thus, in London, parents
in favour not of selection for grammar schools but of a free right to
access to any school usually favoured comprehensive schools, and
began powerful actions which offset many of the decisions made in
individual selections in north London in the 1970s. The arguments
thus became not selection versus comprehensive education but
whether a local authority could press home the comprehensive
policy as far as insisting on all-in community schools from which, at
most, parents could contract out. Again, the development of comprehensive schools coincided with or, as some would maintain, was
casually related to the breakdown of discipline and a more general
alienation of pupils from secondary education. And this in turn set
many teachers, administrators and parents on to testing whether the
policy of creating large comprehensive schools was either right or
necessary. Some Labour leaders had always doubted it [16].

The comprehensive movement began, then, to move back to the
local sites where it had started. Some of its more thoughtful advocates began to raise questions about the general purposes of secondary education [17]. Questions aroused on the periphery of the
educational system by the deschoolers [18] became naturalised in
some of the leading members of the Comprehensive Schools'
Association, who have put up a persistent barrage of information

Chart XVII: *Comprehensive Schools:*
Parliamentary Questions Asked

Year	Local	National	Total
1964	5	4	9
1965	16	21	37
1966	23	22	45
1967	33	20	53
1968	43	23	66
1969	31	18	49
1970	6	8	14
1971	19	14	33

and justification. Other comprehensive school leaders, indeed, determined to show that schools with a poor reputation could be made good if parents and teachers really put their best efforts into change. At least one major comprehensive school in London changed from being almost totally unpreferred by parents to a school which attracted a surplus of first preferences within a few years.

Was Parliament involved? Hardly. Nine Parliamentary Questions were asked in 1964 on comprehensive education. From then on, as Chart XVII shows, there was a trickle of questions about national and local aspects of comprehensive policy. There is no clear connection that we can see between the generation of the policy and parliamentary activity. Between 1964 and 1971 only seven Parliamentary Questions about the abolition of the eleven-plus were asked.

Comprehensives thus demonstrate how issues arise from the conjunction of changes in popular attitudes, perhaps spurred by the consumer boom, and social values. They show how local authorities generate policy changes, at least on schools issues, which become national and social and political. They show how the major interest groups do not easily move on the larger social issues until consensus is evident, but how they then insist that consensual mechanisms are observed. They also show the potential role of the determined minister or local leader.

Part V

SUMMARY AND
CONCLUSIONS

Chapter 12

Summary and Conclusions

Education is not a zone of public policy in which dramatic events are expected. It is not at the centre of the national political stage, though in the last ten years it has become an area of controversy and interest. It is concerned with the day to day expectations of millions of people going about the ordinary course of their lives. It is, therefore, all the more significant that in the period of this study, from 1960 to 1974, educational policy should have changed so much. It thus should provide a good testing ground for generalisations about policy formation.

Our analysis began, as should all political analysis, with history. We have shown how between 1945 and 1965 the education service was largely concerned with expanding and consolidating the system laid down, in a spirit of benign amelioration, in the 1944 Act. At the same time, however, the policies of providing opportunities for potential elites were already being challenged as likely to lead to social division.

In 1964 the Labour Government set in motion the egalitarian policies of comprehensive education, positive discrimination through the educational priority areas, and the overt and systematic expansion of higher education for a mass clientele. By 1968 the pace slowed down as other challenges were made to the system. They mainly concerned educational governance as students and teachers claimed a larger place in decision making. The universities simultaneously faced challenges from the newly-designated polytechnics and from the civil servants, MPs and ministers concerned with issues of accountability, who, in return for increased resources, expected a closer response to the mechanisms of public control.

With the Conservative Government in 1970, expansion continued but under different assumptions. Education, as everything else, was up for more rigorous testing as management technologies, programme analysis review and planning-programming-budgeting systems put programmes, including some previously assumed to have been settled, under scrutiny. The egalitarian trend of the previous government was halted although not entirely reversed. For the first time in decades selective and rigorist arguments were advanced. The liberal consensual and expansionist style of education was broken.

And at the end of the Conservative period, in 1973 and 1974, the same economic troubles that ultimately led to conflict with the trade unions on the wider political scene also led to a reduction in demand for education and a drastic halt to the modestly expansionist programmes still entertained in the 1972 White Paper.

POLICIES AND VALUES

Against this historical backdrop (Chapter 2), it is possible to analyse policy movements (Chapter 3) and, in part, to explain the attitudes of the interest groups in advancing or sustaining policies. Thirty-five policy themes emerged from a scrutiny of the official literature, circulars, speeches, and from the flow of Parliamentary Questions and debates; from a scrutiny of the minutes of three of the major educational interest groups; and from a series of interviews with many involved with decision-making. And from these materials we concluded that policies can be analysed in terms of 'educational', 'social', 'economic', and 'institutional' values (Chapter 3). The values seem to have a relationship to two other calssifications: that of continuity, and that of the institutional status or the degree of legitimisation of the interest groups advancing the policies.

So the educational values underlie policies which are largely continuous. The maintenance of institutional values, which are non-basic and instrumental, are strongly associated with the promotion of the educational values. Where the educational values, or the maintenance of institutional values, are challenged, as by the motives imputed to those who sought to create the Curriculum Study Group, established educational institutions and their interest groups react strongly.

The economic and social values were more volatile and discontinuous as, for example, in the policies of expansion of higher education, and in the proposals of the Labour Government by which the education service might become more redistributive and egalitarian. The participative values, too, were 'new'. The discontinuous values came largely but not wholly from the outside; from the intelligentsia, from research findings, from the press and from the more general political movements, including those associated with the demands resulting from economic growth. Many such movements also developed within the education service itself: teachers challenged the effects of the eleven-plus examinations on pupils. These stimuli created the climate in which ministers could make decisions in the expectation that teacher opinion would not resist them, and public opinion be at least acquiescent. The changes came, too, from local authorities which made the running on comprehensive education between 1945 and 1964.

VALUES AND INTEREST GROUPS

From the analysis of values and the policies associated with them, the roles of the major educational institutions and their interest groups can be more clearly perceived. The educational interest groups preserve the main continuities and appraise gaurdedly any discontinuous policy, whether it be curriculum development by the DES or a private foundation, or education for the disadvantaged, or the identification of the problems of immigrants. They relate to an institutional system which is one of contrived pluralism. Schools and local authorities are viable institutions with authority to sustain their own values, styles and authority. Contrived pluralism and continuity are bedded deeply within the system and support accepted institutional patterns.

For the interest groups themselves, a main line analysis (Chapter 5) is proposed. There are degrees of legitimisation. Some of the 'managerial' interest groups, particularly those representing local authorities (Chapter 6), for example, are consulted fully about official announcements, are party to all the negotiations which affect them and are members of the main consultative bodies. The main teachers' associations are strongly legitimised although their managerial functions are less obvious, and they are also trade unions (Chapter 7). Other interest groups possess varying degrees of legitimisation. The NAS (Chapter 7) and the NUS (Chapter 10) are examples of groups that have come to be accepted by the authority system. Both have a substantive interest in statutory duties and powers, either as teachers helping maintain the system or as recipients of grants which are part of the mandatory framework. Other groups such as parents remain mainly outside the legitimised frameworks (Chapter 8).

Other classifications noted include 'sectional' as against 'promotional' characteristics.[1] All the bodies with which we are concerned are promotional in the sense that all of them believe that education is an unmitigated good to be expanded. The extent to which a group is sectional is another way in which interest groups are differentiated from educational government. Thus, local authority associations hardly disagree with the DES on educational policy but have distinctive views on local authorities' rights and duties in relation to the centre.

Teachers' associations have become more militant but on salaries and conditions of service rather than on the main educational policies; on the latter they, too, have been reactive rather than creative. Their consent makes a policy easier to get through, and their opposition makes it difficult. The changes in policies of comprehensivisation in 1965, 1970 and 1974, and the fate of the Curriculum Study Group, exemplify this point.

Educational interest groups, unlike industrial trade unions, are constrained by the managerial or quasi-managerial roles of their members. They are also limited in the sanctions at their command. A teachers strike or a student sit-in is a serious thing; but it does not compare with a strike by hospital consultants or miners. The teachers' associations, moreover, face public authorities who are elected and thus publicly legitimised, unlike private industrial or business companies. A secretary of state can always appeal to the people or to Parliament for support. The appeal may be rhetorical but political language *is* largely rhetorical.

The more difficult areas of activity to chart are the non-legitimised, non-managerial, or informal, interest groups. Some of them have proved to be the moving edge of policy, even if, or perhaps because, they might not enter the institutional system. CASE and ACE and, to a lesser extent, STOPP have pressed for a distinctive place to be found for parents in both the educational process and in governance. And they have partly succeeded at least at the governing body level. Parent groups have shared with the NUS, the Rank and File of the NUT, the Council for the Defence of Academic Freedom and the National Association of Governors and Managers the function of testing authority on issues such as the breadth of

[1] See ref. [3], Chapter 5.

representation, the style of its decisions on individual students, and teachers' rights and duties. Many such issues have been concerned with individual institutions. But they have sometimes aggregated powerfully to bring parents and teachers on to governing bodies of colleges and universities. They have cast doubts on who are the rightful beneficiaries and what are the proper governing arrangements of education. 'Participatory' as against 'ballot box' democracy [1] are major issues of our time, and local as well as national interest groups have made them so.

We can most easily sum up the range of interest groups by reference to Chart XVIII.

This continuum has a wider range than that of many other areas of public interest. There are those with a greater interest in continuity and amelioration than in radical change. They differ from the permanent elements of government only in the distinctively sectional elements – the position of local authorities, or universities, or colleges of education or teachers – of their terms of reference, and not in terms of their general attitude towards the education system and its policies. Opposition can be, in the words of one senior official, 'ritualistic'. All join company in supporting the expansion and momentum of the system and, in the opinion of both Boyle and Crosland, this is the function of ministers of education as well. (Patrick Gordon Walker [2] disagreed with this 'advocacy' role.)

If the main associations are reactive rather than innovative, this may be because they maintain, as a value, the right of local authorities and teachers to develop education rather than develop it themselves. Moreover, as we have seen, the larger and more broadly based the association, the more cautious it must be in assuming consensus in its membership. It is thus not surprising that they waited for ministers or local authorities to give the lead on the more contentious and socially related policies of the 1960s. Other interest groups not only press for educational change but for radical changes in the underlying assumption about control, government and participation. The pluralism of the system does not extend to many of the main actors in the processes of education. Thus we have shown how parental influence is mainly local, and how the main interest groups themselves find it difficult to bring together practitioner opinion on some of the more important policy issues. All the same, the system is pluralistic inasmuch as authority and power are distributed among well defined institutions at different levels such as the DES, local authorities and schools and colleges. They benefit

Chart XVIII: *Chart of Interest Groups*

Government sponsored	Managerial and legitimised	Non-managerial and legitimised	Non-managerial Non-conflictual	Conflictual
Schools Council	Association of Municipal Corporations	National Union of Teachers*	Advisory Centre for Education	National Union of Teachers*
National Foundation for Educational Research	County Councils' Association	National Association of Schoolmasters*	Confederation for the Advancement of State Education	National Union of Students*
Advisory Committees	Association of Education Committees	Joint Four	Nursery Schools' Association	Society of Teachers Opposed to Physical Punishment
University Grants Committee	Inner London Education Authority	Head Masters' Conference		National Association of Governors and Managers
	Welsh Joint Education Committee	Association of Principles in Technical Institutions		National Association of Schoolmasters*
	Committee of Vice-Chancellors and Principals	Association of Teachers in Technical Institutions		Council for Academic Freedom and Democracy
		National Union of Students*		Child Poverty Action Group
		Committee of Directors of Polytechnics		
		Association of Teachers in Colleges and Departments of Education		
		Denominations		
		Research Community		
		Educational Press		
		Private Foundations: Nuffield Foundation.		
		National Children's Bureau		

Note: This chart excludes Parliament which both creates and receives pressure. And some groups which are both legitimised and non-legitimised, conflictual and non-conflictual, are marked with an asterisk (*).

from the assumption that power should be distributed and they are watchful of encroachments on their access to decision-making.

Because of the distribution of power, any explanations of change must accommodate the way in which local movements affect national policies. The well documented cases of decision-making on secondary education in 'Townley'[1], Gateshead and Darlington, Leeds, Southampton and Bath, and Enfield [3], as well as undocumented studies of change in the quality of comprehensive education caused by parental support and pressure, make us pause to consider where the pressure really started. Education is not like defence or foreign affairs or the Restrictive Trade Practices Act [4]: it is a series of actions conducted in a large number of small institutions. Pressure can be applied to the apex of the system and have no effect. A series of small but continuous actions within local authorities have aggregated over time to produce patterns of comprehensive education for Labour administrators to promulgate nationally [5] community schools concepts in Cambridgeshire, open schooling in a large number of local authority primary schools, and the setting up of a parents' movement in a few places. We have no adequate explanatory framework of how local pressures and decision-making add to the national aggregate, although all the cases quoted here did so, and there was interplay between central departments and local authorities in all of them.

PARLIAMENT

In theory, Parliament exists to promote pluralism. It should help to articulate and aggregate attitudes and beliefs. And it is the most clearly institutionalised of the institutions within the pluralistic system.

Yet from our study of Parliament (Chapter 9) it is clear that MPs do not initiate but at most react to policies, as can be seen by an analysis of Parliamentary Questions and debates against the policies being generated.

If, however, there is no systematic relationship between parliamentary activity and the formation of policies, MPs may still aggregate local interests and anxieties and so keep issues on the educational agenda. Much of their work is finding out and publicising information, bringing up a continuous procession of local items

[1] A pseudonym used by Dr Rene Saran in her case study *Policy Making in Secondary Education* (OUP, 1973).

which help quicken ministerial interest in the workings of the service which they govern. They cause ministers to exercise more powerful 'management by exception' within their own departments. Ministers tend to listen to their own backbenchers, even if Parliament is not as important to them as other influences. But we cannot see any strong temporal or causal links between policy activation and parliamentary activity.

Of the parliamentary instruments, the Select Committees seem potentially most important if only because the process is more exhaustive and overt. Committees do not systematically look at educational policies but, when they do, they enable officials to be questioned by MPs and interest groups to have a say at some length. We can find, however, only a few examples where they have had any clear effect.

Our study of Parliament reinforces the doubts of many commentators before us on the contribution Parliament makes to decisions or to whether it effectively reviews and criticises the authority structure. This point is discussed more fully later.

PATTERNS OF GOVERNANCE AND CHANGE

If the institutional fabric is strong, and interest groups are largely reactive or consensual, where are the loci of national decision-making, and how do policy changes come about? In answering this, we must not underestimate the power, authority and sheer stamina of educational government.

The Secretary of State has enormous authority, although he does not directly manage the schools. He lays down the major policies within which the local authorities and the charter institutions act. Policies are largely formulated and administered by perhaps sixty permanent administrative civil servants. Most of those of assistant secretary rank or higher have served in the DES for more than ten years, and quite a few for more than twenty years. They are a major source of continuity and acquire expertise and authority by virtue of that continuity.

The local authority system, too, is authoritative. It determines the style and quality of education, if not its overall scale, scope and objectives. It consisted, on 31 March 1974, of 162 chief education officers (there are now 101), and some few thousands of other ranking administrators or advisers. The 162 education committees had, perhaps, 5,000 members.

Within the system, many of the decisions affecting the quality of education are delegated to some 30,000 schools and further education colleges and their heads and principals. Other parts of the system, the universities and the colleges of education, influence the ethos, standards and assumptions of the service.

Education is thus a system which has a central and local authority leadership of perhaps 200 public administrators and some 30,000 heads of institutions. And the system itself is a sub-system within the Government in which the Prime Minister, the Cabinet and the Treasury subordinate educational policies to total government policy.

This strong set of government mechanisms is evidently influenced by developments outside itself. But we can see no clear patterns of change, let alone models (or patterns upon which predictions can be based) of change. Yet, obviously, the DES's relationships with interest groups are important, and two questions arise on them. First, how does the Department choose to use its authority in relating to the interest groups and the other authoritative parts of the system? Secondly, is that the only mechanism of change? On the first point, the principal authorities help us. Manzer says that a 'friendly and conspiratorial' triumvirate of Sir Percival Sharp (Secretary, AEC, 1925 to 1945), Sir Maurice Holmes (Permanent Secretary, 1936 to 1945) and Sir Frederick Mander (General Secretary, NUT, 1931 to 1947) entrenched a pattern of relationships which has dominated policy development ever since [6]. And he refers to 'a tripartite structure' of DES, local authority and teacher associations. A Permanent Secretary, indeed, announcing the formation of the Curriculum Study Group, referred to 'the partners' [7].

Certainly there is a set of consensual and well-tried mechanisms but it is not clear that they are the agents of change. The same group of DES officials, local authority association officials, chief officers and councillors may face each other over decades in determining policy. Yet the group is not closed, let alone an elite. They do not have the main characteristics of a closed system, of socio-economic class, of recruitment, or of social integration. Both the Permanent Secretary at the centre and the head of a village school have authority. But they have different educational backgrounds. Even where there is consistency of background or continuity of contact, there is little social communication. The leaders of the teachers' associations, whether selective or mass associations, do not meet the leading HMIs socially but only on somewhat well established official occasions a few times a year. A few senior officials in the DES have a few chief education officers as their personal friends. At one time, DES officials had close relationships with some of the church leaders but that connection, too, has gone. There is virtually no eating of lunches together in London such as one finds among, for example, the academic economics and administrative community.

There are small groups where some opinions may be formed. Sir John Newsom and others established the All Souls Group which meets four times a year at Rhodes House, Oxford to discuss educational matters. A cross-section of academics and DES, local authority and journalist interests attend. There is the smaller Dining Club which until recently met at the Royal College of Art, again quarterly. There are education group meetings of the educational press. But this social network does not include many of the more important of the decision-makers. It reflects rather, the extent to which education is, of all the social services, a fashionable subject.

CHANGE PATTERNS

Our second question is whether an analysis of relationships between Parliament, the DES and the interest groups explains the processes of change.

The changes as reflected by the thirty-five policy movements have been large. Well before our period there was a change in human and educational attitudes which produced the liberal doctrines now so strong in parts of the system. The opening up of the primary schools, teacher rather than university control of examinations, school building design, the equitable distribution of teachers, the attacks on the eleven-plus selective system, the development of comprehensive education, destreaming, the expansion and changing organisation of higher education, were all major changes.

Planning documents, culminating in the White Paper of 1972, applied economic and, to a lesser extent, social criteria to educational and professional assumptions through the means of programme analysis and other 'logical' tests.

The system is strong institutionally and in terms of its historic investments in trained people and buildings. There is inertia in the clientele who like exams and who like selection. Against these institutional continuities, there is no clear or linear process of change.

At this point we look for metaphors. Does educational change follow a helical pattern – that of a staircase in which each step is both a point of advance and an established position? Even this metaphor is too static for it assumes progression from one stage of development to the next whereas the process we have described is multi-dimensional and not linear. The dynamic parts of the process can become stable, and the stable parts can disintegrate or advance. A more appropriate metaphor is that of a kaleidoscope. Colours in a changing pattern move out of view, or get stuck, or change position as the box is tapped.

In looking at the education service and its politics we have to reckon with unpredictable sequences and patterns of changes in ideology, in received concepts of human development, and in the economy.

In these aspects our two case studies are important. Comprehensive education began as an ideological movement, stimulated by socialist teachers and by teachers who perceived that damage was being done by the process of selection. A few local authorities pressed the case hard in the 1940s and 1950s: some were activated by ideology, others by the need to provide secondary education in sparsely populated areas. Their associations took no action, however, until large external forces had their effect. The first was the economic boom which in its turn brought changes: the concept of opportunity. The second was changes, brought about by the social science intelligentsia, in concepts of human intelligence and the social effects of selection. The third was the change in national government in 1964. Since then the policy has taken new courses. Ministers changed. Large schools went out of favour. The environmentalists came under attack. Parental opinion wavered uncertainly. Changes in higher education, too, reflected the build-up of opinion among liberal intellectuals and among social scientists about the 'pool of ability', the influence of transatlantic and European opinion, the economic boom and associated beliefs in the economic benefits of higher education, and the resentment of teachers caused by competition for university places. The decline in higher education's fortunes has about the same ingredients: international student troubles, economic depression and a general pessimism about the usefulness of higher education.

And in all of this there is room for the strong individual: a Crosland or a Thatcher or a Short bring with them decisive power which can make or retard a major policy development. The items on the moving agenda to which we have referred have to wait until the time, and the people, are right for them.

POLICY CONCLUSIONS

Pluralistic, incremental, unsystematic, reactive – how untidy the total system is. Yet those possessing authority are decisive. Programmes are created, promulgated and implemented quickly and firmly. But how does the DES aggregate the knowledge, feelings, resistances and resource feasibility of the 30,000 institutions, the complex political system that we have described, the press and the intelligentsia? The traditional system has been at least as sensitive as most zones of government in its aggregative processes. The Central Advisory Council reports at least made professional education opinion open to explicit questioning. The inputs have been various and increasingly acknowledged. But the process is incremental rather than systematic.

This incrementalism has produced excellent innovations in the schools. But the pluralism might as easily have produced bad schools, and it is difficult to see where in the system any policy-maker can ever be challenged effectively. It is not clear how aggregation of practice takes place. Local examples of good practice, or perceptions of obsolescence, are not well mediated. The DES denies it has power to aggregate or lead [8] yet it plainly does so. So we have a situation in which power is not explicit, in which criticism and discontent have no clear outlet and in which parental opinion still has no adequate way into the system. Effective public review is non-existent.

This policy issue links up with a more theoretical issue. Any single policy takes on multiple guises and is viewed differently at many points of a complex system: pupils, teachers, the head, the chief education officer and his administrative and advisory staffs, councillors, the local electorate, the national electorate, Parliament, the DES, researchers, journalists, teacher educators, the churches, employers and the trades unions.

In this book we have taken a fragment of social concern and are yet still uncertain as to how so vast and complex a structure interacts, creates new policies and somehow moves forward. That uncertainty is, we believe, widely shared and should be a matter of concern for those who feel that education should be under democratic control. The only certainty is that the DES wields determinant authority and great power. Democratic and pluralistic ideals demand more than that, particularly since the Department can itself act as an interest group.

Selected Reading

VALUES AND POLICIES IN EDUCATION

Arblaster, A., *Academic Freedom* (Penguin Books, 1974).
Bilski, R., 'Ideology and the Comprehensive School', *The Political Quarterly* (April/June 1973), vol. 44, no. 2.
Evetts, Julia, *The Sociology of Educational Ideas* (Routledge & Kegan Paul, 1973).
Green, T. (ed.), 'Educational Planning in Perspective', *Futures* (IPC, 1971).
Hirst, P. H. and Peters, R. S., *The Logic of Education* (Routledge & Kegan Paul, 1970).
Pateman, T. (ed.), *Counter Course* (Penguin Books, 1973).
Peters, R. (ed.), *Perspectives on Plowden* (Routledge & Kegan Paul, 1968).
Snook, E., *Education and Indoctrination* (Routledge & Kegan Paul, 1973).
Young, M. D. F., 'The Politics of Educational Knowledge', *Economy and Society* (1972), vol. 1, no. 1.

GOVERNMENT, POLITICS AND ADMINISTRATION OF EDUCATION

Alexander, W. P., *Education in England* (Newnes Educational Publishing Company, 2nd edn, 1964).
Barker, Rodney, *Education and Politics 1900–1951: A Study of the Labour Party* (Oxford University Press, 1971).
Baron, G. and Howell, D. A., *The Government and Management of Schools* (Athlone Press, 1973).
Batley, R., O'Brien, O. and Parris, H., *Going Comprehensive* (Routledge & Kegan Paul, 1970).
Brand, J. A., 'Ministerial Control and Local Autonomy in Education', *Political Quarterly* (1965), vol. 36, no. 2, pp. 154–63.
Coates, R. D., 'The Teachers' Associations and the Restructuring of Burnham', *British Journal of Educational Studies* (June 1972).

Coates, R. D., *Teachers' Unions and Interest Group Politics* (Cambridge University Press, 1972).

Corbett, A., 'The Secret Garden of the Curriculum – Who Should Hold the Key to the Door?', *The Times Educational Supplement* (13 July 1973).

Fabian Pamphlets:

> Blackstone, Tessa, *First School of the Future* (Fabian Research Series, 304, 1972).
>
> Crouch, Colin and Mennel, Stephen, *Universities: Pressures and Prospects* (Fabian Pamphlet 28, 1972).
>
> Glennister, Howard and Hatch, Stephen, *Positive Discrimination and Inequality* (1974).
>
> Harris, Bob, Holmes, Ralph and Wynn, Sandra, *Aspects of Education* (Young Fabian Pamphlet 26, 1971).
>
> Marsden, Dennis, *Politics, Policy and Comprehensives* (1971).

Fowler, G., Morris, V. and Ozga, G. (eds.), *Decision Making in British Education* (Heinemann, 1974).

Gretton, J., 'Cloth Cap Teachers', *New Society* (28 May 1970), pp. 909–11.

Jones, Kathleen (ed.), *The Yearbook of Social Policy in Britain 1972* (Routledge & Kegan Paul, 1972). (Devoted to educational policy.)

Kogan, M., *The Government of Education* (Macmillan, 1971).

Kogan, M., *The Politics of Education* (Penguin, 1971).

Kogan, M. and Packwood, T., *Advisory Committees and Councils in Education* (Routledge & Kegan Paul, 1974).

Kogan, M. and Van Der Eyken, W., *County Hall* (Penguin, 1973).

Lester Smith, W. O., *Government of Education* (Penguin, 1971).

Locke, Michael, *Power and Politics in the School System, A Guide Book* (Routledge & Kegan Paul, 1974).

Maclure, S., 'The Control of Education', *History of Education Society*, Studies in the Government and Control of Education Since 1860 (Methuen, 1970), pp. 1–12.

Manzer, R. A., *Teachers and Politics: The Role of the National Union of Teachers in the Making of National Educational Policy in England and Wales since 1944* (Manchester University Press, 1970).

Parkin, H., *Key Profession* (Routledge & Kegan Paul, 1969).

Parkinson, M., *The Labour Party and the Organisation of Secondary Education 1918–1965* (Routledge & Kegan Paul, 1970).

Peschek, B. and Brand, J., 'Policies and Politics in Secondary Education', *Greater London Papers No. 11* (LSE, 1966).

Richards, Colin, 'The Schools Council – A Critical Examination', *Universities Quarterly* (1974).

Robinson, Eric, *The Polytechnics* (Cornmarket, 1968).

Saran, R., *Policy Making in Secondary Education* (Clarendon Press, 1973).

Short, Edward, *Education in a Changing World* (Pitman, 1971).

Tropp, A., *The School Teachers* (Heinemann, 1957).

Vaizey, J., *The Costs of Education* (George Allen & Unwin, 1958).

Vaizey, J., *Education for Tomorrow* (Penguin, 1962).

Vaizey, J. and Sheehan, J., *Resources for Education* (George Allen & Unwin, 1968).

Wiseman, V., *Local Government at Work* (Routledge & Kegan Paul, 1967).

'Why They Tried to Kill the AEC', *The Times Educational Supplement* (1 March 1974).

'Analysis of an Uncritical Path', *The Times Educational Supplement* (24 May 1974), (published anonymously).

POLITICS AND PRESSURE GROUPS (GENERAL LITERATURE)

Barker, Anthony and Rush, Michael, *The Member of Parliament and His Information* (George Allen & Unwin, 1970).

Barnett, M. J., 'Back Bench Behaviour in the House of Commons', *Parliamentary Affairs*, (1968/69), vol. 22, pp. 38–62.

Bottomore, T. B., *Elites and Society* (Watts, 1964).

Bradshaw, Kenneth, 'A Brief Historical Note on Parliamentary Questions', *Parliamentary Affairs* (Summer, 1954), pp. 317–62.

Bradshaw, Kenneth and Pring, David, *Parliament and Congress* (Constable, 1972).

Butt, Ronald, *The Power of Parliament* (Constable, 1967).

Chester, D. N. and Bowring, N., *Questions in Parliament* (Clarendon Press, 1962).

Coombes, D., *The Member of Parliament and the Administration* (George Allen & Unwin, 1966).

Crewe, L. (ed.), *British Political Sociology Year Book Volume I* (Croom Helm, 1974).

Crick, Bernard, *The Reform of Parliament* (Weidenfeld & Nicolson, 1968).

Finer, S. E., *Anonymous Empire: A Study of the Lobby in Great Britain* (London, Pall Mall Press, 1966).

Franklin, M., 'Voice of the Back Bench: Pattern of Behaviour in the British House of Commons' (Ph.D. dissertation, 1970, Cornell University).

Goldsworthy, 'Colonial Parliamentary Questions', *Parliamentary Affairs* (1970), vol. 23.

Granada Television, *The State of the Nation* (1973).

Guttsman, W. L. (ed.), *The English Ruling Class* (Weidenfeld & Nicolson, 1969).

Hale, L., 'The Backbencher', *The Parliamentarian* (1966), pp. 191–8.

Hanson, A. H., 'The Purpose of Parliament', *Parliamentary Affairs* (1964).

Hanson, A. H. and Crick, B., *The Commons in Transition* (Fontana, 1970).

Hermann, Valentine, 'Adjournment Debates in the House of Commons', *Parliamentary Affairs* (1972/3), vol. 16, no. 1.

Johnson, N., *Parliament and Administration* (George Allen & Unwin, 1966).

Q

Leonard, Dick and Hermann, Valentine (eds), *The Back Bencher and Parliament* (Macmillan, 1972).

Lynskey, J. J., 'The Role of the British Back Bencher in the Modification of Government Policy', *Western Political Quarterly* (1970), vol. 23, no. 2, pp. 333–48.

Mackintosh, John R., *The Government and Politics of Britain* (Hutchinson University Library, 1970).

Parry, G., *Political Elites* (George Allen & Unwin, 1969).

Paterson, Samuel C., review article 'The British House of Commons as a Focus for Political Research', *British Journal of Political Science* (1973), vol. 3.

Report from the Select Committee on Parliamentary Questions (1971–2).

Richards, Peter G., *Honourable Members – A Study of the British Back Bencher* (Faber & Faber, 2nd edn, 1964).

Rose, R. (ed.), *Studies in British Politics* (MacMillan, 2nd edn, 1969).

Roth, Andrew, *The Business Background of MPs* (Parliamentary Profile Service, 1972).

Self, Peter, *Administrative Theories and Politics* (George Allen & Unwin, 1972).

Stewart, J. D., *British Pressure Groups – Their Role in Relation to the House of Commons* (Oxford University Press, 1966).

Wiseman, H. V. (ed.), *Parliament and the Executive* (Routledge & Kegan Paul, 1968).

References

Chapter 1
[1] M. Kogan, *The Politics of Education* (Harmondsworth, Penguin Books, 1971); M. Kogan and W. van der Eyken, *County Hall* (Harmondsworth, Penguin Books, 1973).
[2] For example, Michael Locke, *Power and Politics in the School System* (London, Routledge & Kegan Paul, 1974); and R. A. Manzer, *Teachers and Politics* (Manchester, Manchester University Press, 1970).
[3] R. T. McKenzie, 'Pressure Groups and the British Political Process', *The Political Quarterly* (1968).
[4] For example, Michael Stewart, MP, Edward Short, MP, Lord Eccles.

Chapter 2
[1] Interviews with two Conservative and one Labour MP.
[2] Interview with Lord Eccles, March 1974.
[3] Circular 6/60 (Ministry of Education, London, HMSO, 1960).
[4] Interview with Lord Eccles, March 1974.
[5] Circulars 1/60, 3/60, 8/60, 11/60 (*see* Chart I).
[6] This point has been made by A. Corbett, *Much Ado About Education* (Billericay Home and School Council, revised edn 1974).
[7] These references are from debates and Parliamentary Questions in the House of Commons during 1960.
[8] Kenneth Thompson, MP, House of Commons, 30 November 1960.
[9] M. Kogan, *The Politics of Education* (Harmondsworth, Penguin Books, 1971).
[10] J. Vaizey and J. Sheehan, *Resources for Education* (London, George Allen & Unwin, 1968).
[11] Annual conference, Association of Education Committees, 1963.
[12] For example, Eric Robinson, *The Polytechnics* (London, Cornmarket Press, 1968).
[13] Sir Michael Swann, Chairman of the BBC Board of Governors, formerly Principal, Edinburgh University, speaking at Oxford, 6 July 1974.
[14] Circular 1/68 (DES, London, HMSO, 1968).
[15] Circular 15/68 (DES, London, HMSO, 1968).

[16] *The Reorganisation of Central Government* (London, HMSO, November 1970, Cmnd 4506).

[17] *Education: A Framework for Expansion* (London, HMSO, 1972, Cmnd 5174).

[18] For example, Michael Parkinson, *The Labour Party and the Organisation of Secondary Education 1918–1965* (London, Routledge & Kegan Paul, 1970).

[19] The importance of Sir Fred Clarke's book was pointed out by Sir Toby Weaver (January 1974).

[20] J. Floud, A. H. Halsey and F. M. Martin, *Social Class and Educational Opportunity* (London, Heinemann, 1966); and Michael Young, *The Rise of the Meritocracy* (Thames & Hudson, 1958).

[21] Summarised in Report of the Central Advisory Council for Education (England), *Children and their Primary Schools* (London, HMSO, 1967), Chapter II.

[22] Interview with Dr C. T. Smith, March 1974, and Parkinson (*see* ref. [18] above).

[23] *See* ref. [22] above.

[24] *See* ref. [18] above.

[25] R. Bilski, 'Ideology and the Comprehensive Schools', *The Political Quarterly* (April–June 1973). Also Ph.D. thesis, Glasgow University (1971 unpublished).

[26] *Progress in Reading: 1948–64* (London, HMSO, 1966).

[27] Committee on Higher Education, *Higher Education* (Robbins Report) (London, HMSO, 1963).

[28] Interview with Frank Hooley, MP, April 1974.

[29] Discussed in T. Green, 'Educational Planning in Perspective', *Futures* (London, IPC Science and Technology Press, 1971), Editor's Introduction.

[30] *See* ref. [29].

[31] R. S. Peters (ed.), *Perspectives on Plowden* (London, Routledge & Kegan Paul, 1968).

[32] C. B. Cox and A. E. Dyson (eds), Black Paper One (*Fight for Education*), Black Paper Two (*The Crisis in Education*), (Critical Quarterly Society 1969, 1970).

[33] Interview with Timothy Raison, MP, May 1974.

[34] Interview with John Jennings, MP, October 1973.

[35] Interview with Richard Hornby, MP, September 1973, and Max Wilkinson, March 1974.

[36] Interview with Baroness White (Eirene White), May 1974.

[37] Interview with Max Wilkinson, March 1974.

[38] P. Taylor and F. Musgrove, *Society and the Teachers* (London, Routledge & Kegan Paul, 1969).

[39] For example, M. D. Shipman, *Education and Modernization* (London, Faber & Faber, 1971).

Chapter 3

[1] P. Hirst and R. S. Peters. For example, *The Logic of Education* (London, Routledge & Kegan Paul, 1970).

[2] J. Evetts, *Sociology of Educational Ideas* (London, Routledge & Kegan Paul, 1973).

[3] M. Kogan and T. Packwood, *Advisory Committees and Councils in Education* (London, Routledge & Kegan Paul, 1974).

[4] M. Kogan, 'Social Policy and Public Organisational Values', *Journal of Social Policy* (April 1974), vol. 3, part 2.

[5] M. Kogan and W. van der Eyken, *County Hall* (Harmondsworth, Penguin Books, 1973). The impressions given by the chief education officers in this book were confirmed by conferences with senior officers at Brunel University in 1974.

[6] R. D. Coates, *Teachers' Unions and Interest Group Politics* (Cambridge, Cambridge University Press, 1972).

[7] *Higher Technological Education* (London, HMSO, 1945).

[8] Central Advisory Council for Education (England), *15 to 18* (London, HMSO, 1959), Chapter VI, vol. I.

[9] J. Vaizey, *The Costs of Education* (London, Faber & Faber, 1958).

[10] Hirst and Peters. *See* ref. [1].

[11] For example, Martin Deutsch and Associates, *The Disadvantaged Child of the Social Environment and the Learning Process* (New York, Basic Books, 1967).

[12] M. Kogan, 'English Primary Schools: A Model of Institutional Innovation', *Futures* (London, IPC Science and Technology Press, 1971).

[13] Peters. *See* ref. [31], Chapter II.

[14] *See* ref. [2].

[15] Circular 1/68 (DES, London, HMSO, 1968).

[16] Butterworth, Eric and Weir, David, *Sociology of Modern Britain; An Introductory Reader* (London, Fontana, 1970).

[17] Report of the Central Advisory Council for Education (Wales), *Primary Education in Wales* (London, HMSO, 1967).

[18] The Plowden Report. *See* ref. [21], Chapter 2.

[19] The Plowden Report (para. 746). *See* ref. [21], Chapter 2.

[20] W. K. Richmond, *The Free School* (London, Methuen, 1973) well summarises these views.

[21] D. V. Donnison, 'Education and Opinion', *New Society* (26 October 1967).

[22] J. W. B. Douglas and J. M. Blomfield, *Children Under Five* (London, MacGibbon & Kee, 1958); J. W. B. Douglas, *The Home and School* (London, MacGibbon & Kee, 1964); R. Davie, N. Butler and H. Goldstein, *From Birth to Seven* (London, Longman, 1972).

[23] Maurice Peston in a speech made in 1972.

[24] The Plowden Report (vol. II, appendix 3). *See* ref. [21], Chapter 2.

[25] M. Young and P. McGeeney, *Learning Begins at Home: A Study of Junior School and its Parents* (London, Routledge & Kegan Paul, 1970).

[26] *See* ref. [38], Chapter 2.

Chapter 4

[1] Interview with Sir Toby Weaver, January 1974.

Chapter 5

[1] R. Michels, *Political Parties*, trans. Eden and Cedar Paul (New York, Free Press, 1962).

[2] R. Scase, 'Social Policy and Social Justice: Some Comments on Recent Developments in England and Sweden', Social Administration Association Conference (Nottingham, 1974).

[3] McKenzie. *See* ref. [3], Chapter 1.

Chapter 6

[1] 'Why They've Tried to Kill the AEC', *The Times Educational Supplement* (1 March 1974).

[2] Interview with Lord Eccles, March 1974.

[3] Report in *The Times Educational Supplement* (24 May 1974).

[4] Kogan and Packwood. *See* ref. [3], Chapter 3.

[5] Interview with C. Berry, AMC, April 1974.

[6] Interview with Kenneth Marks, MP, May 1974.

[7] Interview with J. M. MacCall, AMC, April 1974.

[8] Interview with Sir William Alexander, AEC, July 1973.

[9] Kogan. *See* ref. [9], Chapter 2.

[10] Kogan and van der Eyken. *See* ref. [5], Chapter 3.

[11] Interview with Sir Toby Weaver, January 1974.

[12] Interview with Sir William Alexander, AEC, July 1973.

[13] W. P. Alexander, *Towards a New Education Act* (London, Councils and Education Press Ltd, 1969).

[14] Report from the Select Committee on Education and Science, Session 1967–8, *HM Inspectorate* (*England and Wales*) (London, HMSO, 1968), pp. 66–86.

[15] *See* ref. [12].

[16] Interview with Leonard Brown, CCA, January 1974.

[17] Interview with J. M. MacCall, AMC, April 1974.

[18] Meeting with AMC Officers, April 1974.

[19] Interview with J. Swaffield, by then Director-General, GLC, February 1974.

[20] Interview with Peter Sloman, AMA, August 1974.

[21] Kogan. *See* ref. [9], Chapter 2.

[22] Interview with Jack Straw, June 1974.

Chapter 7

[1] Interviews with teachers' association officials.

[2] For example, Circular 5/63 (Ministry of Education, London, HMSO, 1963).

[3] Kogan and Packwood. *See* ref. [3], Chapter 3.

[4] Prospectus (1973).

[5] R. D. Coates. *See* ref. [6], Chapter 3.

[6] Norman Morris, Raymond Ryba and Keith Drake, *How Many Teachers*? (London, NUT, 1973).

[7] Interview with Edward Britton, June 1974.

[8] Report from the Select Committee on Education and Science, Session 1967–8, *HM Inspectorate* (*England and Wales*) (London, HMSO, 1968), NUT oral evidence.

[9] NUT notes of meetings made available to researchers.

[10] Interview with Roy Hattersley, MP, January 1974.

[11] Interview with Alan Evans, September 1974.

[12] Interview with Fred Jarvis, November 1973.

[13] S. Hilsum and B. S. Cane, *The Teacher's Day* (Slough, NFER, 1971).

[14] Interviews with NUT leaders and officials.

[15] Manzer. *See* ref. [2], Chapter 1.

[16] Interview with Edward Short, MP, November 1973.

[17] Interviews with NAS officials, September 1973.

[18] *See* ref. [17].

[19] Report in *The Times Educational Supplement* (5 May 1972). The NUT also took the same stance.
[20] Interview with Terry Casey, September 1973.
[21] Letter from Dame Mary Smieton to the main associations on the foundation of the Curriculum Study Group.
[22] Manzer. *See* ref. [2], Chapter 1.
[23] Interview with Sheila Wood, March 1974.
[24] Coates. *See* ref. [6], Chapter 3.
[25] Manzer. *See* ref. [2], Chapter 1.

Chapter 8
[1] M. Locke, *Power and Politics in Education* (London, Routledge & Kegan Paul, 1974).
[2] H. S. Wolff at the first conference of CASE in Cambridge, 1960.
[3] Interview with Barbara Bullivant, July 1974.
[4] Interview with Anne Sofer, June 1974.
[5] CASE, 'Statement of Objects' (1974).
[6] CASE leaflet (1973).
[7] Interview with Barbara Bullivant, July 1974.
[8] CASE, 'Parents and Schools', information sheet (1972).
[9] Interview with Beryl MacAlhone, July 1974.
[10] Brian Jackson, *1960–1970: A Progress Report*, ACE Occasional Paper (1971).
[11] *See* ref. [10].
[12] Interview with Baroness White (Eirene White), May 1974.
[13] Interview with Timothy Raison, MP, May 1974.
[14] Anne Corbett in a speech to CASE, Cambridge, April 1974.
[15] Interview with Richard Cunningham, September 1973.
[16] Michael Stewart quoting Edward Boyle, interview, October 1973.
[17] Interview with Michael Stewart, MP, October 1973.
[18] Interview with Timothy Raison, MP, May 1974.
[19] Interview with Michael Stewart, MP, October 1973.
[20] Interview with Lord Eccles, March 1974.
[21] Interview with Roy Hattersley, MP, January 1974.
[22] Meeting with John Scott, June 1974.
[23] Kogan. *See* ref. [9], Chapter 2.
[24] *See* ref. [20], Chapter 2.
[25] 'Analysis of a Non-Critical Path', *The Times Educational Supplement* (24 May 1974).
[26] Evidence to the Select Committee on Science and Technology (1972).
[27] Discussion with Department officials.
[28] Meeting with Alfred Yates, Director, NFER, July 1974.
[29] David Donnison (ed.), *A Pattern of Disadvantage* (Slough, NFER, 1972).
[30] Manzer. *See* ref. [2], Chapter 1.
[31] M. Kogan, 'A Reflection on Ralph Fletcher', *The Times Educational Supplement* (3 May 1974).
[32] Anne Corbett, 'The Secret Garden of the Curriculum – Who Should Hold the Key to the Door?', *The Times Educational Supplement* (13 July 1973).
[33] M. F. D. Young, 'The Politics of Educational Knowledge', *Economy and Society* (1972), vol. I, no. 1.

[34] Colin Richards, 'The Schools Council – A Critical Examination', *Universities Quarterly* (Summer 1974).
[35] Much of the information in this section comes from an interview with A. G. Becher, December 1973.

Chapter 9
[1] For example, H. V. Wiseman, *Parliament and the Executive* (London, Routledge & Kegan Paul, 1960), Introduction.
[2] Geraint Parry and Peter Morris, 'When is a Decision Not a Decision? *British Political Sociology Yearbook*, Vol. 1, Ivor Crewe (ed.) (London, Croom Helm, 1974).
[3] Aaron Wildavsky, *The Politics of the Budgetary Process* (Boston, Little, Brown & Co., 1964).
[4] *Control of Public Expenditure* (London, HMSO, 1961, Cmnd 1432).
[5] Described well in *Public Expenditure Survey System*, Memorandum by the Treasury, Second Report, Expenditure Committee, Education and Arts Sub-Committee, Session 1970–1, no. 545.
[6] *Research and Development in the USA* (Paris, OECD, 1971).
[7] Whilst visiting as an OECD examiner in 1968.
[8] Kogan. See ref. [9], Chapter 2.
[9] D. N. Chester and N. Bowring, *Questions in Parliament* (Oxford, Clarendon Press, 1962), Chapter 2.
[10] House of Commons Paper 198 (1969–70).
[11] Neville Johnson, *Parliament and Administration* (London, George Allen & Unwin, 1966), p. 134.
[12] Interviews with Alan Evans, September 1974, and Laurie Sapper, January 1974.
[13] Interview with Alan Evans, September 1974.
[14] See ref. [9].
[15] Kogan. See ref. [9], Chapter 2.
[16] Interviews with Edward Short, MP, Michael Stewart, MP and Dennis Howell, MP, 1973–4.
[17] Mark Franklin, 'Voice of the Back Bencher', Ph.D. thesis, Cornell University (1970, unpublished).
[18] *Hansard* (1 March 1960).
[19] Interview with John Jennings, MP, October 1973.
[20] Anthony Barker and Michael Rush, *The Member of Parliament and His Information* (London, George Allen & Unwin, 1970).
[21] Interview with Kenneth Marks, MP, May 1974.
[22] An amusing account of this is given in R. A. Butler, *The Politics of the 1944 Education Act*, excerpt in G. Fowler and others, *Decision Making in British Education* (London, Heinemann, 1974).
[23] Valentine Hermann, 'Adjournment Debates in the House of Commons', *Parliamentary Affairs* (1972–3), vol. 16, no. 1.
[24] *See* ref. [23].
[25] Interview with Eric Deakins, MP, February 1974.
[26] Interview with Frank Hooley, MP, April 1974.
[27] Interview with Timothy Raison, MP, May 1974.
[28] Interview with Eric Deakins, MP, February 1974.
[29] Interview with Lord Eccles, March 1974.

[30] Report of the Committee appointed by the Minister of Education in November 1958 (Albemarle Report), *The Youth Service in England and Wales* (London, HMSO, 1960, Cmnd 929).

[31] Special Report from the Committee of Public Accounts, *Parliament and Control of University Expenditure*, Session 1966–7, p. 290.

[32] Report from the Select Committee on Education and Science, Session 1967–8, *HM Inspectorate (England and Wales)* (London, HMSO, 1968), pp. 400–1.

[33] Letter from Dr Harry French, *The Times Education Supplement* (26 April 1974).

[34] Select Committee, 1968–9, *Student Relations*.

[35] *See*, for example, the oral evidence reported in the Second Report from the Expenditure Committee. *See* ref. [5].

[36] See ref. [34].

[37] Eighth Report from the Expenditure Committee, Session 1970–1, *Relationship of Expenditure to Needs*, p. 515.

[38] Rodney Barker, *Education and Politics 1900–1951. A Study of the Labour Party* (Oxford, Oxford University Press, 1971).

[39] Interview with Kenneth Marks, MP, May 1974.

[40] Interviews with Sir Gilbert Longden, MP, and John Jennings, MP, October 1973.

[41] Interview with Stanley Hewitt, ATCDE, December 1973.

[42] Edward Boyle, in Kogan. *See* ref. [9], Chapter 2.

[43] Philip H. White, dissertation for M.Phil., 'The Reorganisation of Secondary Education in Bath and Southampton', University of Southampton (1974, unpublished).

[44] Interview with John Jennings, MP, October 1973.

[45] Interviews with two Conservative MPs and one Labour MP, 1973–4.

[46] Interviews with Kenneth Marks, MP, and Timothy Raison, MP.

[47] Interview with Max Morris, NUT, March 1974.

[48] Interview with Sheila Wood, Association of Assistant Mistresses, March 1974.

Chapter 10

[1] ATTI, 'Constitution and Rules' (1972).

[2] Report in *The Times Higher Education Supplement* (27 October 1973).

[3] Interview with Tom Driver, March 1974.

[4] Evidence to Select Committee on Further Education (21 February 1972).

[5] ATTI, 'A Statement on the White Paper' (1973).

[6] Interview with Tom Driver, March 1974.

[7] Much of this section derives from an interview with Stanley Hewitt, December 1973.

[8] Much of this section derives from an interview with Sir Norman Lindop, August 1974.

[9] UGC Report, 1935–47 (HMSO).

[10] Murray Committee 1972.

[11] *Hansard* (1 March 1960).

[12] Report of the English Language Examining Committee, Secondary School Examinations Council, 1963.

[13] Committee on Higher Education, *Higher Education* (London, HMSO, 1963).

[14] Reported in interview with Dr Geoffrey Templeman, May 1974.

R

[15] Interview with Michael Stewart, MP, October 1973.

[16] Interview with Ralph Fletcher, March 1974.

[17] Proposals put informally on ways of providing places more cheaply, such as giving preference to home-based students.

[18] Special Report from the Committee of Public Accounts, *Parliament and the Control of Public Expenditure*, Session 1966–7 (London, HMSO Cmnd 290).

[19] *See* ref. [18], pp. 22–51.

[20] Max Beloff, *Minerva*, vol. V, no. 4, and Sir William Mansfield Cooper, *Minerva*, vol. VI, no. 1.

[21] Proceedings of the Committee of Public Accounts, Session 1969–70, 161-I, 265-I, 297, pages 398–9 (London, HMSO, 1970).

[22] Interview with Laurie Sapper, AUT, January 1974.

[23] Interview with Shirley Williams, MP, October 1973.

[24] Select Committee. *See* ref. [21].

[25] Interviews with Shirley Williams, MP, and A. G. Becher.

[26] Interview with Shirley Williams, MP, October 1973.

[27] Some of the information in this section is derived from an interview with Laurie Sapper, January 1974.

[28] Academic Freedom (London, NUS and NCCL publication, 1969).

[29] Student Rights and Duties (London, NUS and NCCL publication, 1970).

[30] Interview with Jack Straw, July 1974.

Chapter 11

[1] Michael Parkinson. *See* ref. [18], Chapter 2; and Brian Simon and Caroline Benn, *Half Way There* (New York, McGraw-Hill, 1970).

[2] R. Bilski. *See* ref. [25], Chapter 2.

[3] R. Saran, *Policy Making in Secondary Education* (Oxford, Oxford University Press, 1973); R. Batley, O. O'Brien and Henry Parris, *Going Comprehensive* (London, Routledge & Kegan Paul, 1970; H. V. Wiseman *Local Government at Work* (London, Routledge & Kegan Paul, 1967), Philip H. White, dissertation for M.Phil., 'The Reorganisation of Secondary Education in Bath and Southampton', University of Southampton (1974, unpublished); R. Buxton, 'Comprehensive Education: Central Government, Local Authorities and the Law', from R. Buxton, *Local Government* (Harmondsworth, Penguin Books, 1972) (reproduced in *Decision Making in British Education*, G. Fowler and others (eds) (London, Heinemann, 1974)).

[4] J. J. Richardson, *The Policy-Making Process* (Routledge & Kegan Paul, 1969).

[5] Parkinson. *See* ref. [18], Chapter 2.

[6] Interview with Dr C. T. Smith, May 1974.

[7] Parkinson, Evetts and Bilski. *See* refs [18], Chapter 2, [2], Chapter 3, [25], Chapter 2.

[8] Bilski. *See* ref. [25], Chapter 2.

[9] Interview with Edward Britton, NUT, July 1974.

[10] D. V. Donnison, 'Education and Opinion', *New Society* (26 October 1967).

[11] Interview with Michael Stewart, MP, October 1973.

[12] See ref. [3].

[13] White. *See* ref. [3].

[14] Interview with Jack Straw, July 1974.

[15] White. *See* ref. [3].
[16] For example, Eirene White. *See* ref. [12], Chapter 8; and discussions with Dame Evelyn Dennington, ILEA, September 1974.
[17] Interview with Anne Sofer, June 1974.
[18] *See* ref. [20], Chapter 3.

Chapter 12
   [1] Carole Pateman, *Participation and Democratic Theory* (Oxford, Oxford University Press, 1970).
   [2] Patrick Gordon Walker, Review of 'Politics of Education', *The Times* (1 October 1971).
   [3] *See* ref. [3], Chapter 11.
   [4] J. J. Richardson, *The Policy Making Process* (London, Routledge & Kegan Paul, 1969).
   [5] Harry Ree, *Educator Extraordinary; The Life and Achievements of Henry Morris* (London, Longman, 1973).
   [6] *See* ref. [2], Chapter 1.
   [7] Dame Mary Smieton. *See* ref. [21], Chapter 7.
   [8] Research (to be published) by Myron Atkin, A. Becher and H. Simons.

Index